For
my cat
Taz

CONTENTS

Just before you read this book, here's a thought: familiarity makes the incredible seem dull and commonplace. If we saw a man named Frank levitating over a bed of nails down at the Pier Head every day, he'd eventually just be known as "Floating Frank" and we'd unthinkingly accept that he could somehow overcome gravity and think nothing more of it, just as we accept the Moon. We don't think of it as a world as wide as Australia perpetually floating round the world with the same face always turned to us; it's just "the moon" – something that's always been there.

Tom Slemen

A STRANGE SENSE

Most of us are aware of the five main senses of perception in humans - sight, sound, touch, smell and taste. In addition to that we have a sense of time – we know *roughly* what time has elapsed without looking at a clock, and we also have a sense of motion; if we are in a car, or even in the back of a van with no windows in its rear to look out of, we know we are moving. Intuition – when we have a hunch about something or someone that is usually unfounded but often true – may also be a type of sense – and then there is an apparent sense of the supernatural, and that is the subject of this chapter. The alleged sense – and it is one I have experienced and one that is often reported to me by readers - is hard to explain. Here are a few examples of what I mean.

One breezy Wednesday afternoon in March 2018 at around 3:45pm, a 13-year-old schoolgirl named Isla was waiting for the Number 27 bus at a stop on Great Homer Street - located at the Kirkdale Road end of that street, facing the old river buoy and a ship's anchor installed at a cleared site at the junction. Isla had left her school at half-past three, and around this time she usually walked to the bus stop with her two friends, Jenny and Taylor, but Jenny was off school with the flu and Taylor had gone straight to the dentist because of a problem with her braces. Isla was therefore on her own today at the bus stop and there were no other people about. The schoolgirl experienced what she later described as "a really bad feeling" about the bushes to her right, and she did not know why she was so unnerved by them. She'd waited for the bus home at this stop most days from Monday to Friday and had never once had a creepy feeling like this. Isla *was* on her own at the bus stop on this darkening overcast afternoon but was not the type of girl to think about anything vaguely supernatural - and yet - she had the overbearing sensation that someone, or something, was watching her from those bushes to her right. The bushes are part of a green border that runs along an eight-foot-tall brick wall topped with a picket fence which forms the western border of a housing estate, and normally, Isla didn't give the bushes a second thought, but on this March afternoon the bushes nearer to her were causing a growing sense of anxiety. The schoolgirl just *knew* there was something evil in those bushes, and she felt whatever that thing was, it was about to pounce on her. She started to hyperventilate, and she looked up Great Homer Street, longing to see the bus to take her home; why was that bus taking so long? She thought, and Isla decided she was going to phone her mum, as she always felt better when she talked to her. As Isla was going into her contacts on the phone, she saw movement in the bushes out the corner of her eye — and she quickly glanced at the movement and saw a weird grey face peep out from the bushes. That face looked as unreal as a Halloween mask; it had twinkling, luminous eyes and the mouth was shaped like an ellipse – like a zero (0) – and there was something red in that mouth. Isla felt an electric jolt of fear go across her heart, and she was just about to turn and run, when her older brother's friend, Matthew, pulled over at the bus stop in his first car. Isla normally shunned Matthew as she just couldn't take to him, but she found herself trying to pull open the front passenger door – until a startled Matthew unlocked that door - and as Isla was getting into the vehicle, she saw something - something she could only describe as a four-limbed animal similar to a huge greyhound with a man's head jump out of the bushes and run for the car. She screamed for Matthew to drive off, and he did, and he kept looking in the rear view mirror at the thing racing after the car, and he saw it give up the chase after a few seconds and turn to run back to those bushes. Matthew slowed down and Isla took off her knapsack so she could put on the seatbelt. 'What the hell was that?' Matthew asked her, and Isla grappled with the seatbelt buckle and cried, 'I don't know! Just get me home!'

'I'll turn around and see what it was,' suggested Matthew, but Isla swore and told him not to. He therefore drove on and took the badly-shaken girl to her home. Just what that thing was in the bushes is not known, but it is very similar to a 4-legged entity that was seen by a postman, running out of Stanley Park one morning in 2012. In October 2011, a couple walking through Croxteth Country Park almost fell over a terrifying entity that looked like some four-legged animal with a woman's head. I interviewed the witnesses on BBC Radio Merseyside and many listeners contacted me afterwards to say they had either seen the weird entity or heard about it, and many assumed it was just some figure of bogeyman lore. It hissed at the couple in the park that October night and they ran off in terror. It has been seen running across Croxteth Hall Lane, mostly of a night, and seems most active at the time of the full moon. Just what the thing is remains a mystery. It's easy to dismiss the four-legged being seen by Isla and Matthew as a product of imagination or a trick of the light, but Isla struck me as a very level-headed girl, and her parents could tell something had frightened her, and Matthew also backed up the girl's strange story. What I find fascinating about the case on Great Homer Street is the way Isla was filled with a strange sense of fear and an intense foreboding that something bad was going to happen, even before the entity emerged from the bushes. Perhaps her sense of danger is some vestige, some inherited faculty, from the days when early humans relied on their sharpened pro-survival senses to detect a bear or a leopard, lying in wait in a cave or bush for them; and in that case, the sense would be an early warning system working at an unconscious level – detecting faint movement and the scent of a predator before it struck – or it may be nothing of the sort at all. We still know very little about Extra-Sensory Perception – commonly referred to as ESP – and many scientists will not even accept that some people can receive and transmit information on a mental level akin to telepathy. Zener card tests are often carried out in which the subject being tested for

ESP has to guess the patterns on the cards (wavy lines, stars and circles etc) – but the best test would be one in which the subject's life depended on the outcome for real ESP to kick in, but of course, such a test would be unethical and illegal, and I'm just talking hypothetically. Perhaps the being in the bushes on Great Homer Street was itself radiating some malevolent energy which Isla picked up on; it really is hard to say. Another case where a 'sixth sense' type of fear disturbed the mind took place in November 1999. A 35-year-old lady named Patricia started work in a short-lived health shop on Bold Street, and when she had been at work for a week, the boss, Mr Cairns said, 'If you see a girl at the door, askin' to be let in when we're closed, ignore her.' Patricia thought it was an odd thing to say, and she asked Mr Cairns who the girl was but the boss never answered and left the shop. Patricia naturally assumed Cairns had been referring to a troublesome *modern* girl of the type who hung around outside off-licences, pestering adults to buy her alcoholic drinks or cigarettes. At around 5:20pm, just before the shop was about to close, Patricia had an extremely overpowering feeling she was being watched, but by whom she was not sure; all she knew was that the feeling intensified as she stood there behind the counter, and she felt as if something bad was about to happen. Patricia had never experienced such a feeling of fear like this before in her life, and she started to gasp as she was gripped by the strange anxiety. She then noticed a weird-looking girl, aged about eight to ten years old in a jet-black dress with a high collar. The girl had a very pale face and looked really old-fashioned, and she was standing outside the shop with her face close to the plate glass of the door. Her sudden appearance startled Patricia.

'Mama,' the unknown girl said, reminding Patricia of an old doll she'd had as a child which made that sound when a cord was pulled. 'Mama, let me come in!' shouted the girl - then coughed and spat blood against the window of the door.

'Oh my God,' Patricia whispered to herself, seeing how bright and vivid the coughed up blood was as it trickled down the plate glass.

The girl then stepped forward, and slowly came through the *closed* door, and Patricia screamed, now realising the girl was a ghost, and she fled to the back of the shop, where she shouted to an assistant - before recalling he'd gone to the shop next door for something about ten minutes ago. For the past three days, the boss had continually promised he'd hire a security guard soon, and Patricia was now alone in the shop. She hid under the counter, trembling, hoping the ghost would leave the premises, but then she heard the girl say in a well-spoken voice, 'Mama, I can see you hiding.'

The voice sounded close to the counter. Patricia swore and screamed, 'Leave me alone!'

And then she heard the door to the health store open as a customer came in.

Patricia got up in a right state and the customer, a man in his forties asked her if she was alright, as he could see she looked distressed.

'Did you see a little girl in here then?' Patricia asked the man, and he shook his head. Patricia looked at the plate glass door and saw no trace of the blood the child had spat out. She told the customer what had happened and thought he'd think she was crazy but the man said, 'Sounds like something from the Victorian era to me.'

The girl - whoever she was - had gone and Patricia 'sacked the job off' and the boss warned her to tell no one what she had seen, as the shop apparently had a 'history', and he had got the premises at a much reduced rent because of the shop's reputation. The premises are still very hard to let. I mentioned the case on the radio and the estate agents who let the shop complained and said I was scaring potential retailers from moving into the address. I imagine that little girl may have died from tuberculosis a long time ago – back when the disease was called "consumption". I wonder what the history of the girl is concerning her "Mama"?

What intrigued me about the case were the sudden sensations of being watched and the attendant feeling of extreme fear Patricia experienced before the ghost showed itself. An unexplained onset of fear and a feeling of being observed were also observed by a lady in the following uncanny story.

One humid Saturday evening in August 2009, a 33-year-old Wavertree lady named Kate went out for a night on the town with a friend and they bumped into a group of girls Kate knew from her last job, and these girls were having a hen party at a bar on Concert Square, which is located between Bold Street and Fleet Street. Kate got insensibly drunk with them and found herself staggering alone on Bold Street as she swigged from a large bottle of whisky - a drink she never usually touched - but here she was drinking it neat from the bottle; where the large bottle of The Famous

Grouse Scotch Whisky came from remains a mystery to Kate to this day. Next thing Kate knew she was sitting on the kerb, leaning against the base of a lamp post, and now Bold St looked very peculiar to Kate; the lamp posts had flickering flames in quaint-looking lanterns and there wasn't a car about - just horse-drawn cabs, and then Kate saw two bemused men looking down at her.

'Where are your clothes, Polly?' asked one of the men; he wore a cape and a deerstalker hat, and the other man standing next to him, who was also dressed in old-fashioned garb, said something in an American accent, and then his associate, the deerstalker chap, started to sing: 'And you lie there, quite resigned, whiskey deaf, and whiskey blind' and the two men dragged Kate to her feet and the large whisky bottle dropped and smashed on the cobbled roadway and then the man started to sing something Kate recalled as: 'I've a mind to take you out, underneath the water-spout, just to rinse you up a little, so you'll know what you're about!'

The two men then kicked their legs in the air singing and started dancing with Kate between them as if it was all 'some trippy musical' as Kate described it to me. The men in backdated clothes tried to drag Kate into a tavern on Renshaw Street, and Kate struggled and kept asking, 'What year is this?' but received no answer, and at this point, although she was feeling fairly high with all of the drinking, she was suddenly filled with fear, and experienced a panic attack – something that had only ever happened to Kate once before, when she was stuck in a lift in a block of flats and discovered she was claustrophobic. Kate felt malevolent eyes upon her on what seemed to be some Victorian version of Renshaw Street, and she sensed that whoever was looking at her was some threat to her very life – as if the person was some murderer. Kate turned and saw two men in round brimless caps, dark sailor suits with flap collars, and they both wore footwear resembling huge shiny black clogs that peeped out from flared bell-bottomed trousers. One of the men, who had bushy white sideburns, rosy cheeks and wide pale blue eyes, held a small knife, and he was looking Kate up and down, but seemed fixated with her bare legs (as she had on a very short miniskirt). The two men with Kate started arguing with the sailors, and the sailor with the knife lunged forward and tried to grab Kate, and she screamed, ran off, but fell over. She heard the sailor cry, 'Whore!' and she heard the loud footfall of his clogs on the cobbles as he ran to her. Kate picked herself up, lost a shoe - and dropped her handbag - but she kept running, and had to kick off her remaining shoe so she could make a proper break for it. At one point she thought she felt a stone hit her in the back. Upon reaching Leece Street, the year 2009 returned. Kate started laughing with shock. She looked back down Renshaw Street and saw the tavern and the psychopathic sailor had vanished. She flagged down a hackney cab near St Luke's and told the driver what had happened. He gravely told Kate it sounded as if someone had spiked her drink, and said a lot of spiking was going on in the club scene. Kate said the incident had not been drug induced, and she admitted that she *had* drank a lot, but she had not touched ecstasy or any other drug. When Kate told her family and friends about her apparent slip back in time, they all said she'd 'hallucinated' the weird incident because of the heavy drinking - but - I traced the song lyrics the deerstalker man came out with that night, and I discovered that they dated to a popular ballad of 1874 called "Johnny Rich" written by one Will Carleton, an American poet from Michigan. Kate had never heard of him and had certainly never heard of his poems and ballads. All we can do is hazard a guess and speculate that the whole episode was a timeslip, and regular readers of my work will know that Bold Street – where the man picked up Kate – is apparently riddled with such timespace slippages.

In our last story in this chapter, we come to a man who experienced an intense fear of being watched, and how it preceded a materialisation of the terrifying kind. We go back to a sweltering July evening in 1967; a 45-year-old shopkeeper named Bernie finished his stock inventory that night around 11pm and went to bed in the room above his shop in Liverpool city centre. He dozed off, but after a few minutes his much-needed sleep was shattered by the blaring sound of Manfred Mann's *Ha! Ha! Said the Clown* – coming from a bedside transistor radio; a radio that Bernie *knew* he had switched off over an hour ago. He grabbed the radio and turned it off, and tried to settle down to sleep – but Bernie felt the hairs at the back of his neck go up as he lay there, because he felt as if someone was in the dark bedroom, watching him. He tried to counteract his fear by giving a little false laugh and telling himself out loud he was being silly – that it was just his imagination and no one was watching him - but he still felt eyes on him. Bernie switched on the bedside lamp and lay on top of the covers because of the oven heat of July. He closed his eyes – and he heard faint, echoing laughter, and what sounded like carnival music. The laughter became louder, and now there was a sweet smell reminiscent of candy floss in the room. Bernie opened his eyes as the jangly melodies and pipe music of a fairground filled the room, and it was so loud, Bernie heard loud thuds on his wall; the newsagent next door was protesting about the racket.

Then the clown appeared in the space between the bed and the wall, and it was a tragic figure from Bernie's past. In the 1950s, a drunken Bernie had taken his pregnant wife Liz to the fairground, and he had made her go on the ghost train – and Liz hadn't been keen, as she was of a nervous disposition. Bernie pressured her into getting on the ghost train, and in the tunnel, a clown had jumped out on Bernie and Liz. Liz screamed and passed out. She miscarried from the scare – but that was just Bernie's version of events. In reality, Bernie had been arguing with Liz all of that day and he had struck her across the face in a drunken rage and knocked his wife unconscious. That caused the miscarriage – but the clown's employers believed Bernie and sacked the clown – and he took his own life – in the very room Bernie was now sleeping in. Bernie only discovered this after that July night when the clown's ghost appeared. Bernie was so terrified by the ghostly encounter, he closed the shop and ended up moving to London. Every now and then the owners of the shop in the city centre hear echoing laughter, and sometimes sobbing, and it is always accompanied by that sweet candy floss scent and the fairground organ music, and creepier still, the ghost of the clown sometimes tickles people who are sleeping in the haunted room.

Readers often tell me that on some occasions, as they read my books – as *you* are doing now, they get the feeling someone is watching them, especially when they are alone in the evening. One woman told me she felt something breathe down her neck one night as she sat reading my book on her sofa, and then she saw goosebumps appear on her arms – one of the alleged signs of a ghost being close by...

THE MYSTERY OF WHISTON MARY

The following story took place over ten years ago, but I clearly remember interviewing the witness to the events in the strange account as if it was only yesterday. In this story there are no preachy morals of the type you tend to find in most Christmas tales of the supernatural; it is simply a very peculiar and frightening story. The person featured in the account had no belief in the paranormal before the incident happened to him and he has experienced nothing vaguely supernatural since. It all began on the Tuesday afternoon of 21 December, 2010, in the middle of a winter that brought unusually heavy snowfalls and record low temperatures. Travel on the roads, by air and by rail was thrown into chaos, and the Met Office later said it was the coldest winter on record since 1659. The temperature was an unheard-of minus 17.6 degrees Centigrade (0.3 degrees Fahrenheit) when a 39-year-old Huyton businessman named Frank Stevens set out in his brand new Jaguar from his Auntie Joan's house in Halewood, bound for his friend Stephen's house in Tarbock. Frank had just had dinner with Auntie Joan and given her a few Christmas presents and she had given him the usual socks and aftershave and a huge jigsaw puzzle of the Flying Scotsman. Now Frank was taking a few gifts to his friend Stephen's cosy cottage, where the latter lived with his partner Kelly. In his youth, Frank had been nicknamed "Shortcut Stevens" because he was always claiming he knew the fastest way to anywhere, be it on foot or on a bike, and now as a motoring adult, he had not changed. He decided not to go via the Knowsley Expressway; instead, Frank decided he'd take a shortcut to Tarbock and he relaxed, then switched on the Jag's radio and with a cringing expression he listened to the current Number 1 in the pop charts – Matt Cardle's *When We Collide* – as he drove down a black-iced Greensbridge Lane. It was fast approaching four o'clock in the afternoon, and the setting sun was just a hazy incandescent blood-orange disc, glimpsed through the bare silhouetted branches of the trees lining the road. Frank thought a few days ahead to Christmas – the first one he would be spending alone after the break up with his partner Gemma in October. He consoled himself with the thought of the festive season just being a purely commercial venture for capitalists and a traditional excuse for people to get drunk and overeat. He told himself he wasn't bothered at the loss of Gemma one bit, but something must have bothered him because he took a wrong turn onto an eerily deserted Netherley Road, and so he performed a perfect U turn, looked at the detailed GPS map on the screen of his dashboard and got himself onto Whitefield Lane. He cruised down this lane, which was flanked on both sides with vast white acres of snow-covered farmland, and put on his lights.

And then he saw her, and at first he didn't realise what he was looking at. It was a naked woman with black hair, tied to a tree at the roadside on his left. She was alive because he could see the faint spout of exhaled breath coming from her. His first thought was 'Why on earth would anyone tie a woman to a tree?'

Frank switched off the radio and pulled over, but kept the engine running. He looked about in case it was all some ruse by carjackers to get him to stop, and then he put on his hazard lights. He opened the car door, slammed it shut, and ran to the woman's aid, and as he neared her he could see she looked as if she was in her early twenties or even late teens. Her skin was white – almost porcelain-like – and Frank imagined the poor girl would be in the throes of hypothermia.

'What happened, love?' he said, and she turned to face him. She had large blue eyes flooded with tears and a cherubic face, and her teeth were chattering so much, she couldn't get her words out. Frank tried to undo the knots in the ropes binding the girl to the tree, and realised he had his old Swiss Army knife in the glove compartment so he ran back to the car to fetch it. He cut the ropes with the penknife and the girl almost collapsed. Frank carried her to the car, picked up the Christmas presents off the passenger seat and hurled them into the backseat, and then he carefully sat her down. He then took off his leather coat and put it on the unknown girl. Frank pulled off his Christmas pullover and he handed it to the girl and she nodded and tried to smile and covered her lap with it. Frank closed the door, got in the Jag and turned up the heater.

'What happened?' Frank asked, taking his mobile

out, ready to call the police.

'Three men grabbed me – stripped me – and tied me to the tree,' said the girl, shivering and crying. She said she was from Whiston and that her name was Mary, and Frank said, 'Okay Mary, you've been through a horrible experience but you're going to be okay now, alright?'

She nodded and Frank started to dial 999 – but Mary's hand knocked the mobile out of his hand.

A stunned Frank looked at her – and she was now smiling – and her eyes were glowing; not glowing as in some literary expression of enthusiasm or happiness – the woman's eyes were giving off a faint light.

'It's me, Frank,' the girl said in a voice that sounded old.

As a bewildered Frank looked on, the girl's raven long hair slowly turned grey, and the face of "Mary" started to age. Lines appeared in rows across her forehead, and crow's feet appeared at the side of her blue eyes. The instantly aged female reached out and grabbed Frank's crotch with her bony-fingered hand and he reflexively straightened his legs, putting pressure on the accelerator pedal. The sinister woman shrieked with laughter and her other hand put the clutch into first and the car moved off. Frank looked on in terror at the old hag sitting beside him. She was screeching with laughter. He found himself shouting, 'Jesus Christ! Save me!'

'Save me! Save me!' the woman mimicked Frank's outcry in a mocking manner and she went up the gears and kept squeezing at his crotch. Frank saw the car was heading for the tree that the woman had been tied to, and so he turned the wheel right – and she gripped the wheel and turned it back again – so Frank turned it right again and punched the old woman in the face, and some clear yellow fluid shot out of her eyes and spattered the windscreen – and then that woman vanished in an instant.

The driver of a car behind Frank beeped his horn, startling Frank, who realised he was on the right side of the road, and after the car had passed by, Frank drove after it, just to have some company on the road after the terrifying encounter with something that was obviously not of this world, and by the time Frank had reached his friend's cottage at Tarbock he was a nervous wreck. He told his friend Stephen what had happened, and Stephen, who was a complete sceptic towards anything remotely paranormal, asked Frank if he'd been drinking or smoking anything. Frank shook his head and said, 'Stephen, she existed – come and look at this,' and he showed his friend the vile yellowish fluid that had dripped down the windscreen and was now trickling onto the air vent on the fascia. Stephen still looked doubtful, and he spoke his mind, saying, 'You'd be surprised what stress and lack of sleep can do to the human mind.' Frank shook his head and in a raised voice he assured Stephen he had not imagined anything or hallucinated the woman through fatigue.

Frank has no idea what the thing was that metamorphosed before his eyes, or how it knew his name; nor does he know why it was tied to a tree - and to this day he stays well away from Whitefield Lane.

THE HONEY TRAP

For legal reasons I've had to change a few names and details in the following strange but intriguing story. In December 2009 I interviewed a security guard during my slot about the paranormal on the *Billy Butler Show* on BBC Radio Merseyside. The guard, a 35-year-old man named Nick Clarke, had experienced something which had baffled and frightened him. On a humid August morning in 2008, just before 4am, Nick had been doing his rounds on the campus of the Liverpool John Moores University, and had to investigate why an alarm had gone off in the John Foster Building, which is situated on Mount Pleasant. Some security alarms are so sensitive they can be triggered by a fluttering moth being picked up by an infra-red passive motion sensor or even a mouse scuttling about, as well as strong winds rattling windows and heavy vehicles vibrating sensors as they rumble by in the night. There are also anecdotal stories of alarms being tripped by paranormal entities and presences – in other words – ghosts. Nick Clarke had never seen anything remotely supernatural in the ten years he'd worked as a security guard; he'd heard stories about weird cold spots and apparitions in the older buildings on the campus that had been converted into university departments and student flats but Nick himself had not seen or heard anything that could be construed as being paranormal, and he was very sceptical about ghostly and spiritual phenomenon in general – until this particular morning in August 2008. He has, as far as I know, experienced nothing supernatural since – but this one occasion I am about to describe was enough to convince Nick that there are some strange things in this world that defy a logical explanation.

Nick had been alerted to the alarm in the building on Mount Pleasant by another guard who had seen a red LED light flashing on his console at a certain room on campus, and Nick was despatched to look into the matter. He unlocked the main door to the building and locked it behind him, then flashed his powerful 1000-lumens torch down the main corridor on the ground floor. The beam caught nothing; no intruders or any evidence of a break-in. The guard reset the alarm that was echoing throughout the building and radioed his colleague to tell him there was no one about and that some glitch or spike in the power supply had probably tripped the alarm. Nick was then about to do a quick routine inspection of the basement and three floors of the building before exiting the place when he was startled by a song he could hear behind him. The song was one Nick recognised: *The Weekend* by Michael Gray. The song had been a hit in the singles charts back in 2004, and was always playing in the nightclubs Nick had frequented. But who on earth was playing this song at this unearthly hour in the university building? It seemed to be coming from around a corner in the corridor, and what's more, Nick saw faint light coming from a point around that corner. His mind raced; was it intruders – an intruder who might be on drugs? Most burglars go about their business making as little sound as possible for obvious reasons – they don't play songs on the job – unless they are drunk or high on drugs.

And so, Nick Clarke braced himself for an encounter with an unstable intruder, and he had his radio transceiver switched on and was ready to call for back-up if needed. He crept around the corner – and beheld a sight that baffles him to this day. On the white glossy walls in the corridor, to the left of a bulletin board, there was a huge spotlight – about five feet in diameter – and Nick could not see any source of illumination that was projecting this spotlight; his own torch was aimed at the floor. In the baffling spotlight were three beautiful blonde females who looked to Nick to be in their early to mid-twenties, and they were standing shoulder to shoulder in a row, and the projected images of the trio were beckoning the guard with the curling index fingers of their left hands, and in unison the women said to the guard, 'Never mind Alison, we'll have your babies. Come on! [followed by something unintelligible].'

Alison was Nick's wife, and Nick was naturally dumbfounded by the unearthly spectacle before him. His wife Alison could not conceive, and she had recently discussed assisted conception with Nick – but how would these three ethereal women - projected on a wall in the wee small hours by heaven knows what - know about Alison's infertility problem? Who were they? *What* were they?

As Nick stood there in shock at the sight of the women, he wondered if some cruel person was staging an elaborate prank on him; a computer projector playing a video of the women – and yet Nick somehow knew this was not the case and that something very sinister was at work here. Furthermore, Nick was suddenly overcome with inexplicable optimism, and he looked at the blondes as they beckoned him and invited him to come to them again. Nick felt he should walk into that spotlight, which now looked like a real opening – a solid three-dimensional passageway to those three beauties who appeared to be in a sunlit place of greenery – and he was just going to step into the wall, which seemed to be turning transparent, when he noticed something that set an alarm bell off in the back of his mind. Nick Clarke caught a brief glimpse of a man to the left of the trio of blondes - and that partially-hidden man – who had long black hair and a van dyke beard - looked utterly evil. Whoever he was, he swiftly stepped back upon noticing that Nick had spotted him and vanished. The guard swore, and said to the tempters, 'No, go to Hell!' - and the beckoning index fingers of the three platinum-haired women turned to contemptuous middle finger gestures, and the whole vision on that wall went out like a light being switched off – and the song – *The Weekend* - simultaneously ceased. The inexplicable euphoric rush in Nick also abruptly died in that same instant. The guard shone the torch at the spot on the wall where the seductive threesome had been, and now it was just a bare glossy white wall again. Nick turned on the lights in the corridor and walked back and forth, trying to rationalise what had just taken place. He pressed a button on the walkie-talkie, activating transmission mode, as he intended to tell his colleague what had just happened, but quickly came to his senses and decided to say nothing. He checked the basement thoroughly, and the three floors. All of the rooms and toilets and the lift were inspected, and it was clear that no one was about. There were no jokers with a laptop and computer projector to be seen. Nick then realised that he had just experienced something paranormal. He turned the lights off, locked up and was glad to get out of that place. When Nick knocked off work later that morning, he thought about the experience as he drove home, and although he was aching to tell Alison about the uncanny incident, he knew she'd be hurt if he mentioned the way the women had said 'Never mind Alison, we'll have your babies.'

By the time he had reached home, Nick was wondering if he should go and see his doctor about the experience he'd had. He knew he had not imagined it, but he just had to tell someone, but the more he thought about it, the more he worried the word would get out that he was a security guard who had hallucinated three seductive women. Alison could tell he was hiding something from the way he behaved when he came home. He usually chatted to her when he got into bed and told her stories about things the other guards had told him, but on this morning he was unusually quiet. In the end he told Alison he thought he had seen a ghost and made out it was some figure glimpsed out the corner of his eye as he did his rounds.

Nick Clarke told no one what he had seen that morning, and one night a year later, and quite out the blue, an older guard named Des randomly asked the guard, 'You ever seen those three ghosts in the John Foster Building?' - and described the very same three beckoning blondes. Nick looked at his co-worker with a stunned expression that was interpreted as sarcasm by Des, and the latter insisted, 'I'm not joking; I saw them, but I got the feeling it was a trap.'

'Des, I saw the exact same three women last August,' said Nick, and he gave a detailed account of the experience.

'You're not winding me up, are you?' Des asked, narrowing his eyes suspiciously, but Nick shook his head and said, 'I give you my word, Des, I'm telling the truth,' and then he asked Des what he had meant when he said he thought it had been a trap.

'I didn't see someone standing behind them like you;' Des told him with a sombre expression, 'I just had a gut feeling that it was all too good to be true; what would three young blondes see in an old fogey like me? And I just had the feeling it was a honey trap. You know what, Nick? If people heard us talking about this they'd cart us off to the funny farm, they would.'

Nick sipped a coffee and thought about Des's intuitive feelings about the ghostly women – and that man Nick had seen loitering behind them – intending to entrap people. 'If we had gone with them, would it have been just another case of those people who vanish off the face of the earth that you hear about?' Des asked.

THE ENIGMA OF
PHILIP'S GOWNS

One chilly grey afternoon in December 2003, Chris and Aimée – a couple in their late twenties – visited St John's Shopping Centre. Aimée intended to call in on Berketex Bride (a bridalwear retailer) to look at the gowns and wedding accessories, such as veils and tiaras - but Chris was moaning because he and Aimée were both skint.

'We're living on cornflakes and you're looking at wedding gowns;' said Chris, trying to let go of his girlfriend's hand, but Aimée clung on and ended up gripping his thumb. 'Aimée – it's all pie in the sky girl, wake up,' Chris added, and Aimée retorted with, 'We've been engaged for years - we're gonna end up tying the knot in the geriatric ward.'

'If I had the money, I'd love to marry you, but we are brassic,' said Chris, grabbing hold of Aimée's hand again to reassure her that he really did love her.

Aimée then noticed an amazing new store with bridal gowns in. It was called Philip's Gowns, and the decor was more suited to an upmarket store in Beverly Hills than St John's Shopping Centre.

'Hey, look at this;' said Aimée, her eyes aglow as she almost pressed her nose (pink with the December cold) against the plate glass window of the new store, 'how have I never noticed this before? It must have just opened.'

'I'm not going in there dressed like a tramp,' said Chris, looking down at his tracksuit bottoms and no-name trainers, but a manic Aimée dragged him into the place as the doors automatically parted, and warm, perfumed air wafted out to greet the couple. There was a golden brightness in the store, and the layout and furnishings were beautiful in the eyes of Aimée; a veined white marble calacatta floor decked with rugs here and there, and the chaise longue and chairs were all Louis XV, upholstered in gold or orange satin, and sparkling ethereal cut-glass chandeliers hung from a ceiling of elaborate mouldings that Chris – being a plasterer and decorator – noted and admired. A variety of high quality wedding gowns stood there on light grey faceless mannequins which had a spellbinding effect on Aimée. No one seemed to be about though, and the couple stood there as the song *Superstar* by Jamelia was playing in the store. The dresses had no price tags on them, and Aimée was sure that this was probably done so the prospective buyer would not be scared off by the price.

'Come on, Aimée, let's get out of here,' Chris said, and he yawned and nodded sideways towards the doors, then added, 'time to leave Fantasy Island.'

Just then an urbane-looking man in a suit walked out of an archway in the place and in a well-spoken soft voice he said, 'Seen anything you like? I'm Philip, by the way; and you are - '

And Chris interposed to comment: 'She's skint and I'm broke.' But Philip didn't even look at Chris - he seemed fascinated by Aimée, who was blushing, as all she had of value on her was twenty-seven pounds and 32p, but Philip narrowed his eyes, looked Aimée up and down and queried, 'You a 12?' and Aimée replied, 'No, a 14,' and went redder in the face.

Chris sighed and shook his head and said to the man: 'You're wasting your time, "Philip", we're skint, mate.'

But again, Philip ignored Chris and linked his arm to Aimée's arm and led her to various rooms in the store – with an annoyed, mumbling Chris in close pursuit. 'If there's one thing I can't stand, it's the hard sell,' Chris whispered as he followed his fiancée and a man he saw as a silver-tongued ponce.

'My name's Aimée,' she told Philip, her face cooling now, and my fiancé is Chris.'

'You should take a loving interest in this very special lady,' Philip suddenly said to Chris, who was taken aback at actually being acknowledged, 'your wedding day is the most important day of your life after your own birth.'

Chris felt ashamed by Philip's words for some reason; he wasn't usually that thin-skinned, but he explained, 'I *do* take interest in Aimée, but jobs have been a bit scarce recently, and I'm going to save up and have a decent wedding. It might take a few years for the type of wedding I want, like, but we'll get there.'

Philip slowed his gait as he walked with Aimée, and he halted, shook his head at Chris, and said, 'A late marriage – orphaned children.' He then turned away and walked over to another expensive wedding gown.

'Right barrel of laughs you are,' said Chris. He followed Aimée and Philip through several large rooms, and the size of these rooms hinted to Chris that there was something very odd about the store; in his job as a decorator he was good at estimating the dimensions of places, and Chris thought there simply wasn't enough cubic space in the premises to fit between the perfume shop next door and the hobby model kit store; if there were two levels, it would be a squeeze, but this store was all on one level. It just didn't add up in Chris's mind. Aimée meanwhile, was euphoric as she tried on the dress in a booth, and Philip even placed a silver tiara of pearls and emeralds on her head. He smiled at her reflection in the golden mirror and said, 'This brings out your beauty, Aimée, it really does,' and then Philip took hold of Aimée's hand and solemnly told her, 'This marriage will be forever.'

Philip then took Aimée into yet another room where there were shelves of bridal shoes, and he coordinated a pair with the wedding gown Aimée had shown the most interest in. 'Here we are, size 6 shoes,' said Philip, down on one knee, and Aimée slid her foot into the shoe. She tried on the other one, and now she stood there in the dress and tiara, and Chris stood in the doorway, and their eyes locked – and they were thinking the same thing – that they didn't have enough money to buy or hire the outfit – and Aimée became so choked up.

'Every head will turn in the church when you walk down that aisle, Aimée,' said Philip, and Aimée burst into tears. Philip's smile turned to an expression of shock, and he saw her stumble against the wall, and grabbed her gently and sat a sobbing Aimée down.

'We don't – ' she started to say, but was too strangled with sorrow to finish the sentence.

'We don't what?' Philip asked, and he took a folded silk handkerchief from his breast pocket and handed it to the tearful young lady.

'We don't – have the money,' gasped Aimée, 'we can't afford this.'

'Aimée – you don't pay a penny,' Philip begun, and Chris butted in: 'Our credit history is beyond in the red, it's in the infra red, lad, behave.'

'Chris, the wedding first, and all of the worldly concerns come afterwards,' said Philip, and he sat besides Aimée with his arm curled around her.

'Marriage is business nowadays, it's all down to money,' said Chris, and there was bitterness in his voice. 'And for what, like? Just a piece of paper – that's all marriage is.'

'Marriage is not just four bare legs in a bed,' retorted Philip, 'it is forever, Chris, and this one will be forever, there will be no *dismarriage*, and money will not enter into it.'

'So you're not going to make any money out of it then?' asked Chris, sarcastically, plunging his hands into the pockets of his tracksuit bottoms and looking at his reflection in one of the gilded mirrors.

Philip took Aimée back to the reception room and packed the wedding dress, tiara and shoes up in boxes tied with pink glittery bows. At the counter, Philip wrote something in what looked like a duplicate receipt book, and then he tore the white page out of the book and handed it to Aimée.

'As I explained, not a penny,' said Philip, and although he smiled, that smile did not connect with his eyes, which seemed sad to Aimée. Philip then asked Chris to carry the boxes and he walked behind the two of them with a hand placed gently on Aimée's back, and the doors swished open. 'I know the big day will be a dream! Good luck Aimée and Chris!' he shouted, and waved.

When Chris got about fifty feet from the store, he said to Aimée, 'Have you cottoned on yet?'

'What do you mean?' Aimée asked, feeling as if she would wake up from this dream at any moment.

Chris looked back and saw Philip had walked away from the front of his store. He whispered, 'I looked at the receipt, and it says just our first names and what we got off him, but there's no mention of anything else; no figures, no small print, or anything, and he doesn't know where we live or anything.'

'Didn't you give him our details?' asked Aimée, her eyebrows puckered with worry.

'Aimée, you were there with me, every step of the way,' said Chris with annoyance in his voice, 'and you know very well I didn't set up any direct debit or give any banking details, and you know very well we haven't got a credit card, so no – I didn't give him any details!'

'Oh no, have we just committed fraud?' asked Aimée, slowing down and looking back at Philip's Gowns.

'No, we haven't,' said Chris, 'he made a bloomer – or he felt sorry for you and gave you a dress that looks as if it would cost a few grand – '

'And the shoes and tiara,' added Aimée.

'Anyway, we didn't ask for the dress and that,' said Chris, his eyes darting towards a passing security guard, 'he thrust all the stuff upon us, and we assumed he'd taken our details.'

'Shall we go back?' asked Aimée.

'No,' barked Chris, 'and listen, don't you go blabbing to your mam and your sisters because someone might grass on us.'

'How am I going to explain where I got the dress and shoes from?' Aimée asked, startling to walk on again.

'Just tell them I borrowed the money;' said Chris, and then he shook his head and said, 'Aimée just give it a rest for now till we get home and we'll think of something.'

The couple got married in the following year in the cheapest wedding ever, with Chris hiring a suit. The honeymoon was in Talacre, North Wales. Chris won a few hundred pounds on the Grand National, and with his winnings he sneaked down to Philip's Gowns to pay something off, as Aimée seemed to live in mortal fear of being jailed for 'defrauding' Philip.

But Chris could not find Philip's Gowns, and no one in St John's Shopping Centre had heard of the store. Chris went home and told Aimée about the elusive store and she said he must have overlooked it because he had 'been looking too hard for it' – and she added, that, 'shops just don't vanish.'

'It wasn't there!' insisted Chris, 'No one had heard of the place. I went in the perfume shop that was right by it and the girl serving there said there had never been a wedding gown place next door. It's bizarre.'

'Maybe it was a bit too pricey and he moved somewhere else,' suggested Aimée.

'Aimée – listen,' said Chris, gazing hard into her eyes, 'it was never there, according to every trader I talked to.'

'Well that's ridiculous, isn't it?' Aimée told her husband. 'We went in there and I wore the dress and the shoes that man gave us.'

'I've got a bad feeling about this,' confessed Chris, 'I really have.'

'What do you mean – a bad feeling?' asked Aimée; she looked worried.

'Was that Philip fellah a ghost or something?' Chris pondered.

'Chris, there is nothing spooky about this,' Aimée assured him, 'we've got our bearings wrong; we *were* a bit flustered that day to say the least, weren't we?'

'I don't know – I just have this strange feeling about the whole thing,' said Chris.

'I'll go with you tomorrow, and I bet you I'll find the place,' said Aimée, and she smiled and got on her tiptoes to kiss her husband.

The couple went to St John's Precinct, and they could not find the store they had gone into that December afternoon. Chris was right; no one had heard of it. A woman said there was a Berketex Bride shop, but Aimée knew that was not the store they'd gone into. Eventually Aimée told Chris, 'You're right, love – this is creepy, let's go home.'

Then came another mystery which really shocked Aimée. She opened the wardrobe that evening and found the beautiful bridal outfit had vanished without a trace. The idea of something supernatural entering her bedroom and taking back the wedding gown, shoes and tiara really frightened Aimée. She told her mother what had happened and her mum said Philips Gowns had probably closed down and moved elsewhere, and that Aimée and Chris were making a mystery out of nothing. However, Aimée's auntie said Philip might have been the Devil, but Aimée felt that man had been some angel – but she's not sure what he was, and to this day she and Chris often wonder about the strange incident.

A BRAVE UNCLE

In March 1997 a 7-year-old girl in Huyton named Ellie fell ill, and told her mother a "horrible man in black with a scary face" kept visiting her in her bedroom both day and night, and the girl's mother and father were naturally sceptical about Ellie's claims; they thought she was merely having some type of hallucination because of her mysterious illness – until they too saw the apparition, a tall hooded figure in black with a skeletal face which stroked Ellie's head as she slept in her bed one night. The alarming figure vanished when the light was switched on. Both parents sensed the figure was the Grim Reaper, and that he might take away their beloved daughter; her mysterious illness seemed to be getting worse each day and the family doctor was at a loss to explain what was wrong with Ellie. The child was due to go for blood tests soon, but then something very strange took place. When Ellie's Uncle Steve, who worked as a joiner in Liverpool, heard about the ghostly Grim Reaper he rushed to his niece's house straight from work and stayed in her room, and about an hour before Ellie was due to go to bed, the "Reaper" apparition appeared. Steve's sister (Ellie's mum) saw it, but Steve pushed her out the room. Steve's sister managed to open the door about an inch, and her fear of the supernatural entity was countered by the heartfelt concern for her brother Steve, and she watched the unearthly proceedings.

He said to the figure, 'Do you remember me? [and gave his full name]' and the figure, which was facing away, slowly turned to him and in a whispering voice it said, 'I remember you well. You were supposed to be taken thirty years ago.'

'So it *is* you, then,' Steve replied, 'I fell in a canal and almost drowned; they dragged me out and laid me on the towpath - and I saw you leaning over me. Are you death or something? What the hell are you?'

The Reaper looked at Steve with a faint crooked smile on its emaciated chalk-white face.

With a tear in his eye, Steve asked, 'Why are you visiting my niece, eh?'

The Reaper told him: 'I'm waiting for the word, and then I shall take her. It doesn't concern you.'

An enraged Steve yelled, 'I don't know who you work for, but tell whoever it is I want to go instead of Ellie, alright? If you have to take someone, take me you bastard.'

The Reaper turned his back on Steve and said, 'This happens occasionally; people take other people's places; but it's frowned upon.'

But Steve swore and said, 'I'm single, I have no one, I wouldn't be missed, and I'm a selfish bastard! You'll take me; I'm thirty years overdue.'

Outside the room on the landing, Steve's sister was trembling as she watched the weird bargaining. She pinched herself because this all felt so unreal and dreamlike, and the pain in her pinched arm confirmed that sadly, it was really happening. She heard the entity say something that sounded like, 'Oh very well then!'

followed by a loud thump. She went in the room and found her brother lying there with an almost subcutaneous smile upon his face. The Reaper had gone. Steve's sobbing sister was joined by her husband, and he tried to feel for a pulse – there was none. He felt Steve's neck – no carotid pulse either. Steve was dead, yet his sister would not accept it and screamed at her husband, 'Phone an ambulance!'

An ambulance later arrived but they said Steve was dead and they could not resuscitate him.

Ellie then made a complete recovery and the sinister Reaper was seen no more. When I read about the Grim Reaper as a child, my young mind assumed he was just the personification of death – a symbol of the fate that awaits us all in the form of a figure – but I reasoned there would have to be millions of reapers assigned to all of the people who are dying every second of the day on our planet – so the Grim Reaper had to be a myth, along with the Tooth Fairy, Jack Frost and Cupid. That doesn't seem to be the case, though and I have quite a collection of Grim Reaper reports, as well as an assortment of reports featuring that other supposed embodiment of bad news – the banshee. For example, on 16 October 2016 at around 7:15pm, a 20-year-old girl named Clodagh was waiting for the bus on Townsend Lane to go to her Nan's, and the bus was taking forever to arrive - and the roads were unusually quiet. Clodagh thought there was something - something uncanny - hanging in the air on this night, and the full moon hanging over a nearby railway bridge was adding to the eeriness. Clodagh suddenly spotted the weird figure of a woman on the grassy central reservation to her left. The woman had long white hair which covered most of her face, and she was wearing an odd black ankle-length robe. She was almost bent over, as if she was looking for something in the grass, but then she straightened up. When this strangely-dressed woman started crying - and *wailing* - Clodagh had a bad feeling about her; the sounds she made as she wept seemed to be the product of two harmonizing voices, and Clodagh was only too glad when the bus turned up. She got on the vehicle and sat up the driver's end of the bus, still fearful of that creepy woman. When Clodagh reached her Nan's house, she saw an ambulance outside, and started to panic. Clodagh's Nan had suffered a stroke, but eventually recovered. When Clodagh later told her grandmother about the peculiar weeping woman she had seen on Townsend Lane, her Nan nodded with a knowing look and said it was the "Family Banshee" and described her to a tee. 'She always appears when something bad is going to happen,' said Clodagh's grandmother, and Clodagh – who – according to Nan - is of "Irish extraction" - still lives in mortal fear of seeing that sinister wailing harbinger of bad luck - and doom. Where do these Reapers and Banshees hail from? Are they Jungian archetypes – some psychic distillation of our ancient race memory which is found encoded in every human brain as a 'factory standard' of our psyche? Or are they as real as you and I? From the numerous people I have interviewed over the years who claim to have encountered the Grim Reaper, I would say that in a majority of cases, the Reaper doesn't seem to have killed anyone, but has acted more as a guide to a soul that is scheduled to leave the earthly life, and so he acts as an escort in some cases, and these types of shepherds are known in the world of the occult as a psychopomp. The Ancient Egyptian god Anubis, Charon, the ferryman of Greek mythology, the Hindu Deity Yama, and the Aztec god Xolotl are all examples of the psychopomp. I think there is a realm, beyond the confines of space and time, where some of these unchanging beings originate, and they seem to have been coming and going for millennia. We may never know the truth about them – unless, perhaps, they will call upon us one day to accompany our soul to the mysterious life in another realm.

RHEA AND HER SISTERS

In August 2015, a 19-year-old West Derby student named Leah was studying at the City of Liverpool College on Myrtle Street when she started seeing a lad named Sean – a fellow student at her college, and one evening, around midnight, after a night out, the couple got intimate and started to kiss in the shadows of Roscoe Street, which is just off Leece Street, facing St Luke's – the "bombed-out church". A fog rolled down the narrow confines of Roscoe Street as the couple kissed, and from the depths of that fog, Leah heard the easily recognisable voice of her 12-year-old sister, Harper, screaming for her and shrieking "Help!"

Leah broke away from Sean's kiss and said, 'That's my sister! What's she doing down here?' and she went to run up the street but Sean stopped her and said, 'No! It's a trick - phone your sister now! Phone her!'

'What do you mean?' asked a puzzled Leah, 'That's my sister Harper! Let go of me!' and she tried to break away from Sean but he insisted that the voice in the fog was not Harper's and Leah walked up a misty Roscoe Street but took out her mobile and swiftly called Harper from her mobile's contacts - and her sister answered almost immediately. Harper said she was in her room, listening to music - so the voice Leah had heard in the fog had obviously *not* been her sister's cries. Sean said his ex – Rhea - was into the occult - but stopped short of saying she was a witch, and with great sincerity Sean said Rhea was trying all sort of 'spells and tricks' to sabotage his relationship. The couple went into a popular nearby fast-food joint called Hot n' Tender, and they sat down in there and over fries and Pepsi Max Sean went into more detail about his ex-girlfriend Rhea. In the short time Leah had known Sean, he had struck her as a very honest and frank person who did not lie, and yet she had great difficulty believing his story about a former partner using spells to prevent him from having a relationship with her.

'Leah,' said Sean, 'I can tell from that look on your face that you think I'm either imagining all this or winding you up, but I give you my word, it's all true. There are people in this world who call themselves Wiccans and witches and so on, but Rhea is the *real thing*. Her own mother is afraid of her, and her two older sisters.'

'Are you sure you're not just being paranoid and that you might be reading things into coincidences and that?' queried Leah. She really loved Sean and hated the idea of doubting what he was saying; she found it alienating.

'You heard your sister's voice before in the fog – that was no coincidence or just someone else's voice – you were sure it was Harper,' said Sean, his large brown eyes pleading for Leah to believe him.

Leah nodded slowly as she recalled the voice she had heard and then she looked at the table top as she played with a plastic straw. 'Yes, it did sound like her, but – well – it could have just been someone who *sounded* like her.'

'She called for *you*,' said Sean, '– she called your name, and I know there are other Leah's but you were convinced it was your sister.'

The couple left Hot n' Tender and Sean went to his flat on Percy Street after he'd escorted Leah to a hackney cab which took her to her home in West Derby. Leah mentioned the fog to her mother that night, but she soon learned from her mum and others she spoke to that the fog had apparently only been on Roscoe Street - it had not even been misty anywhere else in Liverpool. Leah's older brother Kyle had been out that night down on Mathew Street, and he had seen no fog.

Leah had a long run of inordinate bad luck and weird and quite bizarre things happened to her, including a strange incident where an experienced hairdresser could not straighten Leah's hair at the salon, and red with embarrassment she had to finally give up. In the end, a frightened and frustrated Leah, finally believing she was being jinxed by Sean's former girlfriend, told Sean their relationship was over and he took it bad, but magnanimously said he understood. He dropped out of college, and Leah later saw him with a beautiful Goth girl in town one night in September of that year, down on Slater Street, but the couple didn't see Leah, and she had the overwhelming feeling she was looking at the "witch" Rhea, and that she'd finally got Sean back. Leah was so afraid of falling foul of the strange lady, she went to another area of town that night.

If Rhea was indeed a witch, she has many 'sisters' (for all witches are technically the daughters of Hecate

– the ancient goddess of witchcraft) here in Liverpool, where there are many covens. Here is another alleged incident concerning witchcraft. One night in August 2018, a Nigerian university student named Akin went out with a few mates to Liverpool's city centre and he seemed nervous around a particular group of girls. A friend noticed his odd behaviour and Akin said the girls were five witches disguised as young ladies and he added that in Nigeria, a section of the country's criminal code forbids witchcraft, and that the practice of it is punishable by a jail term. Akin said he had encountered actual witches on many occasions but he noticed that no one in Britain seemed to believe that witchcraft even existed. Akin's other friend, Jack, said it was a barmy superstition, and then Akin saw the five women he believed to be "witches" sit down in a circle on the pavement after they'd been to McDonald's, and Jack marched over to them with a poker-face expression, intending to ask them (all tongue-in-cheek) if they were witches, and he and his friends - and Akin - saw what looked like coloured auras flicker around the seated girls, and Jack felt something like an electric shock that went through his testicles, leaving him doubled-up in agony. The five girls carried on chatting and eating nonchalantly as they sat on the pavement, and Akin turned and walked away, whispering the Lord's Prayer in the Yoruba language of West Africa for protection. Akin's friends followed him, spooked by what they had seen - and Jack was still recovering from the apparent spell cast by the five witches which had left his testicles sore. Over the years I've had a few reports of women who are alleged to be witches, who always go in a group of five (and the number 5 features a lot in witchcraft, from the five points of a pentagram to the head and four limbs of a human which trace a pentagon when they are linked by a line) but beyond the number of the women I have no information on their nature. Here's another strange tale of what seems to have been witches at work.

One warm night in May 1955, a 30-year-old man was walking home from the Railway Inn pub, Wavertree, and as he passed three women standing at a doorway near Wavertree Gardens, he heard one woman mention the name of a woman he knew - a Muriel Brown - and another woman said, 'Muriel dead? No!' and then the other lady said, 'Yeah, she was a pillion passenger, and he hit the bus and I believe she had terrible injuries. She died...'

But the women became quiet when the drinker - Ian - who was returning home, slowed down to eavesdrop. When Ian got home he told his mother what he'd heard about Muriel Brown and she said, 'I haven't heard anything; you've misheard,' but on the following day, Muriel was killed while travelling as a pillion passenger on a motorbike - which hit a bus. Then, in August of that year, Ian was again walking home from a pub when he saw the same trinity of women "jangling" at the same doorway near the tenements, Wavertree Gardens, and on this occasion he heard them talking about a well-known headmaster in a local school who had dropped dead in front of morning assembly. Two days later the headmaster did indeed drop dead from a suspected heart attack in the assembly hall of the school. How had the three women known about the headmaster's death two days before it took place? Ian's mother then said, 'Go a different way home from now on; I've heard those women are three witches.' Ian was so afraid of his mother's words, he always went the long way home when he was returning from a pub. Here's another strange account that features suspected witches, and again, their number is three. On the Friday afternoon of 22 October 2004, a 26-year-old girl named Liv went into a card shop on Church Street and found the place deserted - not even a member of staff was about - and then she noticed three old women dressed in long black calf-length dresses. These women cornered Liv at the far end of the shop and she felt weak and started to panic, for although the women looked as if they were in their seventies, Liv felt they had a very sinister aura about them and they chattered to one another in what sounded like a real rural Lancashire dialect. Liv felt a paralysis in her legs. A young man entered the shop and the women, turned, startled and then the three of them literally vanished; they were there one moment, then gone. Liv felt the paralysis slowly lift and as the man went to walk out the shop she cried, 'Help!' and the young man came to her aid. He had only seen Liv, he said. I have three identical cases like this in my files were three women have been in apparently deserted shops, and one woman, who was pregnant, said one of the old women placed her hand on her tummy and said, 'Aww, she'll be like us,' and vanished. The child - a girl - was later obsessed with the occult when she reached her teens.

Here's another tale of witchery from my personal almanac of the unknown - Friday 30 June 2006 at around 5pm. The clientele of a well-known pub in Liverpool city centre could not take their collective eyes off a young lady who entered the premises with some type of crystal ball. She was joined by an almost identical lady a few minutes later; same bluish hair and similar tattoos - the drinkers said she could have been the first girl's sister. Anyway, a Liverpool businessman had been clockwatching that late afternoon, calculating how long it would take him to get home in the rush-hour - but now he felt as if some great black furry mitten had reached down and grasped the clockwork of time, muffling it - that was the only way he could describe what he felt as he watched that girl holding the crystal ball and sometimes rolling it between her hands. It was mesmerizing and the businessman had never felt as relaxed. It was the same with the two bouncers who had been getting ready for another Friday crowd to contend with soon - they were looking at the blue-haired girl and that crystal ball. All eyes were on that girl and sometimes her sister (or friend). A student couldn't avert his gaze from her, and a solicitor found herself entranced by the girl and that translucent orb, and a young tattoo artist who loved her pint hardly touched a drop as her attention was fixated on those two beguiling girls. Two girls holding hands, who normally had eyes for no one but each other, were also hypnotised by the blue haired woman and that sphere of gleaming crystal.

And then - bang! A boisterous biker burst into the pub with his usual gang and said, 'Did someone die in here? Why are you all quiet?'

Everyone snapped out of some spell, even the barman. The biker said they had all been standing there like statues. And the barman found the till empty, and each of the people who had been under some sort of spell found the cash missing from their wallets and purses. Their credit cards and debit cards were not touched - just banknotes.

The blue-haired girls and the crystal ball had gone. I have an idea who they were because they pulled the same trick in a Chester pub a few years prior. One of the witches has a Welsh nickname: Hwdwinc - "hoodwink" in English. The girls probably used a form of glamour - not to be confused with glamour as in alluring beauty - but its original meaning - a type of hex where the witch cloaks things - often herself - with illusions and the same spell can hypnotise a room full of people.

The biker and the gang had seen two girls rush out the pub before he and his gang went in. The next time you say "I was just going to say something then and I can't remember what it was now" or if you find the clock has jumped an hour or two - there just might be a witch in the vicinity.

There is often a thin line between witches – or the solitary witch who does not belong to a coven (or did belong and was banished) – and ghosts, and the following uncanny story illustrates this difficulty in interpretation.

On the Tuesday morning of 15 August, 2000 at around 4am, a couple in their twenties left a party in a very drunken state - not in the usual manner, via the front door, but by the skylight of their host's residence, because they had lost the keys to their flat next-door-but-one, but being summer they'd left their attic window open because of the heat, and so the couple, Rosa and Dominic, climbed through the skylight and staggered drunkenly across the rooftiles of the Wavertree house, and Rosa remarked on the full moon. Dominic hiccupped and to his girlfriend he said, 'May I have this dance?' and the silly request caused the couple to burst into laughter – but that laughter was very short-lived, because Rosa and Dominic heard someone else laughing; it was female laughter, and Rosa turned, thinking it was her madcap friend Grace - but it wasn't her; it was an unknown red-haired woman, possibly in her late forties to early fifties, and she was floating in mid-air above the rooftop, laughing hysterically now and Rosa was so stunned by the levitating figure she fell, then rolled down the slates of the slanting roof, and only the grip of Dominic saved her from falling to her death. He swore, and opened the attic window and pushed Rosa through it, and she bounced off the bed into a wardrobe, smashing the mirror but luckily she wasn't cut – all she sustained was a bruised forearm. Dominic dropped down onto the bed, and the couple, hearing the laughter getting nearer, ran from the flat and woke up most of the residents. The residents heard the laughter too but when they went upstairs to the couple's flat they saw no one. The couple had been drinking, and Dominic had indulged in a marijuana joint, so no one believed their account of the floating woman. The couple later compared notes regarding the eerie encounter. Rosa recalled the woman had on a long sleeveless black dress, bracelets, and her right arm was in a cast or bandaged and Dominic recalled the woman had on sandals and was red-haired. On the following morning, again around 4am, hysterical laughter was heard coming from the rooftop area of Rosa and Dominic's flat, and the other residents heard the laughter too, but saw no one. Rosa and Dominic peeped through the attic window and saw only the moon. A similar floating figure was seen in October of that same year in Mossley Hill, again on the night of a full moon. Are these sightings that of a witch? Or was the woman a floating airborne ghost? It's a real mystery. You will no doubt find more witches in this book, but let us wrap up this chapter for now with a brief, but intriguing account of a witch that was encountered in the middle of the last century.

Some years ago I interviewed a man who told me how, when he was 11, back in October 1950, he set out to shoot a witch that people had seen in the area where he lived - Deysbrook Lane, West Derby. He borrowed his dad's .22 air rifle and hid in one of the bushes that lined the lane. After a while the boy saw the witch standing on a wall on Deysbrook Lane. She lifted up and off the wall and hovered in the air, dressed in the archetypal pointed hat and long black robe - but had no broomstick. The boy was frightened but he got the witch in the sights of his air rifle and fired. His target cried out and the boy ran off. When he got home his older sister came into the house in tears - dressed in a witch's costume for Duck Apple Night. She said she'd been shot in her left leg, and had to go to hospital to have the .22 pellet removed. She said whoever shot her would lose their hair, and her brother's hair fell out. The boy's parents later divorced and his sister went to live with her mother, and the two of them were known to have dabbled in witchcraft and were part of a large West Derby coven. The man who told me the story was aged 80, and he pointed to his bald head and said 'It never grew back, and it wasn't hereditary baldness as there was no one in the family on both sides who was ever bald, and losing that hair at eleven was traumatising. I begged my sister to reverse the spell but she refused. She was a strange one.'

THE MAN IN RED

I've changed a few names in the following true story to protect the identity of two witnesses.

You have to be so careful when someone reports something paranormal; it takes guts for someone to make a telephone call to a radio station to report a ghost, and if someone mocks the person they understandably hang up. This happened in 2013 on a certain radio phone-in when a woman named Dawn called me on air and told me a man in a scarlet suit was haunting her house in the Swanside area of Liverpool. The DJ asked Dawn where Swanside was and she said it was an area of Knowsley near to Knotty Ash - and the DJ inanely made jokes about Ken Dodd. Dawn, thinking the DJ was not taking her seriously, hung up. I got Dawn's number from the radio station receptionist, apologised profusely to the caller for the idiotic DJ's flippant attitude, and looked into the case. Dawn was a divorced mother who lived with her 4-year-old son Archie on Mayfair Avenue, Swanside, and she told me how a few weeks before, in November of that year, Archie had excitedly told her he had seen "Father Christmas". Thinking her son simply had a vivid imagination, Dawn just smiled at Archie and remarked, 'Father Christmas is a bit early isn't he? He doesn't usually pay a visit until Christmas morning.'

Archie made a drawing of "Father Christmas" – but it was just a sketch of a tall slim man with dark hair in a red suit; no hat and no white fur trimmings, and he carried no sack. Dawn thought there was something eerie about the sketch, but still she put it down to her boy's imagination. A few days later, Dawn's mother Karen arrived at the house to mind Archie. Dawn had divorced her husband Callum a few years ago but he minded Archie every month; today, however, he had called to say he couldn't mind his lad because he had the flu. And so, "Nanny Karen" minded Archie as Dawn went to shop in town, and Karen brought him a big pack of coloured felt tip pens and a drawing book to keep him occupied. At 1pm, Karen went outside to put a bag of rubbish into the wheelie bin, and she was startled to hear the front door slam shut behind her. This was odd, as she knew she had put the safety catch on to prevent the door from locking if the wind happened to blow it shut. Karen tried to open the door without success and panicked. She looked through the letter box and there was Archie with his father, Callum, standing in the hallway, looking towards the front door – only Callum was dressed in a garish-looking red suit.

'I thought you couldn't come because of the flu?' Karen remarked to Callum, but he just stood there with an empty, deadpan expression on his face and did not utter a word of reply. Archie seemed to be cowering behind him, as if he was scared of Karen, and his Nan shouted, 'Archie – can you open the door?'

Archie shook his head and grabbed the left black-gloved hand of his father. Karen lost her patience; if this was some joke, it was a stupid one. She shouted 'Callum, what are you playing at? Open this bloody door!'

Thinking Callum might have had a breakdown, Karen rushed next door to the neighbour's house and a man in his fifties named Sammy answered. Karen told him what had happened and he went with her to the front door of the house, and now when Karen looked through the letter box, she saw Archie and his father had gone; the hall was empty. She panicked and begged Sammy to open the door. Sammy backed up and booted the door twice. The second kick did the trick and the door flew open. Sammy followed Karen into the house, but the father and child were nowhere to be seen. Sammy said, 'Listen! I can hear a child crying!'

The crying was coming from the loft. Sammy fetched a ladder from his house and came back, and he used it to access the loft. What he saw up there was bizarre. The little boy Archie was sitting cross-legged with his face in his hands sobbing, and there was a lit candle next to him. A vertical wooden support beam in the loft had been carved to make it resemble a Native American type of totem pole. The prominent part of this carving was of a scary face with bulging eyes and zig-zagged fanged teeth. Archie was leaning against the weird carved beam as he cried. Sammy carefully took the boy downstairs, and Archie told Karen that the man in the red suit had taken him up to the loft "with magic". Karen telephoned her son-in-law Callum but his girlfriend said he had been in bed all morning with a really bad bout of the flu. There was no way he could have left his home in Prescot and driven down to Archie's house, the girlfriend told Karen, and in a sarcastic tone she added that Callum certainly didn't possess a red suit. Three days later, Dawn had to go to her dentist, and a 17-year-old girl named Olivia minded Archie. Dawn Face-Timed Olivia as she sat in the dentist's waiting room and she waved to Archie on the screen – when she noticed a man in a red suit in the background, standing in the corner of the living room. She asked Olivia who he was, but when the babysitter turned to look, the figure vanished. Dawn's mother saw the man in red on another visit a week afterwards, and this time his face was that of a stranger. Karen screamed as he stood on the landing, and the uncanny visitor vanished. I researched the history of the house and believe the ghost may be that of a man who was in the entertainment business in the 1960s. He dabbled in hard core occultism and is said to have taken his own life because he wanted to see what was beyond this world. Dawn has since moved out of the house but I have a feeling the "red man" will be prowling those premises for some time.

DOPPELGANGERS AND
IDENTITY THIEVES

Regular readers of my books and newspaper columns will know I have touched on the mysterious subjects of doppelgängers over the years. The doppelgänger is a replica – an exact double in looks and often in clothing - of a person who is seen about town while the original person is elsewhere, and of course the activities of these carbon copy people naturally cause confusion and fear, as some believe that the doppelgänger is an omen of impending death for its flesh and blood counterpart – but in reality this is a very rare outcome. I have investigated many cases of doppelgängers and have tried to explain them as unconsciously projected thought-forms or simply the product of proficient impersonators, but the explanations always seem to fall flat, and I get the impression the eerie duplicates are carrying out some hidden agenda which we on this level of reality simply cannot fathom. A case in point is the doppelgänger of Church of England envoy Terry Waite, who was seen by numerous witnesses in Canterbury Cathedral in 1987, but at that time he was being held hostage in the Lebanon (and would not be freed until 1991) – yet people who knew Waite were sure it was him, but like many doppelgängers, the counterfeit Waite seemed to vanish after leaving the cathedral. This chapter is not just about doppelgängers but also other paranormal identity thieves. I'll start with a case that was reported to me many years ago.

The long-suffering Mrs Carson found the private detective Patrick McGinty in the personal services column of the *Liverpool Echo* that afternoon in November 1968. Finding McGinty's terms affordable, she invited the little Irishman to her home in Grassendale and told him she wanted proof that her 45-year-old banker husband Richard was seeing an 18-year-old hotel receptionist named Rose. McGinty was given a few photographs of Richard and a basic outline of the places he frequented with his young lover, along with his car registration. Each day at 5pm, McGinty would wait, parked up in his mustard-coloured Hillman Imp in an alleyway near to the bank where Richard worked off Dale Street, and he would keep a lookout for him and follow him in the hope of Richard leading him to his mistress. On one occasion early in the investigation, something bizarre took place which threw McGinty – he saw that Richard had an *exact double* – and this replica hailed a hackney cab which followed Richard's Jaguar to the Adelphi Hotel. McGinty couldn't be sure which Richard was the real one, and he phoned Richard's wife and asked if her husband had a twin. She assured McGinty he hadn't, and asked the Irishman if he'd been drinking. McGinty took out his trusty old miniature Minox Riga camera and took a picture of the 'two Richards' in the hotel foyer. The flash startled Richard and his dead ringer and McGinty had to pretend he was taking a picture of a young lady. Richard's wife was flabbergasted by her husband's double, but could not explain it. Days later, McGinty discovered the hotel room where Richard and Rose were staying, and cheekily tried the door, and it happened to be unlocked. He went into the room, found the couple in bed, and took a picture of them. Now he had his proof. Richard ran after him stark naked but McGinty was too swift for him. He left the hotel – and passed the double again on Ranelagh Place. He pretended to check his watch, and he turned and saw the double was looking at him with suspicion.

'May I ask if you're related to Richard Carson?' queried McGinty, walking to the living carbon copy. The man produced a knife, but two policemen on the beat saw the weapon and subdued the clone of Richard Carson – and then they realised he was not there. He had vanished into thin air. The police eventually left, completely baffled, but McGinty had a fanciful thought. Had that man been a doppelgänger – or a wraith as they called them in his native Ireland? These supernatural impersonators could commit a murder and vanish, leaving their flesh and blood counterpart to face the dire consequences; had that double been on his way to kill Rose, just to frame Richard for the murder?

The second case in this chapter is rather strange in that the doppelgänger of the story seems to have been some type of entity connected to an object. It really is a baffling one. In December 2017, a student in her twenties named Kate moved into a house on Maiden Lane, Clubmoor, with her boyfriend, and one day she saw a gold-framed picture in a second hand shop, and intended to put a picture of herself and her boyfriend in it but when she removed the original print (of flowers) she saw an oil-painting of a woman who looked exactly like her. Kate's boyfriend remarked,

'Kate - that's you - she looks like your double.'

Kate removed the painting, which was unsigned, and put a photo of herself with Joel, her boyfriend, in the picture, and not long afterwards, Kate's double was seen by Joel and a few friends, walking down Larkhill Lane and Adshead Road (both roads in Clubmoor) - and intriguingly, the double always wore the same clothes Kate was currently wearing on the days it was spotted. Kate thought Joel was pulling her leg at first, but then on Christmas Eve she was out walking to a chippy on Knocklaid Road when she saw the mirror image of her creepy double coming towards her. Kate was so spooked, she turned and ran - and heard the doppelgänger running after her. The living replica of Kate eventually gave up the chase, and Kate took the picture down, put the original picture of her lookalike back in the frame, and threw it in the wheelie bin. After that, the double was seen no more. The story behind the picture therefore remains unknown.

In December 2004, a 17-year-old girl named Molly was alone in her home on Childwall's Okehampton Road while her parents were at a friend's party up in Crosby. Molly's friend Abi (also aged 17) came over to stay with her for company, and as soon as Abi entered the house she scared Molly by saying she'd seen a man with no face standing outside in the drive. Molly thought her friend was joking because Abi had a slight smirk on her face, but Abi said this was with shock. She insisted she had seen a man in a raincoat with no face standing in the driveway, looking up at the bedroom windows.

'Abi, how can he have been *looking* up at the windows if he had no eyes and that?' Molly asked, thinking her friend would admit she was just making up a scatty story to scare her, but Abi suggested looking out the window to see if he was still there. The girls went upstairs and Abi peeped out then said, 'Oh my God! He's still there!' and so Molly shoved her aside and looked out - and there was indeed a man with a blank face, adjusting his collar with his smooth featureless face upturned in Molly's direction. Molly said, 'It's probably a mask,' and she looked very scared. Then the landline rang and Molly picked it up, and a male voice she had never heard before said, 'Molly, put the bolt on your door; your life is in danger. That thing with no face is going to pretend it's your father.' And a suspicious Molly asked, 'Who are you?' to which the man replied, 'My name's Jason - I'm something of an expert on these things. Do not open the door because - ' And Molly hung up and ran downstairs to put the bolt on. She then heard her father's voice outside saying, 'Molly open the door, it's me your dad.' Molly swore at him and said she'd call the police, and the man outside tried to kick the door in. The police were called out, and when they heard about a faceless man and someone called Jason warning Molly her life was in danger - well, they weren't too pleased to put it mildly. Molly's parents came home and saw the dents and marks on the front door, made by the unknown man. Molly's former boyfriend was blamed, but a faceless man was later seen in another part of Childwall. I have several scanty reports about these entities, and they seem to be a type of doppelgänger that can impersonate anyone.

Here's one strange case I remember well, as so many people saw the apparition; Wednesday 26 September

2007 at around 1am, two sisters were returning home from a friend's house, and as they walked down Gateacre Park Drive (which was brightly lit by the full moon), one of the sisters said she could hear a voice shouting her, and the voice sounded like that of her mum, who had died the month before. The other sister then heard the same faint voice calling her name - and then they saw an eerily familiar figure - that of their late mother, waving to them about 100 yards away. 'It's me! Come here!' she shouted, and the sisters just sensed that the person only looked - and sounded - like their late beloved mum - but who on earth was the lookalike? How did she know them? As the figure came nearer the sisters saw it was, without a doubt, their mum but they still sensed it was something sinister in disguise, and the figure ran at the sisters, and they turned and ran. The doppelgänger - or whatever it was - chased them some distance, and the sisters hid behind the hedge of a garden, and saw the shadow of their pursuer loiter by them. 'Why are you hiding from your old mum?' came a voice, and now it sounded a bit 'off' to the frightened sisters - like the voice of an impersonator. The owner of the house came out and asked the girls what they were doing, and they ran past him into his house. They told the man about the weird thing pretending to be their mother and he went to the window and saw her standing on the low front garden wall, gazing at him. She then ran off. Over the next few nights the weird double was seen by a lot of people over quite some area of Gateacre, but just who or what the entity was remains a mystery. Another doppelgänger masquerading as a family member was encountered on Sunday 3 October 1976, when an 18-

year-old girl named Kate was helping her grandfather on his plot at the Thingwall Road Allotments, and around 6pm, Kate decided she'd go home for her tea, but her grandfather shouted from inside his hut, 'I've thrown my back out, Kate, can you rub my shoulder blades please love?'

Kate was just going to go into the hut - which looked darker inside than usual - when she suddenly had the bizarre feeling that the man in the shed was not her grandfather - and she took a step back and did not enter.

'What's to do, love?' came a voice from the hut, and Kate turned her head and looked up the long path on the allotment; and there was her grandfather walking down it. He waved at her as he approached. Who then, was the man in the gloomy interior of the hut? He sounded like Kate's grandfather, but she saw that he had not turned to face her - as if he was hiding his face. Kate ran to her grandfather and told him about the creepy impostor, and he and his grand-daughter heard a bang as the person in the hut closed the door on himself. When Kate's granddad opened that door, he found the hut empty; but one of his old pipes was lit and resting in an ashtray. Kate thought she felt something brush against her in the hut, and so she felt that whoever and whatever that mimic was, it was still there, yet Kate and her grandfather could see no one. The pipe was put out and the hut was locked up. It's possible the impersonator was some doppelgänger who was out to lure Kate into that hut for some shady reason. What scared Kate was the way she had assumed that her grandfather had been in that hut for a few hours, but recalled how he never came out of it -

he had talked to her from inside the hut.

Many years ago in the 1980s, a 20-year-old Wavertree woman named Hailey boarded a bus on Rathbone Road one dismal rainy Saturday afternoon. She was going to her friend Donna's house up in Clubmoor. A woman in her forties was seated opposite Hailey and she was ranting on about how men are no good and how they are unfaithful when she looked at Hailey - and became quiet. The eyes of Hailey and the stranger met, and Hailey first noticed the woman had a birthmark under her left eye – a tiny mole, and it happened to be in the same place as Hailey's birthmark - and then came a surreal shock. Hailey felt she was somehow looking at her older self; it was a bizarre thought, and yet Hailey just knew somehow she was seeing how she'd turn out in her forties. The woman looked at her with such sadness, Hailey cut her journey short and got off the bus at the next stop. Hailey increasingly had the weird feeling that, if she continued going with her current boyfriend, Lawrence, she'd end up having a dog's life and would end up alone and bitter like the woman on the bus, and acrimonious towards all men. Hailey looked at the bus as it pulled away - and could not see the woman she believed to be her future self; it was as if she'd vanished.

After Hailey had given Lawrence the big elbow, she met a man named Greg, and he treated her like a princess, and today they are still married. It's possible that the woman on the bus just *looked* like Hailey and nothing more, but to this day, Hailey believes she had been looking at her older self in some parallel future, and that the encounter had served as a powerful warning. In a way then, if Hailey's theory is correct, then she had met a doppelgänger of sorts that day on the bus.

And finally, the following story about a doppelgänger is unusual in that the double possibly helped save a life. In the summer of 1971, Michael, a 9-year-old boy from Kensington's Molyneux Road told his mother there was a lad who looked just like him and even dressed like him, and he had seen him three times over the past few days. 'God help us, Michael,' laughed the boy's mother as she did the washing up, '*one* of you is a handful enough.'

'Mam, I'm not lyin', honest, he's like my exact double,' insisted Michael. The boy then mentioned that his best friend Jimmy had also seen the boy who looked like him.

'You all look the same with those short back and side haircuts and school uniforms, Michael,' the lad's mum said, dismissively. That very day, Michael went to play with Jimmy, who lived on Smithdown Lane, and they decided to climb over a wall which gave access to a disused railway track and a grassy embankment. The two lads headed for a tunnel, pretending they were soldiers. Jimmy held the leg of an old chair as if it was a machine gun and Michael was ready to throw a large smooth pebble down the embankment, imagining it was a hand grenade. All of a sudden, the lads heard a man's deep voice shout, 'Come here!'

Jimmy sprinted through the deep grass of the embankment in his pumps and was soon scaling the wall. Michael fell over as he ran from the adult, and he turned to see a giant of a man with a huge head of long blonde hair and a sandy beard, and he wore a scruffy grey heavily creased jacket and an open shirt. He had been lying in the grass, and Michael thought he saw a green bottle in the man's right hand. 'Come here, I'm not going to hurt you!' the huge stranger said, but Michael then noticed that the man was fumbling with his trouser zip.

'My Dad's over there!' Michael yelled, but the man was smiling, and Michael was terrified, because he didn't think he'd be able to climb up the wall in time to make his escape. Michael then noticed his exact double – the boy who looked as if he was his twin, run from behind the bearded stranger, and the man noticed the boy too, and because he was nearer to the man than Michael, the boy was chased. Despite the man's large frame, he could certainly run, and he ran down the embankment towards the railway track, gaining on Michael's doppelgänger. Michael turned and ran, and he climbed up the wall and jumped down onto Queensland Street, where he saw Jimmy across the road. The two lads ran off and Jimmy told his father about the man who had chased him and Michael, and how he had been fumbling with his flies – and Jimmy's dad, an amateur boxer, climbed on top of the wall, but could see only swaying grass on the embankment. The man had vanished. When Michael got home, he told his mother and father about the man who had chased him and how his mysterious double had saved him from a fate which was too terrible to dwell upon. Michael's father was furious, and he scolded the boy for playing on that disused railway line and embankment. The boy's parents paid no heed to the account of the double who had saved Michael from a sexual assault which might have ended in the boy being murdered. Michael never again played down on the "Reller" as the local kids called the derelict railway, and he never saw his intriguing doppelgänger again after that eventful summer's day.

STRANGE THINGS AMONG US

This chapter covers strange and bizarre beings that intrude upon our little corner of reality before returning to wherever they originated, leaving behind terrified and disoriented witnesses who, more often than not, are subsequently disbelieved, branded as attention-seekers or told they were dreaming, drunk or hallucinating. The unidentified intruders in this chapter have been perceived as "bogeymen", faeries, goblins, demons, "cryptids", UFO occupants and perhaps even religious visions; they may have various origins from parallel worlds in other dimensions, and some may be from the countless worlds of this vast cosmos. On the scale of the universe, the earth is like a subatomic quark particle in size and significance, but of course it happens to be our home, and we are powerless to stop any extraterrestrials from landing here and mingling with us, sometimes in the guise of a human. There are about 93 international borders on earth, some of which are crossed by illegal migrants every day, but there are no such borders and checkpoints in orbital space to prevent interstellar visitors coming to earth; our world is an open door to extraterrestrial beings, and if they are clever enough to possess the technology to cross light years of space to get here, I am sure they will have no problem slipping unnoticed through our primitive radar. The same situation exists with beings that can travel through time, perhaps from a distant future where time travel has been achieved; they could visit wherever they wished in our history. The vast realms of time and space could not be policed or scanned with our present technology, and hardly a year goes by without an astronomer (and often an amateur one) spotting a previously unknown comet or asteroid swinging dangerously close to the earth from the depths of space. When we look at the total lack of security which exists around our home planet, perhaps it shouldn't be too much of a surprise when we hear of strange beings being encountered among us. That's just on the 'space front' – but what of the other frontier – time itself? For many years, three dimensions of space (length, width and height) plus one of time, were the norm in classical physics, but there are now plausible theories which say that there may be many more *hidden* dimensions, and in one such theory – Supersymmetric String Theory – ten dimensions are postulated (although I personally have doubts about this theory and believe the Kaluza-Klein theory of a 5-dimensional space to be quite likely). We know very little about the very fabric of space and time, and one of the surprising solutions of the Einstein field equations is the wormhole – two openings in the space-time fabric which, if stabilized so they do not collapse, would allow a person, or a signal, or a robotic probe, to travel a few miles or a few million light-years from A to B via the wormhole in a short instant, thus getting round the annoying problem of faster-than-light travel, which is supposedly impossible, according to modern physics. Wormholes are not the stuff of science fiction; they are possible (albeit hypothetical) structures that are scientifically known as Einstein-Rosen Bridges, and they might be the only way we can ever leave this solar system and find other inhabitable worlds in other parts of the galaxy or the universe beyond *within a reasonable time-span*. But such wormholes could also allow travel into the past, future or even parallel worlds. This is a big and very old universe we are living in, and there will be life forms out there that have been around for a lot longer than us humans, and they will be able to travel immense distances in the twinkling of an eye via short-cuts in time and space via wormholes. Once upon a time, we humans only moved about in mostly two dimensions – forwards and backwards - and side to side (discounting trips up mountains and descents into valleys), but when we invented the balloon and later the airplane, we travelled in the third dimension of space, and likewise we will one day be able to move through the fourth and fifth dimensions – but what if life forms from elsewhere are already doing this? They might be responsible for some of the reports in this chapter of the unearthly beings who visit us out the blue. Let's start with a case in point.

On 21 March 2005, at a house on Bentham Drive, Childwall, Leah, a 32-year-old woman who originally hailed from Dovecot, let her 4-year-old daughter Bella sleep with her because the girl had said she'd had another nightmare about "the Wobbly Man" – a mere bogeyman that haunted the child's imagination as far as Leah was concerned. Leah told Bella that Mr Wobbly wasn't real and that no monsters were allowed in the house because the cat, Parker, would frighten them off. Bella said the Wobbly Man was real and that he could get in the house by coming through the wall. Leah eventually calmed her daughter down and she fell asleep beside her as they both watched cartoons on the telly. Around half-past one that morning, Leah dozed off after she'd texted her husband who was working nights as a security guard.

Just after 2 am, Bella woke her mum up and pointed to the wall, and there was a weird shadow of something with two arms and two legs, but the limbs looked long and rubbery, and they squirmed like tentacles. Leah realised something at the window was casting that shadow on the wall and she turned to see what it was - and immediately froze in shock.

"That's him, mummy," said Bella, pointing at the freak pinkish rubbery-looking entity at the window. It was standing on the window ledge outside and its whole body and torso undulated and its arms and legs wriggled and writhed. The surreal, terrifying creature was about six feet in height, from the top of its bald head (which was devoid of ears) to the end of its tentacles. In a state of mute terror, Leah picked up her daughter and swiftly went downstairs. She called her husband and told him what she had seen and he thought she was joking at first. Realising his wife had experienced something uncanny, the security guard got permission to go home, and by now the thing at the window had vanished, but Leah's husband knew his wife – and child – were not liars, but he couldn't explain what the thing had been. Fortunately "Mr Wobbly" never returned.

A being of an identical description to the highly flexible entity encountered in Childwall has been seen right across our region, and a high number of incidents have been in Knowsley, but first we have to go to Tuebrook. In April 2010, a 10-year-old girl named

Chantelle invited her best friend Serena – who lived in Halewood – to a sleepover at her house on Lisburn Lane, Tuebrook. The girls watched their favourite TV shows in Chantelle's room and ate pizza and drank soft drinks until around midnight, when they finally fell fast asleep. Both girls awoke around 3 am to what sounded like a baby crying somewhere, and Serena said the sounds were coming from outside. The girls went to the window and looked through the blinds – and they both saw something which would give them nightmares for years. Standing on the kerb on Lisburn Lane was a weird figure. It looked partly human, only it had long wriggling arms that resembled the tentacles of an octopus. It walked along on all fours with a strange gait, and Chantelle let out a scream.

The unearthly creature jumped, startled by the scream, and turned to look at the window. Serena saw that the head was bald, and looked shiny – almost plastic – and it had two large eyes and a long nose. Before the girls could get away from the window, the thing ran at a phenomenal speed towards Chantelle's house and it tried to climb the wall to the window. The girls became hysterical when they saw the entity do this, and Chantelle's parents and her two older brothers burst into the room. The adults all saw nothing, and the father went outside and said there was a strong smell like ammonia hanging in the air. The whole thing was dismissed as a nightmare, but when Serena went home, she had the continual feeling she was being watched by something. Three days later, Serena saw the terrifying entity with the tentacles for arms and legs outside her house on Baileys Lane as the girl stood on her doorstep, looking for her cat at

9:30pm. It was peeping over the fence at her. Serena screamed, backed into the house and slammed the door. The child's mother looked through the parlour window and saw a head peeping at her over the top of a telephone junction box, but believed it was just a youth messing about.

That night, Serena's father told his wife that he had seen the thing his daughter had described at the end of the back garden around 8pm, and at first he thought he was seeing things. He described the tentacular limbs of the creature – seen in silhouette – as he was getting a breath of fresh air in the kitchen doorway. The weird being slithered over the fence and vanished into the darkness. Thankfully, Serena, her friend Chantelle and the families of the girls saw or heard no more of the creepy entity – but others apparently did. In May, 1974, at a house on Manor Farm Road, Huyton, a 14-year-old boy named Carl was awakened in his bed one night around 11:45pm to the sounds of something metallic. To Carl's ears, it sounded like someone dropping the lid of a dustbin on the floor of his bedroom. The boy turned on his bedside lamp, and the shock of seeing the bizarre and terrifying creature at the bottom of his bed struck him with paralysis; he was literally scared rigid. The thing vaguely resembled a man, only it was standing on four tentacle-like limbs, and it had a long thin pointed nose. It hissed at Carl, before vanishing, leaving a very strong, almost suffocating aroma similar to the smell of bleach in its wake – could this be the same chemical odour Serena's father described as being like ammonia in the Baileys Lane encounter at Halewood? The teenager Carl regained the power to move and ran to his mum and dad downstairs. Predictably, the adults said Carl had just had a nightmare, but to this day, he knows that thing – whatever it was – was real. Another unknown creature that was regarded as equally real was encountered on the glacial evening of Thursday 15 December, 2022 on Liverpool's Lord Street around 11:40pm. Three young men were walking from a pub, having a discussion about what club they should visit, when one of them started mocking an homeless man of about forty who was sitting on a blanket on the corner of Lord Street and Doran's Lane (which is a rather narrow alleyway). The down and out shouted something unintelligible back to the young man, and as a result two of the young men ran to the man and one of them kicked his leg, and right before the eyes of the three youths, the homeless man allegedly changed - literally metamorphosed - into something demonic. The destitute man's eyes started to glow, and his mouth opened wide to show a frightening array of pointed teeth. A group of young ladies passing also saw the terrifying transfiguration of the itinerant, and screamed as he ran off towards Derby Square, where he vanished, leaving a sleeping bag and trilby full of coins behind. The uncanny incident was said to have been captured on a security camera but no more was heard about this intriguing case. Was something from elsewhere living among us under the guise of an outcast of society? For what purpose? And if it was disguised as an homeless man, why did the thing blow its cover by becoming angry at the men who mocked it? Or was it some defence mechanism? Is the thing still among us? We have so many questions that will probably go unanswered.

Some very strange life-forms stalked this world of ours in an unimaginably remote time, billions of years before the Biblical Genesis, and I am not just talking about the dinosaurs; they are recent compared to the things that lurked in the Hadean Eon – an infernal nightmare age when the planet was born out of utter chaos and waged gravitational tidal wars with the dangerously close orbiting Moon. Occultists dating back to Ancient Egypt have alluded to the Ancient Ones who roamed the volcanic continents and radioactive seas in those times, and mysterious long-lost races carved the forms of some of these entities into rock – perhaps to warn us. One of these Hadean races are said to be the most evil things that ever lived, and are invariably depicted as spindly humanoids with seven heads, their seven corresponding necks resembling the multi-branched candelabra of the Hebrew faith. The images of the same seven-headed monstrosity have been found on the cave walls of the Khakassia region of Siberia, and carvings over 5,000 years old have also been unearthed of the alien-looking entity in Mexico, India, South America and many other places. The being with seven heads has a specific name, which I will withhold, because in the occult, it is said that even the mention of the antediluvian abomination's name can sometimes invoke it and bring it into our time period; the invocation of entities and spirits by the mere mentioning of their name is a subject well known in the occult as "names of power" – an ancient belief that the name of a person or spirit contains the essence of their being, and to call out a name in a certain way during a spell is a way of accessing the power of the person or spirit. The name of God has been kept secret for millennia because the mere utterance of the name is said to unleash unimaginable power.

In 2010, a lady who had moved into a semi-detached house on Druids Cross Road (near Calderstones Park), tried to paint over the weird image of a seven-headed figure that had 'bled' through the wallpaper in her daughter's room because the image was giving her girl terrible nightmares. The image of the 7-headed figure came through many coats of paint, and even heavy wallpaper that was put up by a professional decorator. When I saw the seven-headed figure on that wall, I told the woman that the image was of something very ancient that had been seen on walls in various houses across the North West in the 1970s. I also told her that the 7-headed hydra-like figure was feared in every culture. Not long after this, the entity appeared in solid-form in the bedroom of the daughter, and she was so afraid, she suffered a seizure and she and her mother ended up leaving the house. Previous occupants of the house had probably been into the occult and may have inadvertently conjured up the Hadean at some time. I mentioned the terrifying entity on a radio program broadcast by BBC Radio Merseyside in 2008, and a man named Tim called me on air and said he had seen a sinister shadow cast onto the walls of his study at his house on Sunbourne Road, Aigburth, one summer morning in July 1978. The study was on the third floor and the window was facing the east. The sun was rising and throwing its rays through the window of the study onto the walls. Tim had been up since 5am, intending to put in a few hours of study for his Open University course, and around 5:30am as the sun came up, Tim went to the blinds, intending to close them because the solar blaze was dazzling him, and he turned upon hearing his tabby cat hissing at something behind him; the cat was crouched in a state of fear as it looked at the strange clear shadow on the wall. Tim described it as thus: 'The shadow looked bizarre – it was of a man with two arms and two legs, but the neck was about three or four times the length of a normal neck, and branching off the neck on slightly thinner necks were six heads. The seventh head was at the top of the elongated neck, and the heads seemed to quiver. I looked back at the window to see what was casting this creepy shadow but there was nothing there, just the newly-risen sun shining its light in. When I looked back at the wall, the shadow of the thing with seven heads at gone, and the cat hid under my desk. I let him out of the study and he refused to go in there for weeks.'

Tim said he had a very unsettling feeling of being watched after that morning, and there was a bad atmosphere in that room – of something evil being in there – which remained until he moved out of the house a few years later. I traced the family that had lived in the house before Tim and they had never experienced anything supernatural at the place – but – Margaret, a woman who lived next door to the house in question said a decorator who stripped her bedroom walls in 1979 had uncovered paintings of weird figures, described by Margaret as being "similar to the little men you see carved in those Ancient Egyptian walls in the pyramids". Perhaps then, the seven-headed entity which cast its shadow on the wall of Tim's study that morning was from the house next door to his home.

There is one alleged supernatural incident I never got to the bottom of which stands out clearly in my mind from decades ago, and it's still quite difficult to explain, but it belongs squarely in this chapter because it is without doubt one of the strangest things that was ever reported as being among us, and very menacing with it. It was in the winter of 2002, and I was in the studios of BBC Radio Merseyside on a foggy afternoon, ready to go on the Billy Butler Show to talk about local mysteries, when someone told me that the author and presenter Brian Jacques, famous nowadays for his immensely popular *Redwall* series of novels, had mentioned that something strange had happened outside the radio station near Whitechapel – something supernatural. I wondered what this strange thing was, and when I was on air, I mentioned it to Billy Butler, and he in turn asked the listeners if they knew anything about the purported incident. The station's switchboard lit up, and caller after caller mentioned what had happened. On Whitechapel, near to Holy Corner (so called because it is a cross formed by the junction of Whitechapel with Paradise, Church and Lord Streets), a woman in her forties had left the Mothercare store and had been walking through the thick fog in the direction of Stanley Street, when she let out a scream. People then saw what looked like the sinister silhouette in the swirling grey fog of a huge figure in a hooded robe, and it resembled the archetypal Grim Reaper (minus the scythe). This entity seemed to slide out of a wall and lunge at the woman, who fell down onto the pavement, as if her legs had gone weak with terror.

The eerie, unearthly figure, described as being

around 7 feet in height, leaned over the woman on the pavement who was screaming, "Get away from me!"

Those nearer to the creepy entity said they couldn't move with fear because the thing just gave off an aura of utter dread. The woman on the floor screamed for help, and two women bravely started to approach her, when the thing darted away into the fog, but it came back a few moments later, stooped by the woman again, and made several attempts to grab at her with what looked like skeletal hands, but upon seeing the two courageous women closing in on the distressed lady on the floor, it backed away then vanished into thin air. Some thought it was a publicity stunt or a hoax but were at a loss to explain the "Reaper's" literal vanishing act, and the hoaxer would have had to have been about seven feet in height or more. The woman on the floor was helped up, but was so upset, she was sobbing and incoherent, and a thoughtful hackney cabby took her home to the Childwall area free of charge, and throughout the journey the lady babbled incoherently and the cabby could not make sense of what she was saying. Nothing more is known of the woman or the thing that seemed to attack her.

The "Little People" are among the strange beings that occasionally appear among the human clan, and they are included in the 'mythology' of most cultures, from the Native Peoples of North America, to Ireland, Britain, Europe and Africa, to the Philippines and Hawaii, and almost every year I also receive reports of undersized entities remarkably similar to beings that would have once been regarded as members of the Little People - their sizes ranging from just a couple of inches to three feet in height. Here's one of the reports

I looked into a few years ago.

As the clock of the Municipal Buildings struck midnight on Sunday, 12 March 2018, two young women named Kait and Faye, both in their tender twenty-second year, stood swaying on Dale Street, their weary souls longing for a taxi to whisk them away to the comforts of home. However, their journey was far from over, as fate had other plans for them. As Faye stumbled down an alleyway, her body overwhelmed by nausea from drinking too many cocktails, Kait remained behind, alone on the dark street. In a moment of sudden stillness, she heard a voice, sweet and childlike which whispered, 'Hello lovely.'

To her utter surprise, Kait found herself surrounded by a curious band of figures, all of them no taller than a child, wearing colourful pointed caps and clothes of green and brown reminiscent of elves or leprechauns. But what struck her with even greater bewilderment was the realization that these beings wore no masks - their strange round impish faces were real. Some of these little individuals hugged Kait's legs, while others made crude gestures and comments as they looked up her skirt. Panic set in as Kait cried out for her friend, Faye, but to no avail. One of the little men, speaking with a charming Irish brogue, quipped, 'Never mind Faye, we're your friends now!'

As Kait recoiled to the sensation of a forceful kiss to her kneecap, the group of pint-sized people joined hands, encircling her in a chain, and they began to move in a strange dance. The tune they collectively hummed was peculiar, and some chanted, 'You're coming with us, you're coming with us,' with a very hypnotic effect that made Kait believe she was being magically induced to join their mirthful throng. Dale Street faded into the background as the diminutive beings spun around Kait, their voices growing louder, and their movements more frenzied. The ground beneath her feet seemed to shift, and she found herself unable to move. It was then that she heard Faye's voice, swearing in the distance. Faye's voice seemed to break the spell of influence the little people had cast over Kait, and they vanished with a sigh, leaving Kait to gasp for air, bewildered and shaken to her core. Faye, her friend, saw a golden aura surrounding Kait, but, it transpired, she had not seen the strange entities that had surrounded her friend. As the girls made their way to a taxi rank, Kait struggled to articulate what had transpired. She was babbling, her words disjointed, and her friend could hardly make sense of what she was saying. It wasn't until several minutes had passed that Kait was able to convey the events of that eerie encounter to Faye, and she assured Faye that she had not taken any pills at the clubs they had been to.

Days later, on St. Patrick's Day, a surprise visitor arrived at Kait's mother's door - a former lover named Liam, who was, in fact, Kait's real father. Liam hailed from Limerick, and Kait felt that her Celtic blood had somehow drawn the little beings to her that fateful morning. She confided in her newfound father, who listened carefully to her story before issuing a grave warning, 'They've been watching you, and they may have marked you, which means they could try and take you again. Perhaps you should stay with a group of people when you're out, love.' And when she heard that ominous warning, Kait had the unsettling feeling

that her life would never be the same again.

The following story was forwarded to me many years ago, and the witness was a very down to earth lady. The strange incident unfolded around midnight on 7 January 1999 at a house on Childwall's Burford Road. A 5-year-old girl climbed over the child safety gate across the doorway of her bedroom and went downstairs, intending to pinch some biscuits from the kitchen cupboard, but on her way to the kitchen the child happened to see something very odd in the living room - what she perceived as a tiny man in a microwave oven which was lit up inside. The man was waving to the girl and laughing. The girl turned and ran up the stairs to the room of her parents and awakened them to tell them what she had seen. Per usual, the mum - Dawn - told her daughter she'd been dreaming, and scolded the child for climbing over the safety gate. The child seemed very upset and so she was allowed to sleep between her mother and father that night. Just under a week later, Dawn got out of bed at 4am because her cat was crying outside at the front door because of the subzero cold, and after she had let the feline in, it ran upstairs to Dawn's bedroom, and Dawn was about to follow the cat when she saw a light out the corner of her eye. An oval-shaped machine, about four feet in length with a bright yellow window in it, was in the middle of the living room. As Dawn wondered what the thing was, she saw the silhouette of what looked like a man who would have been about 5 inches in height, and he was in the window of the object, waving at her. He said something that sounded like "I've got to get out of here!" but Dawn sensed something bad was about to happen and she switched on the hallway light - and the oval-shaped craft, and the little man, instantly vanished. The window did look like the window of a microwave oven, exactly as Dawn's daughter had described it. What the thing was remains unknown. Was the pocket-sized stranger from some other world, or was he perhaps a traveller from the future? If that 'microwave' was some time machine, it would seem to expand and contract to us if it moved through the fourth dimension, so it could shrink or 'inflate'; which might mean that the man only looked about 5 inches tall because Dawn was looking at him through her three-dimensional eyes. This is, admittedly, pure speculation, and the intruder might have really been 5 inches in height. Another little being that also remains inexplicable is the one which a 22-year-old girl named Lisa encountered one Saturday evening at 7pm on 19 August 1995. Lisa was in the bedroom of her home on West Derby's Eaton Road, getting ready to go out, when she saw what she initially took to be a fly hovering outside her bedroom window - but it looked as if it was giving off light. Lisa took a close look at the thing and saw to her astonishment that it was a tiny female with wings - an archetypal faery - and being such a down-to-earth girl, Lisa doubted her senses for a moment. She was about to shout to her mother, to tell her to come and look at the faery, but she became absolutely mesmerised by the tiny delicate-looking being, and watched her perform what seemed to be a dance in mid-air. After some time, Lisa heard a scream behind her that really startled the girl. It was her mother. She thought Lisa had long gone out, seeing as it was almost 9 o'clock, and was startled to see someone still in her daughter's room. Lisa looked back at the window and saw the faery had vanished. She could not account for almost 2 hours of missing time, and the girl's father earnestly asked her if she had taken drugs. Lisa assured him she hadn't; she didn't even smoke. An old trick of faeries is to spellbind and bewitch humans with their antics and dancing, as they know that control of consciousness is control of time, and for some reason, perhaps to merely amuse themselves, they often tinker with human minds for their own agenda. When I mentioned this case on the Billy Butler Show on BBC Radio Merseyside I was inundated by reports of many faery sightings from right across the city, and what follows is derived from just one of these calls from the listeners.

On Christmas Eve 1965, a brother and sister, aged 6 and 8, decided to get up around midnight while their parents were drinking with neighbours in the kitchen of a house on Old Swan's Woburn Hill, and the kids saw what they later described as a glowing little man - about 6 or 7 inches tall – standing in the living room near to the Christmas tree. The girl asked him, 'What are you?' and the miniature humanoid said, 'You'd never understand,' before walking around the Christmas tree, looking at the multicoloured lights. The girl tried to pick the little man up and received a painful electric shock in her hands and arms, and the tiny figure ran into the fireplace. The children burst into the kitchen in tears, and told their parents what they had seen, and a neighbour named Bob said (jokingly), 'I'll go and give him a hiding.' He went out of the kitchen, and everyone heard his faint cry of 'Jesus!' and when he returned, his face was sparkling, and he seemed to be in a daze. He said, 'There's something in there,' but could not remember what he had seen. His wife said he had what looked like specks of blue and purple glitter on his cheeks and forehead which eventually faded away. On Christmas morning the family found the Christmas pine tree on its side. It had been uprooted from its plant pot, and there were baubles and bells from the tree, smashed in the fireplace. The family had no pets, and lived in mortal fear of encountering the "elf" but never heard from him again. Years later, when the little girl who had seen the tiny man was 16, she saw a Robin Hood film on the TV and said the elf-like man had dressed like one of the Merry Men, in a medieval-looking green, white and brown outfit with black boots. What the thing was is anybody's guess.

From Christmastide 1965 we move forward 31 years to the October of 1996, to clubland in the city centre, where a bouncer was on the doors one night around 11:45pm when two girls came up to him and one said, 'There's a ghost following us everywhere!'

The bouncer looked the girl up and down and replied, 'Go 'ed, what's the punch-line?' but the girl said she wasn't joking; she seemed frightened and claimed a "see-through man" had been following her and her friend and she added that the sub-visible thing had also been "touching" the girls up and the bouncer said, 'You wanna stop taking those little pills you know? You start seeing pink elephants and that,' and a second later there was a bang, and something hit the wall of the club to the left of the door and the girls screamed and one of them pointed at something behind the bouncer and said, 'That's him!' as blood issued from the upper part of something that looked like a partially transparent figure of a tall man.

The figure vanished but there was blood on the door of the club and on the bouncer's coat. He could not see who had fired whatever it was, and the girls were so afraid, they fell over as they ran off. Another bouncer – an older man who had been on the doors for fifteen years - came out the club and asked what the bang was. The first bouncer shrugged - he would not mention the see-through figure with what appeared to be a gunshot wound for obvious reasons. The bouncer was a simple man who never wondered nor believed in paranormal matters, and yet he felt someone had not been targeting him, but that *entity* - and the gunman, or whoever was behind that shooting, had not been visible; he or she had been as invisible as the mysterious being that had been shot. The unseen entity was lustful, according to the two young ladies who claimed it had followed them and touched them up, and this makes me wonder if the being was of the same ilk as the invisible pests which are described in the next report – perhaps one of them is the very same being that was at large in 1996.

Cases of paranormal entities carrying out sexual assaults are thankfully rare, but in the early hours of Friday morning on 12 December 2008, such an assault might have taken place. A 14-year-old girl named Jen was walking home along Old Swan's Broadgreen Road from her friend's house, headed for her home on Durban Road, which was about 100 yards away. The time was 12:45am. There came a ringing from the telephone box Jen was passing, and although she felt she should not answer it, she decided to go against her intuition, pulled open the door of the box, and went inside to pick up the receiver. She heard a noise that sounded like someone howling in pain. Then a voice, which sounded monotone, said, 'Hello Jen.' The teenaged girl smiled, thinking it was Gareth, the brother of her friend Jayne; he was always pulling practical jokes. 'Hiya Gareth,' said Jen but the voice replied, 'It's Denny. I like you and I shall have you.'

Jenny said, 'Will you now? You sound like a saddo.' And "Denny" said, 'I'm there,' to which Jane queried, 'You're where?' And the voice said, 'I'm in the telephone box with you with my friend.' Jen then felt something throw its arms around her, and before the handset dropped she heard a voice shout, 'Told you!' Jen then started to scream, because she felt as if two people were in the telephone box, and one was pushing her from the door, preventing her escape bid, and the other was kissing and biting her leg. She felt a cold hand cover her mouth and a ghastly sweet aroma filled the telephone box. The unseen entity below then started carrying out a terrifying assault on Jen, and the larger invisible presence pushed her head hard against the plexiglass panel of the telephone box. Jen bit the invisible hand hard, then somehow managed to break free from the telephone box, and there was Gareth, walking along the road with his dog. He saw Jen screaming with her skirt disarranged and her thick long hair was in her eyes. She told him what had happened and he escorted her to her home on Durban Road. Jen told her mother her underwear had been torn by the 'ghosts' - and she was not believed. Jen's father naturally grilled her with questions until he was sure something unexplained had happened. The two paranormal beings even visited Jen at home for several days and strange poltergeist phenomena was witnessed by many. Jen was so traumatised by the attack, she still refuses to go anywhere near the telephone box on Broadgreen Road where the two invisible beings assaulted her.

Here's a baffling case of a strange being that terrorised two young ladies, and I still have no workable theory to explain what it was. In 2002, two friends, Emmie and Joely - both aged 19 - went clubbing it in town, but not having that much money that week, they left the club about 1am – which was relatively early for them - and did a stupid thing; they blew the taxi fare home on two big pizzas.

'We'll walk it off, Eddie!' Joely announced, putting on the voice of Richie from *Bottom* - a TV show she and her friend always watched.

'What? Walk home from town?' gasped Emmie, and Joely nodded and said they'd burn the calories from the pizzas off.

Emmie then said a strange and random thing as she looked up at the sky. 'That star's wigging me out; it's following us,' she remarked, and Joely swore and said, 'You didn't take any weird pills off anyone in the club did you?' And Emmie kept looking up till Joely said, 'You're doin' my head in now - it's a star – just a star!'

Emmie narrowed her eyes and her big false eyelashes flickered. She shook her head and declared, 'It's too big - look, it's well weird. See it?' And Joely said, 'That there is a star,' but when the girls walked along Hope Street, close to the corner of Knight Street, Joely could see it wasn't a star; it looked like the figure of a man. She swore and said, 'You've attracted it,' to Emmie, and they ran as the thing descended - towards them. Both girls screamed - and Joely laughed with nerves - and they hid in the one alleyway that wasn't alleygated, and a luminous figure which must have been well over 7 feet in height floated down, and Emmie screamed, 'What do you want?'

The spectacular glowing humanoid hovered there in silence, and then the light from it dimmed slightly, so the girls could see that its body was naked, but it had no genitals, although its build looked masculine. The thing had no face, just a smooth convex area, pale and resembling white marble.

Joely swore at the thing, and shuddered when she saw it had no face. The being then vanished - like a light being switched off.

Joely was that scared by the unearthly encounter she delved into her handbag, retrieved her iPhone and called her father, a tyrant of a man she was always arguing with, and she woke him up and begged him to come and pick her and Emmie up, and he did, but he roared at her when she told him what she and Emmie had encountered and he said they'd obviously taken drugs, either on purpose or through someone spiking their drink, and he told the girls that the so-called "flying man" had been all in their minds. To this day, Emmie and Joely are still best friends, and they often wonder what that figure was; was it an angel of some sort or some abductor? I've heard of UFOs following certain people before, but that humanoid perplexes me. Joely said a strange thing about the entity; she said that when it vanished, she had the impression somehow that the thing had been sad and lonely, and had perhaps just wanted company.

The werewolf is a creature I often come across in my research, and from a biological point of view, a person who can turn into a wolf-like creature and then back into a human again seems an impossibility – yet still the reports come in – and many from witnesses of high reliability. How then do we reconcile our two beliefs in them? The scientist says werewolves are an impossibility and yet people report them. We can make the subject seem more respectable by using the term lycanthropy but that still leaves us in the dark. Some occultists maintain that werewolves are 'psychoplasmic' forms projected by the mind of a person who is directing hatred towards someone, and this theory would explain why werewolves are able to disappear and go to ground in a very short time when they are confronted or hunted – their ectoplasmic-like bodies would merely disintegrate. But some people have been seen to change into animals, and this brings us to the following strange story, reported to me some years ago when I was on a radio programme talking about Liverpool's local mysteries.

On a balmy Friday evening in the spring of 1971, Isla, a pretty young lady of twenty with fiery red locks who hailed from Richmond Upon Thames, was quaffing a pint or two in the Oxford pub in Edge Hill. Little did she know that her innocent revelry would lead to an encounter of a most sinister kind. As fate would have it, a man of questionable character sauntered into the pub and with a brusque gesture he grabbed Isla by her wrist and said, 'I don't pay you to sit on your arse drinking, now get up to Paddy [the Paddington district].' He then dragged Isla outside. This loathsome pimp, who had somehow mistaken

Isla for one of his new girls, had plans for her and was about to make his move when a white transit van pulled up outside the public house and a burly, broad-shouldered chap of thirty years or so got out of the van, eyeing Isla with a salacious gleam in his eye. The pimp slipped away. Isla, being a virtuous young woman, protested her innocence to the lustful stranger, who demanded to know how much she charged. Isla, now quite alarmed, said, 'I'm not what you think,' and the van driver said, 'How much? Get in here,' nodding to the transit. Isla attempted to resist the advances of this brute, and let out a scream, but her cries were interrupted by the sudden arrival of a bobby on the beat. He told the driver to beat it, and the latter walked away. Alas, this constable was not of the true blue variety, as evidenced by his coarse remark to Isla: 'How about a bit for bobby?'

In a sordid display of his malfeasance, he accosted Isla with a lecherous grin and smelt her breath. 'You're pissed, aren't you?' he asked with a smile. Isla, being of sound mind and spirit, refused his advances, and in return, the depraved imposter drew a blade, causing Isla to fear for her life. 'I'll report you! Let me go!' she said, and the copper said, 'Report me, I'm not a real copper, but this is real, real steel,' and he tapped the blade of the knife on Isla's cheek. 'Let's go round the back of the pub,' he suggested.

The muscular van driver, who must have been observing the "policeman" from a distance, sneaked up to him and punched the impersonator in the back of the head, and with such force, the helmet of the ersatz copper came off and hit Isla in the face, while the bogus bobby's head struck the brick wall with a

terrifying the guests, and then it tried to bash the front door in. Screaming guests left via the back garden in terror, climbing over fences in a bid to escape from the freakish beast, but one guest named Simon, aged 17, noticed that his girlfriend Lisa seemed very calm, and he had the impression she *knew something* about the werewolf. She went to the window, and the wild-eyed animal looked at her at very close quarters, and then it became unaccountably calm before turning and running off into the moonlit night on all fours. Simon often asked Lisa why she had been so calm that night when that "thing" had tried to get in the house, and she would never say a word in reply. They split up months later and Simon still wonders just what Lisa knew about the mysterious and terrifying beast. Alas, the answer remains shrouded in mystery. A thousand years ago, when Aigburth was part of Toxteth Park forest, it was known as "the Place of the Oaks" because of the fine old English trees that grew in profusion in the area, in fact Aigburth got its name from the Anglo-Saxon for oak – "ac" – combined with the ancient word "beran" – which meant to bear or produce. Back in those times, wolves prowled the forest of Aigburth, and were extraordinarily numerous in Britain, but by around 1620 they had been hunted to extinction. There have been reports of ghostly wolves – as well as werewolves – in Aigburth and Garston for many years, and perhaps these beings are psychic after-images of the beasts that once roamed south Liverpool millennia ago – but let us return to more recent times, and to another alleged case of an encounter with a werewolf. A couple named Danielle and Stephen went to a party one night in December 2005 at a house on

Chilcott Road, Broadgreen, and towards the end of the party, Stephen skitted at a woman who did Tarot readings - so she smilingly cursed him and Danielle and there was an argument between the Tarot reader and the couple, and Danielle and Stephen left the party in a huff. As the couple walked up Queens Drive, they started to argue, and Stephen said, 'You never stick up for me, do you? That Tarot skank was talking crap and I told her, that's all,' to which Danielle retorted with, 'And she cursed us - well done. We've had so much bad luck and you do a stupid thing like that. I'm not taking you to any parties from now on, you're too mouthy! You've got a lousy attitude problem!'

And then the couple heard a deep growling coming from somewhere close by. They turned to their left to see a huge beast rushing towards them on all fours; it looked like a giant wolf. Stephen ran off and the thing threw itself at Danielle and pinned her against a tree. It sniffed her legs and pulled her knickers down and she screamed for Stephen, but he had vanished.

'Please don't hurt me, please,' sobbed Danielle, and the thing said something that sounded like "sex". Danielle thought she was going to be torn apart by this beast and kept thinking it was all a lucid nightmare. There was a loud beeping of a car horn and the animal turned to look at a car which flashed its headlamps at it - and then it ran off, vanishing down Lexham Road. A white-haired man of about seventy got out the car and ushered Danielle into the vehicle and told her he'd seen the 'huge dog' attack her, and she told him it had not been a dog, but a wolf. The Good Samaritan kindly drove her home and Danielle later threw her cowardly boyfriend Stephen out of her flat. She felt the thing - a werewolf - or whatever it was - had targeted her because of the Tarot reader's curse. The question is: was the thing real or was it a kind of psychically projected form of the type some occultists believe in? Danielle felt the beast pin her against a tree, so she is in no doubt that the werewolf had been a real, physical creature.

Another werewolf was allegedly encountered on Saturday, 14 November, 1970 at 10pm, in West Derby. Betty, a 16-year-old girl, sneaked into the hut in the back garden of her home on Haymans Green with her boyfriend Tim, who had brought along some liquid courage in the form of a bottle of cider and some sweets to sweeten the deal. He and Betty started to kiss, but the couple's amorous activities were abruptly interrupted by a fleeting shadow that darted past the window. They initially thought it was Betty's dad, but it couldn't be since he (along with Betty's mum and grandfather) wouldn't be back home until midnight. Inquisitively, Betty glanced outside into the moonlit garden and was met with the terrifying sight of a huge animal on its hind legs, bigger than any dog she had ever seen in her life. Tim, with a harrowing conviction, proclaimed the beast to be a werewolf, and hastily attempted to slide the rusty bolt across the door as the creature bellowed menacingly and proceeded to pound on the door of the hut. The thing looked through the window, making a low snarling sound, then rained blows upon the side of the hut and the door, which bent inwards during the sustained attack. The couple stood there, frozen with fear, their hearts hammering with the realization that a werewolf wanted to kill them. Finally, the creature moved on, leaping over the garden wall and disappearing into the night. The couple waited, just to make sure the thing really had gone, before running pell-mell into Betty's home. Betty's mother and father didn't believe the couple's story of the werewolf and said it had just been a big Alsatian dog, but days later, a woman in her twenties said a huge animal which walked on two legs had sniffed her underwear hanging on the clothes line in her back garden before tearing the line down and running off. Shortly after this, a neighbour branded as an 'eccentric' said that a man living on Haymans Green was rumoured to be a werewolf, and that his wife had only found out when he had vomited in front of her and thrown up a rat. The man had lived on Hornspit Lane in 1964, and there had been werewolf reports there at that time. Betty later saw the man in question, and he smiled at her in a way that made her skin crawl. Was it all coincidence and hysteria? Or was a real werewolf at large in West Derby in 1970? As Shakespeare said, 'There are more thing in heaven and earth, Horatio than are dreamt of in your philosophy.'

JUST PASSING THROUGH

This chapter chronicles ghosts that appear out of the blue, often in the dead of night, in our homes, in our cars, and sometimes at our place of work, and these are fleeting phantoms that seem to be in transit – on some purposeful journey that originates in the mysterious unknown world that appears to exist beyond this one – and no sooner does the ghostly passerby momentarily brush past us in this reality before it is gone to some unknown destination. This chapter got its name from a remark that was allegedly made by a ghost some years ago; here is the account of this ghost. Just after midnight on Thursday 24 August 1995, a lady of seventy years of age named May was sitting in bed at her home on Carstairs Road, in the Kensington district of Liverpool, and she was enjoying chocolates that a kind friend had bought her, and May was also browsing a magazine (which she read by the light of an orange bedside lamp) as she listened to Steve Madden on BBC Radio 2, which was on at low volume in the background. May's cat Jimmy was usually sprawled out on the bed but was nowhere to be seen, until May saw his ginger tail protruding from under her pillows. Jimmy was laying flat under May's three pillows, as if he was hiding from something. He'd never done this before.

'Come on Jimmykins, what's wrong?' May asked the frightened feline when she heard a noise like a wind blowing through the room. The window was closed and the night was rainy but calm with not even a breeze beyond the window panes, so what was howling through the room? May recalled that the noise tailed off to a sound she likened to blowing your breath through tracing paper wrapped around a comb – something she sometimes did when she was a girl. The baffling sound died down, and then a luminous figure of a bald man in his sixties in a long white nightgown came from the corner of the room to May's left, and Jimmy the cat yowled under the pillows and May yelped, but without turning to face her, and looking straight ahead, the ghost said, 'It's alright love, I'm just passing through,' and then he walked or floated to the wall facing and went through it. The sound of the rushing wind ended abruptly, and May switched the main light on and she and Jimmy went downstairs, both of them in a terrible state. May had lived at the house for eleven years and had never once seen a ghost on the premises or had even the slightest paranormal experience. She went next door to her neighbour the next morning and told her what she had seen and was told the ghost had been encountered at the house over 20 years ago, always emerging from one wall and going into the wall facing. May wondered what the ghost meant about 'just passing through' - passing through to where? Where had he come from and where had he been going? And for that matter, who the hell was he? May never saw the ghost again.

The phantom that May encountered in her bedroom that night was a prime example of the type of ghost this chapter is about, and here is another case in point, only this time the ephemeral entity appeared in a moving car. The incident took place during a Biblical downpour on 23 December 2022 when a 37-year-old man named Greg was driving his 5-year-old son Josh to the house of the boy's grandmother via Queens Drive West Derby, when his son said, 'Dad, there's a man in the car' and Greg said, 'Is there?' thinking Josh was messing about - but when Greg looked in the rear view mirror he saw there *was* someone in the back seat and he swore, and turned to see a young man of about 22 to 25 years of age with large sad-looking blue eyes sitting there in a suit and tie, and he had a flower backed with maidenhead fern in his lapel, as if he'd been to a wedding. Greg also noticed spots of blood on the stranger's face. Before Greg would ask the stranger what he was doing in his car, the young man vanished into thin air. A hackney cab beeped a distracted Greg, who was veering out of his lane and just missed him by a few feet. Greg's son said, 'He's gone. Was that a ghost, dad?'

Greg was stuck for words; he didn't want to scare Josh, so he tried to play it down by smiling and saying, 'Nah, he wasn't a ghost, I think he was a magician.'

Josh was dropped off at his Nan's and when Greg returned an hour later, his mother-in-law said the boy talked about a ghost being in his dad's car all evening and then she asked Greg, 'What are you filling his head with?' to which Greg said, 'Me and him saw a fellah appear in the car when we were on our way here,' but Greg was not believed. His mother-in-law scolded Greg and told him to never drink or do drugs in the car when he had Josh with him. Greg had not been drinking and he did not take drugs, but he gave up trying to convince his mother-in-law that he and her grandson had encountered a ghost.

I've heard of ghosts appearing in cars before; I wonder what the back-story is to the unknown phantom that appeared in Greg's vehicle? I am equally interested in another car-riding phantasm which thumbs lifts on a motorway in the dead of night. It was around 1:20am on a windy Tuesday morning, 18 March, 2014, when a Huyton man in his fifties named Jack was driving home from a school reunion down the M62. He saw a man waving frantically on the hard shoulder near Ikea, and Jack did what he normally wouldn't do - he stopped for the hitch-hiker. The bearded hitcher wore a black anorak, dark pleated trousers and Doc Martens, and getting into the car he said, 'Ah cheers lad, thanks for stopping mate; ah, can you take me anywhere near St John's Road in Huyton?'

Jack nodded and said, 'I'm going home to Huyton so you're in luck,' and the man said, 'Ah, nice one lad, I don't do this often like but I've had a bit of bother like, which I won't go into and bore you with, like. I'm Bazza by the way.'

Bazza then asked, 'You a red or a blue lad if you don't mind me asking like?'

'Blue, why?' replied Jack, and the hitcher said, 'I don't really 'folly the game lad but the blues have got a good squad at the moment. I like erm, Southall, and Ratcliffe and that Steve McMahon, and good old Reidy - he's a case isn't he? Oh, and erm, Sheedy...' And Jack thinned his eyes and said, 'That's going back a bit, mate; that's the Eighties.'

Bazza said, 'As I say I don't folly the footy now, like,' and for some reason, Jack felt a cold tingle in his stomach – some warning from his subconscious perhaps - and he reached into his glove compartment, took out rosary beads from it and said, 'You're a ghost, aren't you?' And he heard a faint, 'Yeah.' And the man was gone. Jack slowed the car and kept looking at the empty passenger seat; he *had* gone, and only a ghost could do that, he thought. He kept the rosary beads in his hand as he held the steering wheel.

When the car was travelling over that part of the M62 which crosses Clock Face Lane, Jack heard '*Sheedy*', close to his left ear, and this naturally startled him, and he swore and made the sign of the cross. He saw - and heard - no more of the ghost, but so many have encountered him over the years, although his identity is unknown. Jack is an accomplished illustrator and he sketched a picture of "Bazza". I showed this drawing to a lady named Carol, and she identified him as the person she had given a lift to one night in March 2002 – and she had a witness – her son Mark, who was 15 at the time. The hitcher had asked to be dropped off at Huyton, said nothing throughout the journey then vanished at the Jubits Lane flyover. Carol had been looking at the road when the ghost vanished, so she did not see him dematerialise – but her son Mark did, and he described how the hitch-hiker's eyes widened, as if he was receiving a shock, before vanishing in an instant.

On the 24 January, 1902, two faintly luminous young ladies appeared in a bedroom at Croxteth Hall, terrifying a guest who, upon seeing the figures, ducked his head under the covers and shouted, 'Begone, spirits!' He kept his head under the blankets and heard one of the ethereal ladies apologise in a well-spoken voice; she said she and her companion had come to the wrong house - then vanished, along with her colleague. Some thought the apparitions were somehow connected to the death of the Earl of

Sefton, which had taken place at Croxteth Hall in the previous month. An elderly female cook at Croxteth Hall opined that the visitants had most probably been witches, merely "passing through" on their way to another residence; if this *was* the case, the passing through on this occasion would perhaps be achieved through some type of teleportation. From Edwardian bedroom visitors we next move forward to the early 1970s to another bedroom where two teenaged girls purportedly had a fleeting encounter with a supernatural character of old who is known to the world - yet paradoxically remains unknown. This intriguing but nevertheless frightening encounter with a transient figure of fear took place on the night of Friday 8 March, 1974; 13-year-old Lucy and her friend Helen (same age) were up late at Lucy's home, a large Victorian house on Ullet Rd, close to Sefton Park. Helen loved these sleepovers, because Lucy was an amazing storyteller, and on this night, Helen asked Lucy to tell her a story about Jack the Ripper, and Lucy told Helen all she knew about the case, and ended the tale with: "...well, whoever Jack was, by now he will have taken his awful secret with him to the grave forever.' And the girls heard a noise outside the window, so Lucy turned off the lights. A silhouette of a man in a top hat and cape; thrown by the light of the full moon onto the net curtains, startled the teenagers; then they heard a rich, sonorous voice from outside which said, 'The grave can wait,' followed by deep laughter. The girls hid in the corner and heard the window rattle, as if the man outside was trying to get in. They ran out the room screaming and Lucy's father and uncle, who had been watching a late-night film on the TV, went outside - and saw a tall top-hatted man casually walking away into the moonlit night as he whistled the nursery rhyme, *This Old Man.*

'Some idiot's idea of a joke,' said Lucy's father, watching the oddly-dressed man walk off into the darkness - but then the figure seemed to fade away, although this could have been a trick of the light. Lucy and Helen were sure the man had been no prankster, but - Jack himself. We are left with two possibilities; someone was on the prowl that night, dressed up in a top hat and opera cloak, and he just happened to hear two teenage girls talking about the Ripper and thought he'd play a prank on them – or the visitor was a ghost, perhaps even the ghost of Jack himself, but what would he be doing up in Liverpool? Surely he'd haunt the East End? And a similar question mark hangs over the next ghost of the 'just passing through' variety – a monk haunting a place where no monastery ever existed.

It was Tuesday 14 February, 1978; a woman in her thirties named Lorraine was in bed with the flu, and at 10pm her husband Mike brought her a hot mug of Oxo, the only thing Lorraine could bear to sip; everything else made her nauseous. Mike went back downstairs and Lorraine dozed off at 10:30pm, but was awakened by someone muttering in what sounded like Latin. Lorraine didn't understand Latin but remembered bits of it from her schooldays. She opened her eyes and saw a hooded monk kneeling at the foot of her bed, his hands clasped in prayer, and she could feel those joined hands resting on her feet. The monk stopped praying and looked at her, then slightly shook his head, as if he disapproved of something. Lorraine screamed, and Mike came bounding up the stairs as the monk shook his fist at Lorraine in anger, then vanished. When Lorraine told Mike about the Monk he said she'd had a nightmare, and Lorraine insisted she'd been wide awake.

Mike laughed: 'Lorraine, what would a monk be doing haunting this house? There was never any monastery round here.' The house was on Deverell Road in Wavertree, incidentally, and Mike was right - there had never been a monastery in that area. Lorraine pleaded with Mike to get in bed so she'd feel safer, and she reminded him it *was* Valentine's Day - so Mike begrudgingly got into the bed, and was soon fast asleep. Lorraine was awakened by the monk spouting Latin again at 2:20am, and she nudged Mike and said, 'Mike - he's back,' to which her husband replied, 'I know,' he'd been awakened by the ghost too and had been slyly watching him with his bleary eyes. Mike jumped out of the bed and switched on the bedside lamp - and the monk vanished in an instant. Thankfully, the monk never returned, but - a year later, Mike and Lorraine were in the Oxford Pub, Edge Hill one night, and overheard a man saying he had awakened one night a few weeks back at his home in Heywood Road, Childwall, and he had seen a monk at the bottom of his bed, praying in Latin. The man took the visitation as an omen of his imminent departure from this life but fortunately nothing happened. Why a ghostly monk is doing the rounds praying for people in the dead of night is unknown. I wonder if he might be the very same monk that was reported to me some years ago? On Saturday 16 October 1982, a 19-year-old man named Jimmy awoke in his bedroom at his home on Doric Road, Old Swan at 3:30 am to feel someone massaging his right foot, which had been badly sprained during a five-a-side footy game the day before. Jimmy felt tremendous heat in the injured foot and looked to the bottom of his bed to see a ghostly monk massaging his injured foot. The hands of the ghost were somehow passing through the blankets to rub Jimmy's toes and sole. Jimmy withdrew his foot from the hands of the ethereal monk and ran in terror from the bedroom before realising that his foot had been completely healed. The ghost was never seen again, and might have been one of the many phantom monks said to haunt the area around St Oswald's Street. Jimmy's mum said a prayer, thanking the monk for 'fixing' Jimmy's foot, and a smell of incense filled her room. Another random intrusion by a monk takes place in the next account. A lady named Izzy who now lives in Spain told me about the ghostly monk of Doric Road, Old Swan. Izzy recalled that in November 1995, she was aged 6, and was visiting her Nan's house in Allenby Square, Old Swan at teatime, when she saw a tall figure dressed in a monk's cowl which appeared in the corner of the living room as Izzy's Nan was in the kitchen. She ran and told her Nan about the monk, and when the two of them went back into the living room the ghost was still there, but it had its back presented towards them as it faced the wall. The child's Nan said, 'You'll have to go, you're scaring the child,' and the monk slowly vanished into the wall. The girl's Nan then told her, 'Don't be scared, he's probably just lost.' The girl never saw the ghost again and her Nan died a few years later.

In the first sentence of this chapter I mentioned that

some of the ghosts 'just passing through' sometimes appeared in the workplace; well, the following case concerns an incident where a person was at her place of work when she encountered an entity that did something *very* rare in the sphere of the paranormal – it stabbed her.

In September 2010 a security guard named Helen was patrolling a building site in the Low Hill area of Liverpool one Sunday morning at 11am with her dog, and she had gone through this routine many times. Ghosts were the furthest thing from Helen's mind on this crisp sunny morning; phantoms and spirits are associated in most people's minds with the dead of night, not a sunny autumnal morning, but it was in the broad daylight of that morning, just after eleven o'clock when Helen saw a man, dressed in what looked like 18th century garb with the powdered wig, dancing on the site. She initially thought the "oddball" might be a student messing about as part of some practical joke, but then the stranger asked, 'Do you know who I am, young lady?' to which Helen replied, 'A divvy - come on, get out of here,' and her dog - a trained Belgian Malinois - laid down.

The bizarre-looking intruder pulled a dagger from a scabbard and leapt forward in a type of fencing lunge - plunging the dagger in Helen's chest in one swift movement. Helen felt the cold blade go in - and simultaneously the man vanished. Helen felt her chest - and was convinced she'd been stabbed. The dog got up and Helen hurried to a portakabin and took off her sweater and yanked her bra apart, expecting to see a wound which blood would soon seep out of – but the guard saw there was not a mark on her chest. No one had reported any ghosts on the site before this shocking incident and Helen saw nothing remotely supernatural after that, but the dog was always reluctant to go near the spot where the incident occurred. The identity of the violent ghost remains a mystery; I wonder if he'll ever 'pass through' the building that now stands on the land where the attack took place?

Here is a particularly eerie account of another ghost that was fleetingly encountered, and this one had a grim warning to the woman who saw the entity. On the chilly grey Friday afternoon of 5 October 1979 - a 32-year-old woman named Anne was putting flowers on her Nan's grave in West Derby Cemetery, and as she stooped to say a prayer, she was startled by the appearance of a lady in black about ten feet away. This lady, who looked as if she was about six feet in height, had her back to Anne, and she wore an odd dark-grey quilted beret of some sort, a long black coat that almost went down to her ankles, and a pair of black high heels. She stood there motionless to the right of a gravestone. In a well-spoken voice the female stranger said, 'Anne, stop seeing that married man or you'll be in that grave with your grandmother soon.' The woman then vanished in an instant, which naturally scared Anne, for she realised she had just seen an actual ghost. Anne *was* seeing a married man named Sam, and so she told her mother about the ghost's apparent warning. Anne's mother was more shocked at her daughter seeing a married man than the report of the graveside ghost, and she sternly told Anne to stop seeing the man immediately, which Anne did, and she was so scared to tell Sam in person, she telephoned him to tell him it was over. He asked if there was someone else, and Anne said there wasn't, and after ignoring Sam's pleas for her to change her mind, Anne hung up. Less than a week after this, Sam was seen with another woman, and they were in a well-known pub on Lime Street one evening when Sam punched his new girlfriend because she'd allegedly been looking at another man. Over the next six months Sam went through four other partners, and each time he showed violence towards them until he was finally arrested for assault and battery. Anne felt that the ghost of that woman in West Derby Cemetery had foreseen Sam killing her, but who she was remains a mystery to this day.

An unknown blond-haired ghost of a man who seems to date back to the days of Queen Anne and the Georgian era, sometimes passes through bedrooms in the Woolton, Garston and Halewood areas in the dead of night, and has been known to get into bed with men or women. He gives his name as "Richard" sometimes, and is said to have striking blue eyes. I have the sneaking suspicion that he is one and the same ghost I once saw at Woolton Hall during an interval in a talk I was giving, and many who saw him on a staircase thought he was some hired actor who was part of the talk. This means he may be one of the Molyneux family who once lived at the hall, but admittedly I may be wrong and the ghost may not be the same lecherous Richard who does the rounds over quite an area, which is very unusual for a ghost (they usually stay put in one place). The lustful bedroom visitor was last encountered by a woman at her home on Manor Road, Woolton in September 2017 at 3:50am. The woman woke up as she was kissed, and realising her husband was working nights, she drew back and saw a man with long blond hair in a long nightshirt leaning over her. He vanished, but returned on the following night when the woman's husband was in bed but flitted through a wall when the husband chased him. A ghost matching the same description - long blond hair and blue eyes - was seen a week later in the bedroom of a 21-year-old girl on Hunts Cross Avenue at 5:10am but vanished when the girl screamed. She later discovered she had love-bites on her neck and other parts of her body.

Here's a classic case of an entity that eerily passed through the life of a woman one night, and it imparted a sombre message then departed. On the Saturday night of 10 August 1985, at around 7:15pm, a woman in her forties named Jackie got out the bath in her home on Mackets Lane, Hunts Cross, dried herself in a leisurely manner, and dressed in some comfy clothes, intending to have a bit of peace for a few hours. Her husband Mark was at the pub with his brother-in-law, the kids were out at their friend's houses, and the only company Jackie had was the dog, Bruce, knocking about somewhere, either under the stairs in his basket or in the back garden on the lookout for audacious cats. Jackie sat down with a cup of coffee and an unopened packet of McVitie's chocolate digestives and decided Saturday night was pig-out night. She watched *Winner Takes All* with Jimmy Tarbuck, and then made another coffee and sat with a magazine, half-watching *Murder She Wrote* at 7:45pm. As Jackie was watching one scene in the TV crime series, she thought she saw an eerie figure - it looked like a woman in a white robe, standing behind a character on screen, but then with an icy shudder on this warm August evening, Jackie realised the figure wasn't in the TV show - it was a reflection on the telly's screen of someone standing in her living room - and whoever it was, they were standing behind her armchair. She slowly turned and saw it was a woman in a hooded long white robe with scary glowing eyes, and the apparition seemed to be phosphorescent. The apparition said 'Anne,' and then it was gone. There came a howl from Jackie's dog, Bruce, in the hallway. Jackie switched the living room light on, as well as the lights in the hallway and kitchen, and she stood there in the doorway of the living room, and she felt numb with shock. The only Anne she could think of was a friend she'd known since junior school and she now worked at a filling station. At 11:20pm, Mark, Jackie's husband came back from the pub and stood there with a carton of curried chicken and rice, something he always brought in from the chippy on his way back from the pub. It was for Jackie. He had a strange, sad serious look on his face, and Jackie just knew he was going to tell her some bad news. 'Love, I heard that your old mate Anne, [and he gave her surname] died tonight.'

'What – 'Jackie immediately thought of the ghost uttering her friend's name.

'She had a heart attack in her bath, and her nephew found her,' added Mark, and he put the carton down and held his wife's hands. 'You okay?'

'What time was it when she died?' Jackie asked, a tear in her eye.

'I think they said she was found around ten past eight, why?' Mark replied.

She told him about the woman in the long white robe with the sinister glowing eyes, and how she'd appeared around the time of Anne's death and mentioned her name.

Jackie had never had a supernatural experience before this, and she has not seen or heard anything remotely paranormal since that night in 1985. Why a ghost came to tell her about her friend's death is unknown, although Jackie was very close to Anne. People said she had imagined the ghost, but Jackie was not even thinking about anything supernatural that evening; she was just enjoying a coffee, biscuits and a telly show. She knew she had not imagined it because she had seen the reflection of the ghost in the screen of the TV, and the dog had howled when the ghost had mentioned Anne's name.

And finally, here is a case of not one but *two* ghosts who casually passed through the bedroom of a young lady one Saturday morning at 1:20am on 20 October 2018. A 23-year-old girl named Callie awoke in the bedroom of her home on Rocky Lane, Childwall. She heard unfamiliar voices and listened carefully, then she distinctly heard a male voice whisper, 'Come, Roger, the coast is clear,' and out of the wall on the right of Callie's bedroom came a man, and he hesitated, with half of his body still in the wall, and he licked his lips. He wore old fashioned clothes; a starched white collar and dark waistcoat. As a scared but equally curious Callie watched stock-still from her bed, she saw part of a second face emerge from the wall and this ghost, who looked younger than the other one said, 'I feel she's about.'

The older ghost went to a drawer in a dresser,

opened it, and lifted a pair of Callie's knickers up to his nose; he was either sniffing them or perhaps he was short-sighted and was looking at them; whatever the case, Callie screamed, and in a flash, the ghosts flitted back into that wall.

Callie's father came upstairs and asked what the screaming was for and Callie told him. She was told she'd been dreaming. Callie was normally out on Friday and Saturday nights but had found herself low on funds (skint) this week so she'd stayed in. Had the ghosts - whoever they were - thought the girl had gone out? The phantom duo has not been seen since, and Callie hopes she never sets eyes on them again!

TEMPTERS FROM BEYOND

'I can resist everything except temptation,' wrote that inimitable lord of language Oscar Wilde in his scintillating four-act comedy *Lady Windermere's Fan* (based on the life of Lillie Langtry), and that line is an excellent introduction to the subject of this chapter – temptation. One of Satan's many names is the Tempter, and we see him at work in the Old Testament as the Serpent who tempts Eve to take a bite of the Forbidden Fruit in the Garden of Eden, and then the Tempter reappears in the New Testament, where we read of the temptations of Christ in the wilderness. There are tempters in other religions too; in Islam, Iblis is the Tempter of humanity, and in Buddhism, the demon Mara tempts Siddartha Guatama. Temptation today comes from more mundane sources: the dieter who is tempted by an advertisement for some chocolate cake, the alcoholic who has become abstinent but reluctantly accepts an invitation to a party and struggles to stay on a non-alcoholic beverage, and so on. But over the years I have looked into cases where the tempter seems to be of a supernatural and sinister nature, attempting to lure the prey for some unspeakable gain – possibly even the soul of the tempted victim, and what follows in this chapter is a little distillation of some of these cases in the form of several stories of paranormal tempters.

Let us start at the tail-end of the Nineties.

One drizzly afternoon in September 1999, 18-year-old Penny was strumming her acoustic and singing one of her self-penned songs in the bedroom of her home near Sefton Park. She had retreated into her room because some relatives were visiting and she didn't feel like mixing with them downstairs. As Penny was singing her song, *I Hate Everyone*, the door opened and in walked a man of about twenty-five years of age with dark curly hair and dark brown penetrating eyes, and Penny stopped singing and glared at him. He wore a long knee-length grungy coat. With confidence he closed the door behind him and stood there, gazing right into the girl's eyes.

'Who the hell said you could come in here?' she asked the man, who said his name was Gabriel, and she assumed he was some boyfriend of her cousin Andrea, but he said, 'No, I'm with a band. That chord change in your song from G to C at the start would sound better if you went from G to C-Add-9.'

Penny was puzzled; 'You're with a band?' she said, posing the question with narrowed eyes, her head tilted back a little, and Gabriel nodded and answered, 'Yeah, we're called The Little Tin Gods and there are three other members but we need a female singer pronto, and your voice sounds boss.'

'That's bullshit,' sneered Penny, 'you're Andrea's latest fellah. You're not in any band; play the guitar then.' Penny lifted the acoustic up and took her head and shoulder out of the rainbow-striped guitar strap.

Gabriel took the acoustic from Penny, tuned it (which really annoyed the girl because she believed it was already tuned), and then he said, 'The working title of this one is *Antisocial* and he played an amazing circling 4-chord sequence as an intro to a song which sounded as if it was about Penny's unsociable antics; and although Gabriel's singing voice sounded whiny, Penny was impressed. She naturally asked. 'If you're not Andrea's boyfriend, what are you doing in this house? And you sound like a wool.'

'Never mind all that, we want you in the band; your voice is just right, and we've heard some voices,' said Gabriel, and Penny just sensed there was something eerie about him; his eyes looked cold, dead. She looked at the newly-risen goosepimples on her forearms; it was as if she had reacted to someone rubbing a steel fork's prongs on a china plate.

He seemed to read her mind, and said, 'Yeah, big deal, I am something out the ordinary, but if you can just have the balls to step outside of your boring little mundane world and come with me, you'll be in the band; you'll live forever.'

'Who *are* you?' Penny asked, backing towards the door, and Gabriel produced a long golden pin from the inside pocket of his shabby coat, and said, 'If you let me respectfully stick this in your head, you'll know it all - you'll be one of us, and I give you my word, it doesn't even hurt.'

Penny swore at Gabriel, then she lunged at the bedroom door handle and yanked open the door. 'Dad!' she yelled, exiting the room, and she ran downstairs and told them all in the living room and kitchen about the man upstairs and her father and uncle went up to the bedroom and found it empty. Penny's cousin Andrea had seen Gabriel go up the stairs and had wondered who he was, so Penny had not imagined the weird stranger. Penny grew out of the songwriting phase and ended up a hairdresser, and she still wonders who Gabriel was and why on earth he wanted her – and furthermore – why did he want to insert that long golden pin into her head? Gabriel is a perfect example of a supernatural tempter, and on that occasion, he claimed he would bestow immortality on Penny. In the next story, we meet another tempter who appeared in quite a bizarre place in the 1930s.

The strange incident happened at a huge house on Aigburth's Parkfield Road. Amy had been looking forward to the Moochi – a fun "couple dance" that was a form of the Foxtrot – on Christmas Eve at the State down in Dale Street, but now Eddy had told her that his wife Julia *was* going to the seasonal dance, and so Amy didn't know what to do. This was in the Yuletide of 1930 by the way, six decades before the State Ballroom was synonymous with House Music. Something very strange happened that Christmas Eve in Amy's bedroom as she tried to decide whether to go to the Grafton or the Rialto. At 8pm she heard music coming from the wardrobe. The 24-year-old divorcée gingerly opened the wardrobe door, and there stood an exceedingly handsome debonair man in a tuxedo, and behind him was a bright room lit with sparkling chandeliers and peopled with young men and women.

'Yes,' said the attractive but mysterious man, 'a Christmas party in a wardrobe, but don't be too perplexed and alarmed, Amy, come and have a jolly good time. My name is Percival.'

Understandably, Amy backed away a little from the wardrobe and felt herself fall into a type of trance. It was like those dreams she had where she met an uncle who had died years ago, yet she never thought to ask him how he could be alive again. Amy faintly wondered how a huge room could fit in her wardrobe.

'Come on, Amy, come to the party,' said Percival, reaching out to her, and she saw his hand was tanned, and that he had long slender fingers and well-manicured fingernails. 'Come on Amy – the party has only just started,' he said, and now his voice almost sounded melodious.

Amy walked forward, halted, smiled at Percival, then willingly stepped into the room in the wardrobe and he gently took her hand as a pretty willowy girl of about eighteen who Percival referred to as Cheri took Amy's other hand. A band was playing and someone was singing last year's big hit, *Tiptoe Through the Tulips*. Percival took the disoriented Amy to a bar and she was served strange sparkling, fizzing champagne cocktails she'd never heard of, and then the jaunty Percival asked her to dance to a dreamy waltz that kicked off; Amy recognised the tune - it was called *Pagan Love Song* by The Troubadours. Amy gazed into Percival's dark eyes, and felt utterly seduced by this unfathomable man. His cologne, like his charisma, was intoxicating, overpowering, and Amy had never been so strongly attracted to a man.

'Where – where is this place?' she asked, her head craned back, looking up at his smiling face.

'The Majestic - a place I hope you will never leave, Amy,' said Percival, 'and tonight it's your turn to live; you've done so much for people – I know that much – and they have taken you for granted and abused your good nature – but tonight you will be on the receiving end, beautiful Amy. All of my life I've looked for someone like you, and was ready to give up, and I know this will sound silly, but – well – I'm in love with you.'

'But you don't even know me,' Amy replied, trying to stifle a grin. She had always dreamt of having a man like this, but he didn't seem to exist outside of a Ronald Colman film.

'I've admired you from afar,' said Percival, and he leaned in close to Amy – so close that she felt his breath on her face as he spoke; he continued, 'always from afar – but afraid of rejection – afraid that you'll stab me in the heart with a mere few words of rejection.'

Alarm bells started to jangle at the back of Amy's mind; this dialogue sounded pretentious, stilted – scripted. She recalled where she was again and asked, 'How can all of this exist inside my wardrobe; I don't understand – '

'There's nothing to understand here except that I love you, dearest Amy,' said Percival holding her so close now as they waltzed, and as Amy doubted the phoney-sounding patter again, one of the women waltzing by in the arms of another man cried to Amy, 'Get away! He killed us all!'

And the band slowed and then the music came to an abrupt halt.

Amy saw Percival's eyes bulge at the woman's claim, and she felt his large hand, which had been so gently holding her hand suddenly close hard like a vice. Amy then felt as if she had snapped out of a spell. Fearing Percival was some devil that had hypnotised her, she pulled away from him and ran to the door. Two men in tuxedos tried to block her escape but Percival cried,

'Let her go for now!'

Amy pushed at the door and fell out of that strange wardrobe, and she heard one of the men that Percival addressed shout back at him, 'No! We shouldn't let her go! She'll tell people about us!' And this man reached out and grabbed Amy by her foot. He tried to drag her back into the wardrobe but she screamed for help and kicked her other foot at him. She felt the heel ram into his face and she heard him cry out in pain.

He pulled off her shoe, and Amy slipped from his grasp, crawled across the floor to the door and got up, and then she looked back as she opened the bedroom door. She saw that brightly lit dance floor and all of the well-dressed men and women standing there, looking at her, and Percival was standing in the centre of the crowd. A strange cacophony of moaning, echoing voices came from the wardrobe as the scene within it dimmed, and Amy left the house and went to stay with her brother. She told him what had happened and he had known Amy long enough to be able to tell that *something* had happened to her from the look on her face alone. His wife – Amy's sister-in-law – believed Percival had been the Devil, out to take her and her mortal soul, but Amy believed there was something more to Percival than that; she felt he was some visitor from elsewhere, and if that woman who warned Amy was telling the truth, perhaps he really had killed all of the women in that dance hall, but she simply couldn't fathom out how or why. Amy had recurring nightmares about Percival for years. The wardrobe, which had belonged to Amy's ex-husband Edward, was smashed up in the backyard of the house on Boxing Day and Amy's brother used most of it as firewood.

We now move 85 years into the future, to a tale of another eldritch enticer, and I can't help feeling that this story has an uncanny parallel with a story in an earlier chapter in this book called *The Enigma of Philip's Gowns*; read it (if you haven't already) and see what you think.

On 25 March 2015, a couple in their twenties, Louise and Matt, were returning from B&Q in Warrington, and as Matt drove down the M62 Louise said the "B&Q" in the DIY store was meaningless, but Matt said it stood for Block & Quayle, the store's founders, and they argued – and the outcome of the silly tiff was that Louise sulked for a while and looked out the window to her left - until she saw a shopping complex called "Neverdale" or "Neerdale" that she'd never noticed before. Although the couple was skint, Louise pestered Matt to drive to the shopping centre and so their car slowed and left the M62 and they travelled through an immense car park that was empty except for one dark blue car. The centre inside the squat building was huge, and looked like an upmarket mall. Louise dragged Matt around the place and he noticed there was no one about - just a smartly-dressed man who, according to Matt, bore a resemblance in looks and manner to the late Bob Monkhouse. The man explained that the store had just opened, and as Louise and Matt were the first customers, they each could have any first item that took their fancy for free - be it expensive shoes, a mobile phone, etc, and Louise and Matt were excited at this astounding offer. Everywhere they went, that man would turn up at whatever store they visited, and Matt noticed that most of the stores had a name from a Liverpool district or street - Tuebrook Coffee, Lime Street Gin House etc, and he just sensed there was something 'off' about the shopping centre, and that smiling man was following them everywhere. In a low voice, Matt told Louise about his suspicions, and she whispered back, 'You just took the words out of my mouth. That man's creeping me out as well.'

'When we drove through this area a few weeks ago, I clearly remember nothing being here,' recalled Matt, his eyes darting about, 'and now there's a big shopping mall here. Maybe we should just leave.'

Matt and Louise then simultaneously experienced a feeling of utter dread – that something very bad was going to happen. The couple decided to leave immediately but it took Matt and Louise ages to locate the exit, as there were no signs – and as they walked about with a mounting sense of panic, that smarmy man kept following them, uttering permutations of, 'You're not leaving are you?' and 'Why are you leaving without your free gifts?'

When the couple finally found the exit to the vast store, the man stood in front of them with his arms stretched out and he sounded desperate as he said, 'Look, let me tempt you with this offer: instead of one free gift each, you can also have one free gift that would suit the two of you, be it a brand new washing machine or the very latest giant TV screen with Dolby and everything thrown in – or even a fitted kitchen.'

'No ta,' said Louise, pushing past him. Matt halted and took a picture of the man on his mobile, and the man glared at him, then turned and walked away. The couple hurried to their car and Louise said the experience had kicked her anxiety off. Matt then tried to start the car – but the engine seemed to be dead.

'I don't believe this,' he said, trying the ignition again. Nothing.

'I can't breathe,' said Louise, her hand on her chest. Matt saw that hand move because her palpitations were that strong.

'The battery's just been changed as well, I don't understand it,' Matt told Louise, and turned the key again. Still nothing.

'Lord, please start the engine,' said Louise, and she panted with the acute uncontrollable anxiety.

Matt turned the key again. The engine started. He drove out of that car park and rejoined the motorway, and after about ten minutes, Louise's anxiety faded away.

When the couple got back to Liverpool they went to the house of Louise's parents and told them what had happened - and Matt could not find that picture he had taken of the man - just the last picture he'd taken in B&Q of a product, and the couple searched for that shopping centre, but found nothing but farmland. Louise still has nightmares about that excessively suave and ingratiating man in the weird mall, and wonders who the hell he was, and Louise also wonders what he wanted in return for the free gifts he was so eager to give to her and Matt.

And now for a strange story of a paranormal persuader who might have been the original tempter from the Bible. Many years ago, I wrote about the Devil's alleged appearance at the subterranean Cavern Club (in *Haunted Liverpool 3*) one night after the crowds had gone and the bouncers and staff started messing with a ouija board. I had so much feedback from the reading public and also from the million-plus listeners to my regular slot on BBC Radio Merseyside. From the accounts I received, it would seem that the Cavern Club was visited by a Mephistophelean character on quite a few occasions. This is just *one* of them. It was the Wednesday night of March 27, 1963, long after The Hollies and the other bands had left the club, when – perhaps through boredom or because someone was looking for kicks - there was said to have been a deliberate invocation of Lucifer at the Cavern by five men. Someone, (who never actually said he was the Devil) appeared in a pall of pale blue smoke, with tiny flames flickering behind him, and a handsome young man who had designs to become a singer – even though he was said to have possessed a rather mediocre voice - asked the supernatural visitor if he could bestow great success and fame upon him (perhaps of the magnitude the Fab Four were starting to experience at that time). There was no reply for about ten seconds, and then the tall dark man said, 'Yes, of course - as long as you call yourself Cain [or possibly Caine].'

'Cain?' the young man queried the name, and told the sinister man his full name and how it was also his stage-name, and the stranger said, 'I know what your real name is – it's a dreadful name. If you want to be world-famous, you must call yourself Cain.'

'Yeah, alright,' said the fame-hungry young man, then he asked, 'and is there anything I've got to do in return?'

The man told the wannabe pop idol to meet him at a certain secluded spot up at Ince Blundell on 9 April.

The young hopeful nodded nervously and said, 'I'll be there,' and then the inauspicious visitant vanished, leaving an aroma in his wake that was reminiscent of church incense. The young man bottled out and never kept his appointment and started to attend church as much as he could. He abandoned his singing career and settled for the mundane job of a driving instructor.

The tempter in the following account is unusual in that he apparently communicated with a woman from an old oil painting. At noon on Saturday 4 February 1967, a 24-year-old married woman named Maureen left the city centre newsagents where she worked part-time, and in her handbag she carried her little brown envelope pay-packet. She met up with her 34-year-old lover Jimmy at the Bon Bon Coffee Bar on Renshaw Street. He slyly pecked Maureen's cheek as she embraced him and muttered in her ear, 'Pipe down, Mo, you don't know who's in here; one of them might be your fellah's hoppo,' and Maureen looked about at the customers in the coffee bar, then smiled, 'I don't care if any of them are his mate - you're my fellah now.'

Maureen's husband had used her as a punch-bag once too often, and now she had finally seen the light and left him, and she wanted this relationship with Jimmy to work, but he *did* like his gambling.

Jimmy scanned the declared runners for today's race meetings in the newspaper, and he asked Maureen if she wanted to pick a horse in the Hopeful Hurdle meeting at Stratford-on-Avon. She picked a runner called "West of the Border", even though Jimmy tutted; but that horse later won. Jimmy said it was beginner's luck. The couple then went to the Melrose Hotel on Mount Pleasant. This was a small hotel – what we would now call a boutique hotel with less than 50 rooms – and at this hotel there was a group of guests in the lounge, and one of them asked Jimmy if he fancied a few games of poker. Jimmy felt pressured to take part in the game and borrowed money from Maureen to play, and Maureen sat in the lounge, bored, and she tried to keep track of the game, but her eyes wandered about and settled on a faded old painting of a man of bygone times. Maureen then went into what we vaguely call a 'brown study' – a state of consciousness in which we daydream at some depth and forget our surroundings for a while. While Maureen was in this state of reverie, she heard a voice from the painting on the wall, and she soon realised the voice was purely in her mind; no one else seemed to hear it. The well-spoken voice of a male told her that the men playing poker with Jimmy were all card sharps, and that the origin of the voice she was hearing was the man in the picture. He told Maureen she should join the game and that he would use his skills to make her win the money back, for he was a professional master gamesman and card-game strategist. Maureen knew nothing about poker but asked the players if she could join the game - and despite Jimmy's objections - the players said they'd love female company, but Jimmy knew they just wanted to fleece Maureen. Maureen, however, kept winning each round, and even asked to shuffle the pack, and Jimmy was astounded at the way she rapidly dealt the cards. After she won the pot, she left the game and an Irish player remarked to her, "hit and run, eh?" and another player, a Scotsman named Hugh, said he suspected Maureen of being a cheat and Jimmy asked him to go outside but Hugh swore and stayed seated.

The couple retired to their room, where Maureen told Jimmy about the spooky advice of the man in the old picture. Jimmy asked the hotel barman about the painting and was told "It says John Gully on the back of the frame but we haven't a clue who he was. The picture has been there for years." It so happens there was a John Gully back in the Regency era, and he was a prizefighter, racehorse owner - and an accomplished gambler who died in 1863. Maureen went into the lounge on the following morning after the breakfast while Jimmy left the hotel to go and get the Sunday newspaper and cigarettes, and once again, as Maureen gazed at the picture of John Gully, she heard his voice in her mind say, 'Maureen, buy this picture with the money you have won and take me with you and we shall make a fortune – you shall enjoy a life of wealth beyond your wildest dreams.'

Maureen thought about Jimmy, and wondered if the thing in that picture included him in the promised life of wealth, and the voice told her: 'If you remain with Jimmy, he'll be forever dipping into your purse.'

'No, I'd rather be poor with Jimmy by my side than be rich and lonely,' said Maureen, and an elderly hotel guest standing nearby thought she was addressing him, and he said, 'What was that, sorry?'

'Nothing,' said Maureen, 'just thinking out loud,' and the picture of John Gully fell from the wall. She then heard the voice cry out in anger: 'Then go and be poor for the rest of your days!'

That afternoon, Maureen and Jimmy left the Melrose Hotel and something strange happened. Maureen thought Jimmy would go straight to the betting shop with the poker winnings on Monday, but he had a 'Road to Damascus' moment on Sunday evening as they sat in the Vines pub on Lime Street. He'd been looking into his pint of bitter and Maureen had said, 'Penny for your thoughts, Jimmy,' and he had replied: 'Was just thinking – when you come to think of it, in a bet is a fool and a thief. I was the fool and the bookie is the thief, but come Monday you'll see a new man, Maureen.'

'Is it the drink talking, though?' Maureen asked, bringing her face close to his, and Jimmy said, 'No, this is me talking, it's not ale talk; I think the best throw of the dice is to throw the dice away.'

And Jimmy was true to his word – on Monday he started scanning the Situations Vacant column of the *Liverpool Echo* - and after doing this for a few days he found a job – just a factory job – but it was a start. Maureen eventually divorced her violent husband, and after living with Jimmy for two years they got married. The whereabouts of that painting of John Gully are unknown.

The tempter in the following short account did not use her persuasion to bring some monetary reward to bring about the desired result – this was a much more sinister type of temptation.

One night, around 11pm in March, 2017, a Hackney driver named David was hailed on Thomas Lane by a lady who looked about 20 to 22 years of age, and she got in the cab and the driver made a remark about a female caller on a radio phone-in programme he was listening to. 'Women should have stayed in the kitchen - they've got too much to say,' he said, and the fare glared at him. The lights were on red at the Thomas Lane/Thomas Drive junction, and as the idling cab's diesel engine rattled, the cabby was about to ask, 'Where to, love?' when he saw the image of the woman in the rear view mirror getting closer and closer until he could see her reflected eyes, and they looked huge in the mirror, and then they started to shine. David was mesmerised by the sight, and he heard the passenger say in a Liverpool accent, 'Let me out, and then drive your taxi into that wall as fast as you can.'

David then unlocked the doors and let the lady out and then he had an overwhelming urge to drive across a traffic island and smash the vehicle into the sandstone wall at the corner of Holly Bank Avenue. He fought hard in his mind to stop himself from what would be a sure suicide, and he looked at the tiny photo of his grandson dangling from the rear view mirror, and he experienced a feverish cold shudder. 'I can't do this,' David said to himself, 'I want to live,' and he kept seeing the eyes of that passenger – who had now gone – in the mirror, and he had the overwhelming feeling that death would be a lovely state of being in which he'd be free of any health or money problems. It was hard to put into words, but the idea of ending David's life was very seductive to him. To the photograph of his grandson, David said, 'I'm sorry, but I've got to go – I'll meet you again one day,' and he felt tears rolling down his cheeks. David took the handbrake off, ready to smash the cab, and himself, into the sandstone wall, and the thought of an imminent cessation of his life was so tempting, and yet a part of the cabby's mind was trying to prevent the act of self-destruction. 'Well, here comes my death,' said the cabby when he suddenly heard a loud car horn next to him. David's friend, another hackney driver named Roy, had pulled alongside him, and he was swearing at David, and then Roy drove in front of the cab, preventing David from accelerating into that wall. Roy got out, opened the driver's side of the taxi and punched David in the right eye. That seemed to break him out of his 'death wish', and David cried out and asked, 'What was that for?'

Roy threw another punch that missed, and David lifted his size 12 foot, placed it on Roy's abdomen, and kicked him onto the pavement. He wasn't sure whether he should close and lock the door to prevent a further barrage of blows or whether he should get out and restrain his violent friend. Thinking Roy might throw a brick through the window of the cab, David jumped out the taxi and as Roy got up and ran at him he stepped aside and caught his solar plexus with his left fist. Roy bent over, winded, and David asked, 'Now, would you mind telling me what's brought all this on?'

'You! You gossiping about me in that coffee bar in town!' came the reply from Roy, his face twisted in pain.

'I haven't mentioned you playing away with anyone, you paranoid bastard;' said David, 'now will you calm down before you come to some real harm?'

'Calm down?' gasped Roy, 'She's walked out on me.'

'Who?' queried David, keeping his distance, just in case Roy kicked off again.

'My wife, who do you think?' said Roy, 'I think

you've ruptured my colon.'

David eventually convinced Roy he had not been jangling about him, and that it had most probably been a friend of the woman he'd been seeing. Roy went home, and so did David, and he thought about the strange woman who had somehow convinced him to take his own life. He had the eerie feeling that young woman had been some type of witch, perhaps upset by his sexist remark, and he realised that, only for Roy attacking him, he would have driven the taxi into that wall. David has not seen that woman since, and he hopes he'll never set eyes on her again.

Now for an account of a very strange – and sinister temptation – that of a schoolgirl who found herself drawn to a spellbinding spectacle. One windy afternoon in March 1966, a 13-year-old schoolgirl named Jackie, a pupil of the Liverpool Institute High School for Girls (a grammar school) on Blackburne Place, felt an urge to go into the playground, even though it was not yet officially playtime. Jackie was a quiet, well-behaved girl and not the type of person who would suddenly venture out into the playground between lessons. On this day she had been fully occupied with the school's production of the Shakespeare play *The Tempest*, which would be staged at the school's hall on 30 March. Jackie was overwhelmed by the urge to go outside and she hurried to the western side of the playground, the part adjacent to Hope Street, and there she saw her late grandmother inside of what looked like a huge floating, faintly glowing semitransparent sphere, very similar to a soap bubble. The figure in the sphere beckoned Jackie, and the girl was about to run to her when a teacher shouted at Jackie, and the teenager looked back - and the sphere - and the figure of her grandmother inside of it, vanished. The teacher had also seen the strange 'apparition', but later backtracked and said it had been 'something like St Elmo's Fire' (a poorly understood atmospheric phenomenon where an electric field seems to cause a display of glowing plasma) when Jackie told another teacher about the weird incident. Jackie felt as if she had been in a trance when she had experienced the irresistible urge to go out of the school to a certain part of the playground. The figure in the 'bubble' might have been something impersonating the girl's deceased grandmother, perhaps as a way of abducting the schoolgirl. The Institute closed in 1984 and is now Blackburne House Centre for Women.

Some stories of a mysterious tempter have a happy ending, such as the following one, but they are a rarity.

On the Friday afternoon of 11 November 2016; a 42-year-old lady named Hannah felt so down, and so she got in her little car and drove from her home on Greenhill Road, Mossley Hill, and found herself bound for the Childwall Fiveways pub - a place she'd only ever driven past - and Hannah was baffled as to why she felt the need to visit this pub. She often went for a 'therapeutic drive' (as she called these excursions) when she was feeling anxious or depressed, and today, for some utterly bizarre reason, the prospect of visiting the Fiveways was lifting her gloomy mood. She parked up outside the pub, and by now she was wondering if she was losing her marbles. If she'd wanted a drink, she could have gone to the Greenhills pub at the end of her road. She went into the Fiveways and bought herself a diet coke and a bag of scampi and sat in a corner of an almost deserted pub. She thought of her life, and her disastrous relationships - all two of them - and now she was sinking back into depression when a man walked in and looked about. Hannah watched him ask for a diet coke, and then he sat about ten feet away and Hannah smiled at him out of politeness, and the man smiled back, looked out the window - then slowly turned his head until he faced Hannah. He gazed hard at her.

'Excuse me,' didn't you live on Molyneux Road in Kensington?' he asked Hannah and this query startled her, for she had indeed lived on that road in Kensington till she was twelve. The man came over, his eyes thinned and his mouth a wide smile now, and he said, 'Hannah - Maureen and Ken's girl? You haven't changed a bit.' The man then said his name was Chris, and Hannah recalled him; he had knocked about with her brother and lived next door. The two long-lost neighbours chatted, and Chris said a strange thing: 'You know what? It's strange us bumping into one another - I just had the *urge* to come here, it was bizarre.'

Hannah couldn't get her words out quick enough, and she said she'd had the same urge to visit this particular pub. Then she saw her mother - just for a split-second in the mirror behind the bar, but when she turned her head, she'd gone. It had been her mum's birthday today, and then Hannah recalled something else: her mother was a Childwall girl who'd married a "Kenny" (Kensington) lad, and she had met him in this very pub. Hannah started seeing Chris and they ended up married. Hannah believes her late mum was a matchmaker that day in November.

The enigmatic enticer in the following peculiar account seems more like a force than a being, but of course, it's sometimes hard to distinguish between the two in the world of the paranormal.

The story is derived from a lady I interviewed in 2019. Gillian worked in the Dolcis shoe store on Church Street in the 1980s. She said she went up to a room above the shop that hadn't been used for years and there, hanging from the ceiling was an old mirror ball, of the type you often see suspended from the ceilings of dance halls and discotheques (where they are referred to as disco balls). Gillian pressed a switch on the wall of the dusty and gloomy old room, thinking it might turn on a light, but instead the switch activated the mirror ball, and as Gillian looked at it spinning she became mesmerised by the glinting colours of light the sphere gave off and she felt herself being drawn into it; her very consciousness seemed to move upwards and she had what we could term as an out-of-body experience. Gillian tried to resist the force pulling her up into the mirror ball, but she went into the globe of hundreds of mirrored facets and through a tunnel of light, feeling she was going to pass out from intense vertigo. Gillian likened the sensation she was feeling to that of the butterflies she felt in her stomach when she was on a roller coaster. Gillian then found herself for a few seconds in Liverpool's Church Street in the 1960s. She felt the cold wind on her face and a sense that she was really there; it was no dream or some hallucination. She heard a woman say, 'Where did she just come from?' and then Gillian experienced a sensation of falling backwards and she was back in the room above the shoe shop. She cried out, 'Oh!' and steadied herself by leaning against the wall. The mirror ball was now slowly rotating, ready to stop, and the switch on the wall was in the off position. The experience really shook Gillian, and when she told her workmates, her advisor got wind of the story and advised Gillian not to go into that room again and it was locked up. Why a mirror ball had been installed in the room above the shoe shop is unknown, and no one could remember when it had last been used. The mirror ball was removed by two workmen not long after Gillian's experience, and one of the workmen made a curious remark about the room upstairs, saying, 'There's a few spooks upstairs,' but he did not elaborate on why he had made the comment. I'm still looking into the incident.

If you should feel tempted – not by the lure of a bar of chocolate, a cream cake, an alcoholic drink or a cigarette – but by some inexplicable urge that seems to have a *supernatural* hold on you, then try your utmost to resist it, because you never know what that temptation may lead to...

NINE GREEN LADIES

This is a story I can't get to the bottom of; it's open to a few interpretations, but for now here's the account as it was given to me by the two main witnesses – the couple in the tale. The time was 3:20 in the morning that February in 2013, and a couple in their twenties - Theo and Erin, were about to go asleep in their flat on Canning Street in the Georgian Quarter, but Theo just couldn't settle down in the bed. His fiancée Erin stroked his arm reassuringly, urging him to relax, but felt the goosebumps on that arm. 'What's up?' she asked, to which he replied, 'I keep feeling a cold shiver.'

'A virus,' Erin opined, and eventually the two of them fell asleep, but awoke thirty minutes later to the sound of women's voices talking excitedly in the lounge, which was next door to the couple's bedroom. Theo got up but Erin was that tired she lay in bed with her fatigued eyes squinting at the doorway, through which she could see some blurry greenish figures. Theo peered into the lounge and could not believe his eyes, for there were nine women, all around 5 feet and 5 inches tall (Erin's height in her bare feet), all dressed in outlandish green skin-tight costumes, and Theo had never set eyes on any of them before in his life. One woman was smoking a thin cigar – his Henry Wintermans Panatella, one was knocking back what looked like vodka, neat from the bottle, and the others were drinking everything from the cocktail cabinet. Theo coughed but the strangers never reacted and chatted among themselves, so he went back to Erin and in a low voice he told her about the oddly dressed women. 'Erin, you're not going to believe this but there are nine women, all dressed in bizarre green clothes in our lounge, and they are smoking my cigars and knocking back all our drinks.'

'You're half asleep, Theo; how would they get in here?' Erin asked with an annoyed tone, and with a groan she sat up in the bed. She saw the nine outlandishly dressed women in green through the gap in the door, which Theo had left ajar. Then the grandfather clock in the lounge struck four - and the women were all suddenly gone - yet the couple could still smell the cigarette and cigar smoke.

'Oh my God, they were ghosts,' said Erin, and now, with the shock of seeing them she was wide awake.

'I'll check the front door in case they're not ghosts,' said Theo, and Erin jumped up out the bed and walked close behind him, scared of being on her own in the bedroom.

Theo and Erin could clearly see that the front door was locked and bolted, and then they went into the smoky lounge and Erin shuddered at the sight of the lipstick marks on the glasses which the mysterious visitors had used, plus an abandoned panatella, still smoking in the ashtray.

Theo picked up the stub of the slender cigar and looked at the lipstick smudge upon it and he also brought it close to his nostrils and gently inhaled. He could smell a faint sweet scent.

'Theo, I'm scared;' said Erin, clinging onto his left forearm, 'why are they haunting us? Is it an omen?'

'I don't know,' Theo admitted, putting the cigar butt back in the cut glass ashtray. 'I've never seen a ghost before in my life, and if I hadn't have seen them with my own eyes I wouldn't have believed it. It's well weird.'

'Maybe we should move,' Erin suggested – she was serious; Theo could see how serious she was by her huge frightened eyes.

'With our credit history?' he replied, trying to smile, 'And where are we going to get a deposit and rent in advance from and all that?'

'We could stay in me mum's,' replied Erin, but straight away Theo shook his head and said, 'Will you calm down? I've read about these things and nine times out of ten you never hear of them again once they put in an appearance.'

Erin clung on to Theo all night. As they days passed, Erin came to believe the ghosts would never be seen again, but then eight days after the incident, Theo got up to go to the toilet at 3:20 am one morning - and there were the nine women in green again. This time, Theo wasn't as afraid as he had been during the first encounter, and he shouted, 'Oi!' and the figures vanished. He went in and shook Erin awake and she said, 'Who was shouting then?'

'Me,' said Theo, 'I was shouting at the ghosts – they were back!'

'What!' Erin sat up in the bed in a flash and looked at the bedroom door, but it was shut.

Theo looked at the door and said: 'I shouted at them; I yelled "Oi!" and they vanished. They weren't drinking or smoking this time.'

'We need to get a priest in or we are moving,' said Erin, sternly, 'and I don't care about our credit history – we'll move in with my sister or me mum!'

Fortunately for Erin and Theo, the nine women have not been seen since and who they are and why they were all dressed in green is still a mystery. When Theo told his grandmother about the incident, she cryptically remarked, 'Not all fairies are like Tinkerbell – some really like to drink and eat.'

I've heard of phantom green visitors in the wee small hours before, and I'm inclined to agree with Theo's Nan.

MISS MERCER

One lunch hour in March 2016, a 50-year-old store detective named Tony was standing on Church Street smoking a cheroot and getting a little sun and fresh air (when he wasn't inhaling the cigar smoke), and then he intended to dart into the Grapes pub on Mathew Street, have a swift half before getting back to a job that was increasingly dissatisfying to Tony. The thought of being half a century old and not being at a place in life he had imagined when he was a kid filled him with a little sadness, but then Tony looked up from the pavement and beheld a sight that made him smile: an old tramp directing traffic on Hanover Street, his arms moving about like semaphore flags. With a great earnest expression on his bearded face, the vagrant now had his palm presented to a bemused hackney cab driver and he was using the other hand to beckon an annoyed bus driver. The busman beeped his horn and even from here, Tony could hear the driver yelling, 'Get out the way you stupid old get!'

Upon hearing this insult the tramp took out a piece of paper and pulled a little blue pen he'd probably got from the bookmakers and walked to the bus to perhaps take down the name of the offensive bus driver. 'What a city,' Tony said softly as he exhaled from the cheroot, and then he noticed an elegant lady in black, dressed in a large old-fashioned hat; her attire looked Edwardian; Tony knew a little about history to date those clothes. He followed the woman out of pure curiosity – and perhaps something else at the unconscious level, and he wondered if she was an eccentric, or perhaps even some girl with a liking for Gothic fashion, but something told Tony he was tailing a ghost. Ghosts were something Tony had never believed in. When his father died, he was told by an aunt who was into the supernatural that he'd see him again as a ghost, but Tony saw nothing, and so he became bitter to the whole concept of spirits. And yet, here, today, not in a foggy cemetery, but in a bustling thoroughfare of noisy life, on Church Street, in broad daylight, he had a sneaking suspicion that this woman was a bona fide ghost. She seemed to be looking for something near Top Shop, and she peered in the window of Dorothy Perkins and Burton. She then halted, and with great grace in her movement she walked back towards Hanover Street, and was almost hit by a car as she crossed to go up Bold Street, and her behaviour piqued Tony's inquisitiveness, so he went to the outdated lady, ran a little ahead of her, feeling so foolish as he considered the age of fifty to be old, and then he stopped in her path and said, 'Excuse me,' and she looked at him with unusually clear olive green eyes; her complexion was porcelain; she was beautiful. She stopped.

'Can I help you?' he said, 'You seemed to be looking for someone before up on Church Street. I hope you don't mind me trying to help you; I'm not trying it on or anything; I'm old enough to be your dad.'

The lady smiled but her eyes seemed sad, and she

nodded, and said she was looking for a certain café, and Tony couldn't quite make out the word, but it sounded like "Kardomah"; he had vague recollections of that name being connected to a number of cafés in the 1960s and he recalled his mum talking about them. Tony pointed to a nearby café and he asked, 'Can I get you some refreshment in there?' And that lady stood there still as a statue for what seemed a long time – probably just ten seconds - and then she walked silently with Tony to the café, and he pushed the door open and held it for her and then he escorted this strange but lovely lady to a window seat and the woman asked for tea. The waitress asked Tony and the lady if they wanted anything else, but he was so captivated by the potential ghost, he didn't answer and the waitress stormed away in a huff, and minutes later she returned, bringing a pot of Earl Grey and Tony asked the lady who she was as he stood up and served the tea into her cup.

'Miss Mercer,' she told him, 'my fiancé is Mr Thorburn, a cotton broker, but I cannot find him, and we were supposed to meet at the Kardomah Café on Church Street; but he wasn't there; he is never there.'

Tony now wondered if he should ask her an obvious question, and something deep down – some warning voice - said, "No!" - but nevertheless he found himself posing the query in an awkward way: 'Are you a ghost?' he asked, and something strange, yet very sad took place; the woman closed her eyes, gave a very faint smile, bowed her head - and vanished. The waitress and two members of staff came over and looked at the empty seat in shock; they had seen the lady disappear. Their eyes then travelled over to Tony, as if he would have some explanation for the incredible vanishing act. He felt so sad for some reason, and he gasped to the staff of the café, 'I blew it – I blew it – what an idiot!' and they didn't know what he meant. It was so completely bizarre, but Tony felt as if he was *in love* with that ghost - a ghost he now so desperately wanted to see again. He had no one in his life; he got up each day, sometimes at the weekends too, and ate, went to work, came home, ate, watched TV and slept, and that was it – but this lady – had she been some form of promise? Had love come to his empty life in a very unusual way? Would Miss Mercer return to him? After that day, Tony would linger around Church Street at lunchtime and after work, and this went on for years, but he hasn't seen Miss Mercer since that day. A long, long time ago, in Victorian times, there had been a Kardomah Café that had stood where Top Shop, Dorothy Perkins and Burtons had been located in 2016, but it had long been swept away by the great tides of change, and here in our own time we have seen the places we frequented erased in the name of progress, and what precious keepsake memories, bitter and sweet, are obliterated by the 'developers'.

HOTEL IN ANOTHER DIMENSION

On Boxing Day in 1994, at around 8:20pm, a 26-year-old Huyton lady named Georgina was sitting on her sofa with her snoring boyfriend Ray slumped beside her as she watched an uninspiring seasonal episode of *The Bill*, when the landline telephone warbled. Georgina leaned over the arm of the sofa and answered the call. It was Chipper – the nickname of Alec, her colleague in an electrical engineering firm. He'd got his nickname because he had an encyclopaedic knowledge of every make of silicon chip, its serial number and what it did, from op-amps to complex logic gates.

'You busy, Georgie?' Chipper asked, and Georgina said she wasn't and asked where they were needed. 'There's some electrical fault in the alarm down in the Adelphi;' Chipper told her, 'I asked Roger first [another employee in the electrical firm] but he's got the flu.'

'On the ale, more like,' Georgina remarked, and within the space of five minutes, she had left a note on the refrigerator door for boyfriend Ray – who was still sparked out on the sofa – telling him she'd been called out on a job, and her Vauxhall Corsa was travelling down Lordens Road. Georgina turned onto East Prescot Road, and the traffic lights seemed to be against her tonight, so what should have been a half-hour trip took forty-five minutes. She arrived at the Adelphi Hotel a few minutes after Chipper, and she went into the foyer with her usual tools, continuity tester, spare electronic components and so on. Despite it being Boxing Day, town was super busy, and a few drunks were singing at the entrance to the hotel.

'Something keeps tripping it, I'm told,' said Chipper, 'but I'm not too au fait on these new alarms but I know you are.'

'So you called me out,' said Georgina, and she smiled and added, 'I could have come down here on me tod, Chipper,' but her colleague said, 'Nah, not on barmpot night. Anyway, you can educate me.'

'Boxing Day used to be so dead once,' said Georgina, opening the control panel after trying unsuccessfully to reset the alarm, 'but now everyone goes to town. Oh, what's this?' She noticed something odd; there was a lot of static electricity around the alarm console. Her blonde hair stood on end with the charge and Chipper giggled and asked, 'Is that with the static?'

'Yeah, I've never seen this before,' said Georgina, 'what the hell's causing it?'

'Well, that's for you to find out. I'm just going to check on the van, Georgie,' said Chipper, eyeing a rowdy gang of lads through the panes of the hotel's revolving door. 'Be back in a mo,' he added and he went whistling out through the revolving door to guard the van, which was parked round the corner on Copperas Hill.

As Georgina was testing the components of the alarm, she overheard a quaint-sounding conversation going on somewhere behind her. Two well-spoken men were talking, and one of them said, 'He tipped the chambermaid and the parlour maid and even the hall porter, but he was not very forthcoming with the rest of the hotel staff.'

The other voice said in reply: 'So, he did not leave any gratuities for the others? Well that is most disgraceful for a man of his standing, Mr Jones. Now, I trust you will excuse me, for I must make sure everything is perfect for the dinner to celebrate the Royal Wedding.'

'Royal Wedding?' muttered Georgina, and she wondered what regal wedding that would be. Georgina turned – and received quite a shock. *The place had changed.* There were candlelit dining tables and elaborate, expensive chairs around them, set for what was obviously some important event. A tall immaculately-attired waiter stood there holding a silver serving tray, and he was gazing at Georgina with an intense puzzled expression. 'What on earth are *you?*' he asked Georgina, and she recognised his voice; he had been one of the men she'd just heard talking about a Royal Wedding.

'I'm the electrician, what are *you?*' Georgina retorted, peeved at the man's strange question.

'You're a *woman,*' the waiter replied, setting the tray down on one of the set tables, 'is this some silly practical joke?'

'What the f-' Georgina almost swore; 'I'm fixing the alarm,' Georgina told him, and turned to point at the control panel hanging from a spaghetti-like mass of multicoloured wires – but the alarm's panel had gone; there was just wood panelling there. Georgina couldn't help but swear, and the waiter said, 'Really! I think you should leave now, before it becomes a matter for the police.'

At that precise moment, Georgina realised she had somehow gone back in time to the hotel as it must have been decades ago, and a numbness inside of her welled into panic. A young rosy-cheeked male of about fifteen years of age came into the vast room, and he had on a round brimless drum-shaped hat held on a by a strap that went under his chin – like the bell-boy's Georgina had seen in films of bygone days, and the tall waiter said to the lad, 'Martin, you will eject this – this vagrant immediately.'

Georgina then heard a voice cry out what sounded like a name in the next room and the waiter shouted back, 'Coming, Mr Towel!' and then he left. The bell-boy meekly asked Georgina to follow him out of the hotel, and in a daze of confusion the electrician walked outside – and she saw trams trundling along Ranelagh Place and Lime Street with a clanging noise. Stunned at the sight of these vintage vehicles, Georgina turned to the boy and asked, 'What *year* is this?'

The boy looked at her in a perplexed manner.

'I said what's the year?' she yelled at him, and the boy stepped back and said, 'It's 1922. You're potty.'

And then he went back into the hotel. Georgina walked past people dressed in the fashions of the 1920s, and received some strange looks, because she was in jeans, a tee shirt and trainers, and had a tool belt strung around her.

'Oi!' came a voice from behind the electrician, and she turned – and saw a policeman hurrying towards her. Walking with him was the bell-boy. Georgina ran around the corner and her ears popped, and then she heard a strange loud noise – it sounded like all of the noises of the busy street being played on a reel to reel tape recorder that was being wound backwards. Georgina was so relieved to see Chipper's van on Copperas Hill – 1994 had returned. Chipper had been looking everywhere for Georgina for the last ten minutes. Georgina fixed the alarm, and told Chipper what had happened, and how she believed she had somehow gone back in time. Chipper was a superstitious soul, and he didn't think his colleague had been in some timeslip – he thought ghosts were to blame and said he always thought the Adelphi had a spooky atmosphere about it. Georgina said the experienced had been so real – as if she had actually been in the past. She recalled the static electricity; had that caused the slip in time or had the timeslip caused the static? She later discovered there had been a Royal Wedding in February 1922 when a Princess Mary had married a Viscount, and furthermore, that year a Mr Towle - pronounced "Towel" had been the manager of the Adelphi - and Georgina had distinctly heard the sexist waiter call his name.

EMOTIONS AND
THE SUPERNATURAL

After studying ghosts and the paranormal for many years, I have come to believe that emotions are a big factor in the whole phenomenon, whether it is a bond of love or a longstanding vendetta of hate between two people, the emotions involved seem to be part of some arcane equation that plays a major part in hauntings, telepathy, precognition and so on. The bond between a couple who loved – or hated – one another unconditionally seems to be a connection that even death cannot break. I know of numerous cases where ghosts have had a romantic interest in the living, and what follows are two excellent examples of this scenario.

On the sunny afternoon of Sunday 20 September 2020, two girls in their early twenties, Arabella and Luna, went to have a look around Speke Hall, one of our better tourist attractions, and during the visit, Luna took a shine to the Hall's guide dressed as a cavalier. 'I think the cavalier guy's hot,' she told Arabella, who said, 'You think everyone's hot.'

'He's got midnight blue eyes and long hair like Viggo Mortensen,' Luna went on, and her friend dared her to make a pass at her latest crush. Luna took the guide's picture on her phone and he must have heard Arabella call Luna by her name and he said, 'Luna' in a sort of sigh before adding, 'Beauteous thou art, Luna. Upon my soul I shall win you, golden-haired maiden.'

And Luna, looking at her phone with a smile said, 'Shurrup.'

The guide, who seemed to be keeping up the act, said "One hour shall feel like ten when you have departed, sweet Luna.'

Luna was startled by a colourful orange, black and white butterfly (most probably a Painted Lady) that landed on Arabella's nose and she turned to take a picture of it with the phone, but Arabella exclaimed a swear word and the butterfly flew off, spoiling Luna's shot.

'He vanished!' Arabella told Luna, 'The guide! Oh my God!'

Luna turned to see that she was right - the guide had gone - but there was nowhere he could have gone in such a short space of time – literally seconds - and so Luna checked her phone and saw that the picture she had taken of the guide was just one of a sandstone wall. Luna asked two people who worked at Speke Hall who the guide dressed as the cavalier had been. Yes, you've guessed right: there was no guide dressed as a cavalier. There have been a few sightings of the cavalier in and around the Hall and in the attic, both night and day. Many of those who have encountered the unidentified ghost have spoken of how solid he looks – so solid in fact, he is often taken as one of the living. Many years ago I did two talks at Speke Hall and noticed him standing at the back of the room near a doorway, and people who saw him thought he was some actor who would take part in the talk, but instead he vanished, and such was the commotion that ensued, I had to suspend the talk for a few minutes. A woman in the audience later told me she had felt a phantom kiss on the left side of her neck.

And here is another account of a ghost that had feeling for one of the living.

For several weeks in April 2010, a 30-year-old barmaid named Kath often saw a man 'dressed as a Victorian' as she described him, following her when she was going to work or returning home. The stalker wore a top hat, a long coat that went below his knees, and shiny black boots with studs that made a clicking sound when he walked. Kath lived in a flat on Wood Street with her boyfriend Neil, and when she told the latter about the oddly dressed man following her, Neil said it was probably just someone trying to spook her; he didn't offer to accompany his girlfriend to her workplace, which was just a five minute walk away. For a fortnight, Kath would see the man in the quaint attire standing in doorways, eyeing her or blatantly walking behind her, and then one night there was an unexpected break in the pattern of stalking as Kath was on her way home from work. Upon reaching the corner of Wood Street and Hanover Street, the barmaid was confronted by a young man who casually asked her, 'Can you just give me whatever you have on you?' and he kept his right hand in his pocket, and Kath, sensing the man had a knife, or even a gun, felt her legs turn to jelly. She was just about to open her handbag to hand the man her purse when the top-hatted "stalker" who had been following Kath seemed to appear out of nowhere and he lunged with both hands at the would-be mugger - who turned and ran across the road and narrowly missed being knocked down by a hackney cab. Kath thanked the stalker and he said, 'I have watched you from afar, and followed you,' and then seemed stuck for words, and Kath said, 'I know,' to which the man said, 'I love you,' and he muttered something else but Kath couldn't quite make out what he said. Then she saw that the man had a faint blue glow around him, and he started to fade away, and she backed away, ready to run, but then something told her to stay put – and although she knew he *was* a ghost, he obviously genuinely loved her. The spectral man smiled and vanished into thin air, and a stunned yet moved Kath found herself on a rainy Hanover Street, gazing at mid-air. She never saw him again, and she told me: 'It was strange; no man had ever said those three words to me before – and here was a ghost telling me those words. Besides being shocked by encountering a ghost, I was also a little taken aback by him telling me he loved me.'

Alas, after that eventful rainy morning, Kath never again set eyes on her admirer from beyond. I wonder who he was.

An emotional bond between two people was picked up by an apparently genuine fortune-teller in the next story.

In the early 1970s, a 24-year-old Childwall lady

named Clare went to see an old self-proclaimed fortune teller in Knotty Ash named Rose Mary who used to scry in a crystal ball for just 50p. Rose Mary was booked for months in advance as she was said to be very accurate, but she let Clare jump the queue because she knew the girl's mother well. Rose Mary looked into the crystal ball on the table for a while, thinning her eyes and humming to herself, and then she told Clare, 'You're going to dye your hair blonde but you must not or you could come to very serious harm - or worse.' Well, Clare went cold, as she'd just bought a 59p box of Clairol Nice 'n Easy blonde hair dye. The fortune teller went on: 'There's a man - his name begins with a D; oh, if only I could see the rest of his name – but, anyway, your paths cross near a bridge but there's something strange about this man - he has two faces, like the old Roman god Janus, and he keeps one face hidden. He loved you once, Clare, I can see the silver line of a lost love between you and him.'

Clare opened her purse and gave Rose Mary the 50p and she gave it begrudgingly as she was not very impressed by the fortune teller, but a week later, a dyed-blonde Clare was walking home from her friend's house on Childwall Valley Road at 12:40am, and as she passed under the railway bridge, a man with a frightening hooded mask stepped out and blocked her path.

'Oh my God!' gasped Clare, 'Don't hurt me! All I have is a quid!' and she heard the masked man faintly mutter, 'It's *you* - I didn't recognise you with your...' but without finishing the sentence the would-be mugger turned and ran off into the moonlit night, and Clare thought she saw a knife in his hand. Clare had definitely heard his voice before somewhere but couldn't place it - until later that morning. She sat in the kitchen with her mother, drinking tea, eating cheese on toast and smoking cigarettes at two in the morning, and Clare was still in shock from the knifeman encounter when her mum said, 'Could that man whose name begins with D be that Davy fellah who used to be mad on you? He lived in Netherley.'

'Mam, you're right,' said Clare, 'I think it *was* his voice!'

Clare didn't go to the police, because she could not prove Davy had been the man who had confronted her that night, but rather coincidentally, she saw Davy walking near her house days after the encounter with the masked knifeman and she glared at him, and somehow Clare just knew from the way he looked at her that he had been the would-be robber – and perhaps even a rapist – that she had met under the railway bridge, and not long after, Davy suddenly moved from Liverpool and was heard from no more, although someone told Clare he had moved to Cardiff. Clare realised Davy hadn't recognised her that night because her usual jet-black hair had been bleached to an almost platinum blonde. The fortune teller's prediction had been spot on.

We sometimes hear the adage, 'You can't *make* somebody love you' but the following weird account seems to suggest otherwise. Someone – perhaps using witchcraft – literally mesmerised a married man, and the victim of this emotional hijacking, now in his eighties is still in the dark about the strange unexplained attraction.

It was a typical English summer's day that Saturday

afternoon on 27 August 1977 – drizzly and humid – and a 39-year-old Garston man named Terry Golding got off the bus at Renshaw Street and felt his wife Thelma's note in his coat pocket. Thelma had a bad case of summer flu and so he had been given the task today to get some of his children's clothes at Blacklers and TJ Hughes for their return to school – and he also had to get a certain sized pair of Eastex slacks for Thelma. Terry thought about nipping into Yates's Wine Lodge to make the shopping mission more bearable but then he saw a pretty redheaded woman pass by – and the strangest change came over him. He had a powerful urge to follow this woman, who looked as if she was in her late twenties. Terry couldn't help himself; he had been happily married to Thelma for fourteen years – but this woman seemed to have an almost hypnotic hold on him. He walked, zombielike after her, as far as Church Street, and she ran across the road and turned to look at him outside of the shoe store Dolcis – and Terry could see only the redhead in his tunnel vision. He walked towards her – and found a huge stocky man dragging him backwards by the scruff of his shirt collar.

'Gerroff!' yelled Terry, but the man yanked him back – and a bus roared past – and it would have slammed into Terry if that man had not restrained him from walking after that redhead. When Terry snapped out of the strange spell, the woman with the red hair had gone. Now he had a real excuse to go and have a swift half a pint in a pub – to steady his nerves – and at the pub he wondered why he had been entirely smitten by that redheaded lady. At the age of 39, was Terry experiencing one of those male mid-life crises he had recently read about in the newspapers? He looked at himself in the pub mirror in an introspective way, and shook his head slightly. He loved his wife, and he could not understand why he had been so bewitched by that woman. After the quick drink, Terry got on with the shopping and returned home.

Weeks later in September, Terry had had a bit too much to drink at a social club in Garston one night when he decided to go home. His best friend Frank told him to stay a little longer because the barman was going to bring out a big plate of fried chicken drumsticks, but Terry shook his head and in a slurred voice he told him, 'Frankie, you are a single man, and it's different for you; you can stay out all night, but I have a tasty wife waiting for me at home with a lovely supper.'

'Don't you mean a lovely wife with a tasty supper, Terry?' laughed Frankie, patting his friend on the back as he headed unsteadily for the door. Terry walked - or staggered - out of the pub and straight into a thick fog, and that night there was a power failure in the area, so all of the lamp posts went out. Terry stumbled drunkenly along the pavement, cursing the darkness and the fog, when he saw that redheaded lady again – and she was holding what looked like an old lantern.

'Come on, Terry!' the woman shouted, and walked off, and Terry found himself unable to resist. He blindly followed her through the thickest fog he'd ever encountered – and she vanished, along with her lamp, and Terry ended up stranded on a sandbank somewhere off the Cast Iron Shore. The silhouette of an enormous ship passed by Terry with its fog horn blasting and its closeness terrified him; he could hear its bows moving through the waters. The tide was coming in, and Terry was disoriented in the darkness. Two people heard his frantic cries that night and one of them bravely rescued him. Terry saw the enigmatic woman one more time in town – walking towards him with an unsettling smile on London Road, but Terry turned and ran. Who this mesmeric lady was remains a mystery to this day.

The bond of love between two brothers in the following story seems to have formed some type of telepathic channel. I've changed a few names in the account for reasons of confidentiality. In August 1971, 9-year-old Alec was enjoying the school summer holidays exploring Sefton Park with his 5-year-old brother Jake – a very special boy who, according to Alec, could see things no one else could. Jake drew pictures of squirrels, birds and butterflies as well as little green elves in yellow pointed hats and toadstool-shaped houses. Jake also loved music; he cherished a small transistor radio he'd received for his birthday, and he would always smile when a recently released song came on the radio called *My Brother Jake* (by the band, Free). Alec and Jake lived just across the road from the park, and on this day the brothers were making paper airplanes. Jake was clever at making "airies" as Alec called them; the lad would put a paper clip in the nose of the plane to make it go straight. One day, Jake smiled at Alec and pointed at his own forehead, and in Alec's mind he heard a voice say, 'I love you, Alec.'

Alec was amazed, it had sounded like Jake's voice only much clearer. Later that year when Alec was at school, he heard Jake crying for him in his mind, and

Alec just knew something had happened to his brother, so he got up from his desk and left the class in front of the flabbergasted teacher and ran home. Jake was nowhere to be seen. Alec's parents had decided to have Jake sent away to a 'home' (as they called such institutions back in those times).

'But he's *got a home* here!' cried Alec, and his father explained that Jake had Down's Syndrome – and they used that dreadful "M" word back then. Alec kept hearing his brother shouting his name and saying he was scared, and he begged his mother to take him to see Jake. The parents took Alec to a grim old building on the outskirts of the city and Jake clung to his brother when he saw him and wouldn't let go. Alec's parents suddenly had a change of heart and they took Jake back. Jake seemed to live in mortal fear of being sent away from his beloved brother, and after a few years the mind to mind communication faded away as Jake started to speak more. Today, Alec and Jake are still inseparable, and live close to one another. Alec says the telepathy he experienced between himself and Jake was not imagined, and he cannot explain it, although I have noticed on many occasions that a bond of telepathy often occurs between couples and members of closely-knit families.

In the following story, which was related to me a few years ago, it would seem that sometimes a telepathic cry for help can be picked up by a complete stranger. I have seen this phenomenon in action. Years ago, a girl I was seeing told me that a very unusual name had just come into her head out of the blue. I wrote the name down and agreed it was an unusual one. The next day, I saw that name on the front page of the *Liverpool Echo* because the bearer of the name had decided to end it all by jumping off a block of flats in the city. He had committed suicide because – according to the note he left behind – he had no friends and felt isolated. The girl had picked up his name just before he had jumped. Here's another example of one of these psychic S.O.S. messages.

During a heavy fall of snow one arctic morning at eight in January 2011, a 20-year-old Mossley Hill girl named Rhianna was standing at a bus stop on Menlove Avenue, wishing she was in bed instead of hanging round in sub-zero conditions, waiting for the bus that would take her to work. The passing council gritter lorry with its yellow flashing lights startled her and the pellets of salt struck her Uggs and stockinged legs. An elderly man, one of six people standing at the bus stop, shouted to the gritter driver, 'Bit late now, aren't ya? You should have been out last night!'

Rhianna smiled at the ranting old man, but then she suddenly felt very anxious, and for a moment she thought she was going to have a panic attack, but no, this was different; this wasn't an anxiety issue about herself, but for a man she had never seen before in her life. He was standing about ten feet away. He was bearded, had on a dark brown woollen hat that was flecked with snowflakes and he wore a green parka. He looked as if he was in a trance as he gazed down at the slush in the gutter. Rhianna somehow knew this man, who was around her age, intended to throw himself in front of the petrol tanker thundering up Menlove Avenue. The brooding young man shuffled slowly to the kerb. Rhianna - usually a quiet girl - swore at him and bellowed, 'No you don't! Stop!'

The gaggle of people at the bus stop naturally assumed that she knew the man she was yelling at. Then she threw a punch; her fist in a mitten slammed into his face, and she slipped and fell backwards into the arms of a huge man, and David fell sideways almost on top of Rhianna, stunned. The petrol tanker rolled past the bus stop. The violent 'incident' ended up holding the passengers up as they tried to get on the bus. The bus driver asked what had happened, and Rhianna apologised to David and said, 'I thought you were going to jump in front of that tanker,' and he said, 'I was.'

It transpired he had been cheated on badly and had decided to end it all; he'd been so depressed he could not see any future for himself.

Rhianna took out her mobile and phoned her boss to say she was sick, and she and David went to Speke Retail Park and he had a heart-to-heart with her over coffee and a bite to eat. He thanked her for saving his life; and they both cried. It was the strangest thing; the two young people felt as if they had always known one another.

'You must have picked up some type of distress call that my mind was sending out – a cry for help;' theorised David, 'I asked for someone to help me in my mind.'

Rhianna and David started seeing one another, as friends at first, but they became engaged in 2012 and later married. I actually believe the two of them are soul mates.

It is my opinion that the bond of affection between two people who are in love, or two people who *were* in love, can often transcend death, and I think the same is true between a human and their pet – if one of them dies, there will still be a type of channel open between them, although for some strange reason, there are people who think animals do not possess souls when nothing could be further from the truth. One of the strongest bonds of love exists between a parent and their child, and I have had so many firsthand experiences of this phenomenon, sometimes occurring many years after the parent has died, and this brings me to the following story.

I've changed one name in this story to protect someone's identity. A few years ago a man in his sixties named Joey had a win on the Lottery which amounted to almost a million, and on the same day his doctor broke the news – he had about six months to live. Joey took refuge in the past. His friends asked him if he was going to Florida, and Joey cryptically answered, 'Somewhere better,' and he was delighted to discover that his old house in Everton was up for sale. He bought it and he and his wife Julie trawled eBay for vintage 1970s furniture – replicas of the sideboards, tables and chairs they could see in the old photographs of Joey's childhood home. Julie even obtained old still-sealed rolls of the same living room wallpaper pattern. 'You can't turn the clock back though, Joey,' she sighed, tearfully, and Joey said, 'The whole of the cosmetics industry is based on that longing, Julie, or you wouldn't dye your hair and plaster your face with make-up, and I wouldn't shave and dress young.'

And so the clock *was* turned back at the house in Everton, and one Saturday morning as Joey watched DVDs of Hanna-Barbera's *The Banana Splits*, *Robinson Crusoe* and *The Flashing Blade* on a black and white telly, he felt very ill, and warned Julie not to call for an ambulance. He went to a replica of his single bed in the mock-up of his old room upstairs, and as he lay there, Julie sneaked out to fetch Joey's younger brother Michael, who lived a few streets away. Michael broke down in tears when Julie told him Joey had taken a turn for the worst, and the two of them eventually reached the old house fifteen minutes later – and they found Joey, sitting up in bed – smiling, and his torso was wrapped in brown paper and there was a sharp odour of vinegar hanging in the air. Joey said his Mam had put the brown paper, doused with vinegar, on him, after rubbing goose grease into his chest. Joey and Michael's mum had died 32 years ago, so Julie assumed her husband was hallucinating because of his illness – but Joey made a steady recovery – and his illness went into remission. His doctor said these remissions sometimes happened for reasons unknown, but Joey was convinced his mum had returned from beyond to somehow cure him with one of her old offbeat remedies. Like Julie, Michael said his brother Joey must have hallucinated his mum because of his condition, but if that was the case, where did the brown paper and goose grease come from? To this day, Joey believes his mother came back from the hereafter to save a son she loved, and every week, Joey goes to Mass and says a prayer for his beloved and much-missed mother.

You will find more cases in this book where love, or some paranormal Cupid has altered the course of a living person's life, but the collection in this chapter were bundled together because they struck me as being of a similar vein. If love comes your way – and by that

167

I mean a true love – grab it with both hands. Sadly, in this world today, there is so much hate knocking about, and finding love is like finding a rare jewel, but there's someone for everyone out there.

THE FIVE EMILIES

I have changed a few names in this peculiar story to preserve confidentiality. Some years ago a retired headmaster who had served at a very well-known Liverpool school in the 1990s told me a very strange story concerning five of his pupils. The five girls were named Andrea, Lisa, Erica, Lily and Emily, and they were all aged fourteen. In January 1995, something strange took place regarding these girls; they all started to dress identically – and adopted the same voice and hairstyle – and four of them asserted *they were their friend Emily*. Their teachers and schoolmates thought this was just a cringey joke or a silly fad at first, but the girls even wrote their identical names on the front of their exercise books in the same handwriting style, and the parents of the four new Emilies told their daughters to stop messing about – but the four of them assured their families they really were now Emily, and seemed to regard the girl they had based their identities on as some guru. Whenever the four new Emilies needed advice or were unsure of something they would look at the original Emily or go and visit her. An educational psychologist named Chris Marker heard about this strange case, and so he visited the school and interviewed the five Emilies and jokingly asked them why they had all 'become one', and the original Emily of the group said they were now a 'group mind' and that more might be joining up with them in the near future. Asked to elaborate on this statement by Marker, the original Emily said the other four were 'sisters in spirit' and that their souls had merged because they were so alike and so empathic to one another. The 'proto-Emily' also claimed the group were telepathic, and sure enough, when Marker tested the alleged telepathic abilities of the five girls, he was shocked to see that there was indeed a mind-reading talent at work, and one which he could not explain. Marker told the headmaster about his findings and then the girls started to apparently read the mind of Marker, and told him they knew of his many embarrassing secrets and sexual kinks. Marker was so perturbed by the quintet's unearthly faculty, he told the headmaster he could not explain the phenomenon and promptly abandoned his investigation of the five Emilies. In the meantime, the psychic powers of the five clone-like girls were manifested in poltergeist activity in the gymnasium of the school. When a P.E. teacher named Mr Kayes was vaulting over the pommel horse in the gym, something pushed him into a group of male pupils. The same unearthly force sent a gaggle of boys who had pestered the five Emilies hurtling backwards down the school corridors one morning as they returned from playtime, and one lad who tried to come between the carbon copy girls was pinned against a pillar in the school playground by some force that injured his ribs and diaphragm. And then, in March of that year, the dominating member of the quintet, the archetypal Emily, was suddenly put in another school, and Andrea, Lisa, Erica and Lily slowly regained their identities. Various explanations were put forward to explain the Case of the 5 Emilies; the girls were all anxious and had taken refuge from reality by some type of psychological defence mechanism that involved adopting the persona of the 'Alpha Female' –

Emily – but friends of the four girls and their teachers said none of them were the anxious type, and they were all extraverts and head-strong girls who were not easily controlled. The educational psychologist Marker said the whole thing was a classic case of disassociation – a state of mind where the girls felt disconnected with their everyday world – but that theory did not fit the facts, and in the end the headmaster thought the whole thing might have been play-acting by the girls, but the families of the four Emily clones disagreed, and said their personalities underwent a complete change and that not even the greatest method actor could have put in such a performance. The Case of the 5 Emilies therefore remains a mystery.

Just before I end this chapter, let me tell you another story of a group of girls who became drawn together in a strange camaraderie which resulted from an apparent occult force.

In November 1975, three 18-year-old friends named Suzy, Tracy and Cathy, were starting to fall out over silly arguments, and yet they were paradoxically the best of friends, always sticking together and sticking up for one another, and although a few girls tried to split them up by claiming one of the trio had said something about another member of the threesome, the trinity remained solid friends – until recently, that was, with the arrival of some male admirers. Tracy had heard of this before – the closest of friends who had fallen out when lads came on the scene to complicate matters. Tracy's mum said it was just a natural outcome of friends going on to have relationships – but - Tracy's Nan said there was a way to bond friends, but hinted that something akin to witchcraft was involved. She told Tracy that there was a wise old woman named Mrs Archer who lived off Copperas Hill down the town, and she could cast a friendship spell on people and couples to 'bind them together'. Tracy convinced Suzy and Cathy to visit this woman, who had a tiny house near the Vines pub, just around the corner from Lime Street, but when the three girls called at Mrs Archer's house, a young girl named Nancy, who was around the age of Suzy, answered the door and said her aunt - Mrs Archer - was in hospital having a minor operation. Suzy said she had come on the advice of her Nan, and that she and her two friends wanted to be bound together so their friendship would never end. Young Nancy smiled and nodded, and then she confidently assured Suzy she'd bind her and her two friends together so they'd never split up. Nancy explained, 'It's easy-peasy – all I need to do is put a special tattoo of three interlocking circles on each of your palms, and each of the three circles has got to be the colour of each of your eyes.'

'Tattoo?' Suzy queried with an anxious expression, as she was terrified of needles, but Nancy laughed and said, 'Yeah, but you'll be alright because no needles are used; we use a special ink you can never wash off. The ink is as indelible as the Mark of Cain.'

'Can we just discuss it a mo?' Suzy asked Nancy, and the girl said, 'Yeah, of course – come in and I'll make you all a cup of coffee and get some Eccles cakes that me auntie made.'

The girls discussed whether they should get the 'painless tattoos' done and they conferred with Nancy again, and she put their minds at ease, and said she'd carry out the job for just one pound - instead of the

usual three quid - and so the three girls, seeing their combined pocket money would easily finance the tattoo work, unanimously decided to go ahead with the plan. The whole thing was over in half an hour. Each girl had her palm carefully stamped with precisely positioned interlocking circles of brown, green and blue – Tracy's eyes were brown, Suzy's irises were olive green, and Cathy had midnight blue eyes. 'Those three interlocking circles are called the Borromean Rings,' said Nancy, 'and they cannot be broken; if one is removed they fall apart, and, if one of you died, it would be the same for the other two.'

Suzy felt faint when she heard this, and she later tried to scrub the permanent tattoo off with Lifebuoy soap – but it was ingrained – it didn't even fade with repeated scrubbing – her palm just felt sore. The girls pined for one another after that, and enraged their parents as they took turns at staying over at each other's homes, and when Cathy began to seriously date a lad named Ian, Suzy and Tracy always accompanied her, and when Ian slept with Cathy one night, he awoke with her two friends on his bed. Some lesser men wouldn't complain about this arrangement but upright Ian gave Cathy an ultimatum: 'Listen love, you have to decide – right? It's me or your two friends!'

'Then I choose my two friends,' said Cathy straight away.

'What?' Ian recoiled, and when he saw that Cathy was serious, his round face became flushed and he said, 'Frig you, then! I'll find someone normal!' And he marched off, out of Cathy's life.

When Suzy fell ill with tonsillitis, the other two became sick and developed sore throats, but a year later Mrs Archer (of Copperas Hill) visited the girls when they were at Tracy's house and she apologised about her niece Nancy's "incorrect and dangerous spell" – and the tattoos – and the close friendship of Suzy, Tracy and Cathy – faded almost overnight.

CUPID

In December 1999, just a week before Christmas, a Liverpool couple in their sixties went into a little well-known restaurant in the city centre for a quiet meal. The couple were Bob, a retired chef, and Betty, a former club singer, and, unknown to one another, each was going to tell the other they were calling it a day with their relationship, which had started when they were both in their late twenties. They'd both seen other people between those early days and now, but somehow they had always gravitated back to one another. Betty felt some fire had gone out in the relationship with Bob, and on top of that she wasn't feeling as young in her outlook anymore – and recently she had taken to avoiding mirrors – and when she *had* to look into a mirror to brush her teeth or put on her foundation, she tried her utmost not to look too close at the crow's feet and the laughter lines and the sagging hooded eyes under the unconvincing eyebrows. Bob said he loved those 'character lines and features' on her face, but Betty hated them, although she was reluctant to go for cosmetic surgery as she just knew some procedure would go disastrously wrong. So much for the surface of Betty; she had loved singing on the clubs, but nowadays she found she just didn't possess the confidence to sing to even a few friends; where *had* her self-esteem gone? Betty didn't know, but what she did know was that she was going to tell Bob they were parting ways, albeit in an amicable manner, over dinner. Bob, meanwhile, was going to tell Betty he felt like a burnt-out ageing loser who would soon be a burden, and felt she should remain a friend but should also feel free to look for someone younger if she felt so inclined. The couple had never got round to marrying somehow, and thought a wedding was a long-vanished pipe dream by now.

Anyway, as they sat at the table, waiting to order, an old smiling man grabbed Bob's left hand and placed it on Betty's hand - then left. Betty, forever the hypochondriac, went to wash her hands and Bob, who was so used to Betty's germophobia, smilingly said the old man 'didn't have the plague'. With Betty away in the loo, Bob sat there, his mind drifting down the timeline into the past as his out of focus eyes almost attended the multicoloured bokeh lights of the city centre through the restaurant windows.

Betty returned. For a brief instant, Bob saw Betty as she had looked when she was about 30; he thought he was seeing things - but Betty - when she'd had a few drinks - said she had seen Bob as he had looked when he was younger. 'That's bizarre, because I saw the exact same thing when I looked at you earlier,' said Bob, and she smiled and turned her face away from Bob and gave a little dismissive wave of her hand as she said, 'You're just saying that because I said it.'

'Betty, I swear on my life I saw you – I dunno – as you looked in your late twenties, early thirties – ' Bob insisted, and Betty cut in with, 'Oh well we must have had acid flashbacks.'

'I've never done acid,' said Bob in all seriousness, and Betty said, 'I did – once - at Tina Gallaeri's flat – just sat there for twenty-four hours with a sore arse looking at weird paisley patterns. A complete waste of a whole day.'

'Maybe someone spiked the wine,' Bob joked, and he saw Betty try – but she couldn't even fake a brief smile to his trite remark, and he knew something was wrong. He avoided going down that negative road and said, 'That guy before, who put our hands together,' and Betty said, 'What about it?'

'Dunno, just struck me as odd, and when my hand touched yours I felt a tingle.'

'Bob,' Betty grimaced, 'that's like something out of a Mills & Boon story.'

'I suppose it is, but I'm telling the truth,' Bob replied and smirked, and he started to fidget with a beer mat.

'This is like the last meal they give the condemned convict on death row,' said Betty, at last, and Bob said, 'It's not that bad. You think we're drifting apart, don't you?'

'No, more like full steam ahead to the iceberg,' Betty told him, and she smiled and said, 'stop playing with that beer mat, you look immature.'

And then something happened to the both of them simultaneously – they looked at one another – their eyes locked, and Betty said, 'You look as if you're going to cry; don't – I can't stand seeing a man cry.'

'I'm not going to cry – I actually feel the exact opposite – happy - and I have not felt this happy in a long time,' said Bob, and he exhibited his old toothy smile; not a smirk – but a proper smile.

Betty felt the same happiness welling up inside of her but she didn't tell Bob because her hypochondriasis was leading her to believe she was having some mood disorder, but as the night went on at the restaurant, the couple were steadily filled with a strange optimism, and they could both see it welling in each other - and they both felt as if *something* was renewing their love. Both were sure it wasn't the wine – so what was it? Was it merely what the poets used to call "the vicissitudes of love" – or was it – as Bob (the more open-minded half of the couple) suspected - some metaphysical force at work?

'It's baffling isn't it?' remarked Bob, referring to the way some Phoenix of new love had arisen from the carbonized wreckages of their past affairs. 'I am intrigued by this,' Bob went on but Betty reached out across the table, held his hand, squeezed it and said, 'Don't start dissecting rainbows, Bob – just enjoy whatever this is.'

'Good advice,' Bob conceded, and looked about the restaurant, trying not to dwell on this mysterious change of mood. He overheard the manager saying he was understaffed and so Bob went over to him and in a whispering voice, he offered his services, and although the manager said it wasn't the done thing to let someone in the kitchen, he knew Bob, and he knew he had been an ace executive chef in his day who had worked at the Savoy and some of the greatest kitchens on the Continent, and so he let him cook Beef Wellington and some difficult dishes that night, and to top it all that strange evening, a young couple in the restaurant was celebrating their first wedding anniversary, and Betty sat at the old piano in the place and started to sing the old Al Green song, *Let's Stay Together* - and the couple said they were very moved, because they had two songs which meant a lot to them - George Harrison's *Something* and *Let's Stay Together*.

Betty was surprised she had rediscovered her confidence to sing and play the piano that night, and Bob said she had been magnificent. He did, however, have a personal request – he wanted his long-term love to sing *Amazing Grace*, because that was a song she had once sung to his grandfather as he lay dying in hospital many years ago. Just the memory of that incident often brought a tear to Bob's eye, and he knew it would tonight - *if* Betty would sing it, that is; Bob thought her confidence was a fragile thing, and he almost begged her to sing it.

'I don't know the chords to it,' she told Bob, and she glanced at the manager, wondering if he'd think she was putting off the customers in the restaurant, but the manager said, 'Then sing it *a capella* then.'

'Are you sure I'm not boring the diners here?' Betty asked, and Bob felt she was on the cusp of losing her confidence again, and someone groaned, 'Oh put a sock in it,' and Bob glared at him, but the diner – a man who happened to be a young music student - smiled and said to Betty, 'I'm joking – I'm joking, take no notice; you have an amazing voice.' And then, the same student put his hand up in a meek manner and said to the manager, 'I play the piano; I know the chords to the song; there're only five chords.'

The manager looked at the student and tilted his head sideways, gesturing for him to get behind the piano. The student left the table wiping his hands on a napkin and sat at the upright piano – an old Barratt & Robinson model. The student played an intro, and then Betty came in right on cue; it was obvious that she was a professional singer. People passing by outside the restaurant slowed and some stopped, and

179

they gazed at the source of the haunting voice through the windows.

Bob felt the tears on his cheeks as he listened to the first verse.

Amazing grace! how sweet the sound,
That saved a wretch; like me!
I once was lost, but now am found,
Was blind, but now I see.

What an evocation it was for Bob; he saw his beloved grandfather, a man who often played this song in a haphazard way on his harmonica when Bob was just a boy, and it would later become the deathbed song of his grandad. The song brought that lovely innocent period of Bob's life back for a while, and he listened to the student who had made the jokey remark; he was doing a fine job – a gospel rhythm, and it sounded celestial. There was a standing ovation by the diners when the song ended, and even the people outside in the street clapped as they gazed at Betty through the windows, and the manager clapped and he gave the thumbs-up to the student pianist, who smiled self-consciously, then clapped as he nodded at Betty.

This was one of those nights – one of those memories – that the couple would enjoy to the end of their days. What a strange night it had been; from the oncoming despair of a parting between two lifelong lovers to a renaissance of their love that was completely out of the blue and unexpected. Bob proposed to Betty that night; they married in the summer of the year 2000. Bob and Betty often chatted about that night in the restaurant and they would try and look at the strange episode from various angles, but always they would come to the conclusion that the old man who had linked their hands had been some otherworldly Cupid.

TIME TRAVEL REFUGEES

Regular readers of my books, newspaper articles and columns will know I have written extensively about time-travel and reported on numerous alleged timeslips in Liverpool – especially in the Bold Street area. I will devote a chapter to local timeslips later in this book, but within *this* chapter I would like to detail four timeslip cases where people have purportedly sought refuge in the past. Since I started documenting the many reports of timeslips which I have investigated, I have been somewhat surprised by the amount of people who have expressed a desire to live in the past, and some readers have written to me to ask if there are any local "portals" or timeslip areas where they might have a good chance of stepping into another time. These are serious enquiries from people who seem to be looking for a way out of the modern world. It would seem that for many, this period we are living in is unbearable for a variety of perceived reasons; some say the entertainment is cheap and banal, the music is dreadful and lacking in soul, the politics is Orwellian, Draconian and oppressive, and the fashion is neither here nor there. What's strange is that people who were not even around in the 1960s and 1970s are hankering for those decades, and many young people have told me they would willingly emigrate from the bleakness of the 21st Century to live in the Swinging Sixties of The Beatles or the Seventies of *Saturday Night Fever*, *Starsky and Hutch*, the 1976 Heatwave, Elton, Bowie and *Jaws*. It says a lot about today's society when a sizeable amount of its citizens are yearning for a life in bygone times, and this leads me nicely to the first strange story in this chapter.

Around the year 1999 I was on a local radio phone-in on BBC Radio Merseyside's *Billy Butler Show* talking about mysteries of a paranormal nature, including ghosts and timeslips, when an elderly lady named Ann, who had worked for the Salvation Army and a number of other charity organisations, called me live on air and told me that in the 1970s she often helped the many vagrants and discards of humanity who congregated at the back of the Metropolitan Cathedral of Christ the King on Brownlow Hill, and there was a very strange and intriguing 'tramp' named John who stuck out in Ann's memory. He was known to some of the other tramps by the nickname of "Steptoe" because he bore a striking resemblance to Wilfred Bramble, the Irish actor who was well-known for playing Albert Steptoe in the highly-popular sitcom *Steptoe and Son*. John was quite cagey about the whys and wherefores of his descent into poverty and always seemed to be hiding from someone. When he got to know Ann, he relaxed a little and opened up somewhat, and often talked of escaping a 'tyranny' and Ann initially thought that he had fled from some satellite state of the USSR (as it was then called), but it soon became clear that John was bizarrely referring to the future, and spoke of it as if he had lived there, and Ann clearly recalled John talking about the Falklands War, years before it happened, and when his guard was down in drink (for he was fond of whiskey) he told her how everyone in the future had a phone - a preposterous claim in the Seventies when the only phones were accessible via red public telephone boxes or via a rental system run by the GPO (the General Post Office, which served as the state postal system and telecommunications carrier). John said the telephones everyone owned in the future were tiny flat portable devices that people carried everywhere they went. The intriguing vagrant also mentioned a mass-brainwashing incident in the 'next century' that had left everyone like mindless zombies who followed orders from a totalitarian government, and he often talked of "the tangled web of minds" that had caused a type of widespread insanity and loss of identity. He made many predictions that have since come to pass, and chillingly described a 5-figure IQ World Government advisor called Counsel that used phenomenal artificial intelligence to blackmail world leaders, and this supercomputer also played a life-and-death Chess-like game with whole nations and individuals. John also pensively talked of nuclear attacks that had decimated Moscow and several cities of the 'British Republic'. The tangled web of minds John referred to seems to have been the outcome of some sort of social media on a technological telepathic-device level.

Ann was not sure if John was merely an imaginative fabricator of science fiction or whether he really was a time-traveller, and she asked him outright: 'John, if you are telling the truth, how did you get back here? How did you go on the run from the future?'

John's reply consisted of him spouting technical

jargon that Ann could not fully understand, but she gathered he was claiming he had been some physicist who had found a way to travel backwards along the fourth dimension of time, and John hinted that others had escaped with him, and he said that these 'refugees' had used their knowledge of the future and their superior technical knowhow to create lucrative businesses in the fields of commerce and computer technology.

Ann told a priest about the fascinating claims of the thought-provoking vagrant, and the clergyman dismissed John as a fantasist - but then, one foggy afternoon in 1983, with her own eyes, Ann saw John disappear into a mist at the back of the cathedral, and she never saw him again. Perhaps the fugitive from future horrors had returned to his 'own time' or maybe he went even further back in time, to escape the dystopia he described; the way things are going nowadays, I can fully imagine the coming terrors John might have been running from.

I had been talking about unsolved mysteries on the *Billy Butler Show* in March 2002 and afterwards a well-spoken lady named Penny called me at the radio station and here is a summary of what she told me. It is one of the most seemingly far-fetched stories I have ever been told, but there seems to be some evidence to suggest that there might be more than a grain of truth in the account. At Christmas Eve, December 1974, Penny's Liverpool-born father, Richard, was visited in the dead of night at his farmhouse near Javron-les-Chapelles in North-Western France. Penny's father was a retired inventor who had worked for the Ministry of Defence on top secret weapons and gadgets that were decades ahead of their time. The caller at Richard's farmhouse was a man named Bill, and he was Richard's regular Bridge partner; Richard had known him for about ten years, and upon this freezing December night, Bill had someone waiting in his car outside – someone who was in "a bit of trouble"; a well-to-do man Bill referred to as "John". Now for the unbelievable part of the story: Richard had been working on a way to travel through time for twelve years and had sent animals to unknown destinations on miniature prototypes of the large time-machine he was working on. Not one of these guinea pigs ever returned. Bill wanted to know if Richard would send John through time to escape the consequences of some awful crime he had committed – before Interpol closed in on him. At first Richard said the machine wasn't ready, that even if it had been ready it was unsafe, and then he stated that he would not be involved in enabling a criminal to escape justice – but something changed his mind, and Penny is not clear on what this something was that changed her father's attitude to John. Richard told Bill he would require an expensive computer – and was given one – because the calculus needed to get the machine to work was mind-boggling. John – a tall dark-haired Englishman with a moustache and – according to Penny - an aristocratic bearing – was introduced to Richard, and he inspected the machine. John told the inventor he desperately wanted to go back to 1950 to 'make a new start' and Richard aimed for that year. After working round the clock on the prototype time machine for three days without any sleep, Richard said the machine was charged up and ready to go. John sat in the globe-shaped machine, which had an oxygen supply and was hermetically sealed, and Richard and Bill left the room where the machine was housed and closed the door. Richard operated a control panel in another room and gazed through a narrow long window with Bill, and then he flicked a row of switches and the machine seemed to go out of focus as it was activated - and then it silently vanished. According to Penny, a few hours after this alleged incident, Richard supposedly realised the calculations were wrong and said that – the machine – if it managed to reach its geographical destination at all, would have gone back to the days of the French Revolution instead of the year 1950. Now, this might be a coincidence, but it just so happens that on 12 June 1790, a metal globe of unknown origin appeared on a hilltop in Alencon, France in a flash of light, and was so hot it caused a grass fire. A strangely-dressed man got out the sphere and motioned for the peasants to get back. Some reports say he shouted what sounded like a warning and the curious people standing around drew back. The metallic sphere exploded with a muffled bang and the man vanished into the woods. There was a subsequent search for the man from the metal globe but he couldn't be found and his fate is unknown. An Inspector Liabeuf travelled from Paris to investigate the incident – which is recorded in France's National Archives. Now, let us think; who could have been that English aristocrat fleeing from justice in late 1974? No, surely not him? Well, Penny never named Lord Lucan in her story, but who else could it have been? I have tried to make enquiries and it is true that some military research and development geniuses who worked for the Ministry of Defence – people like the fictional gadget-designing "Q" character in the James Bond films - did retire to live in France, but it's difficult to say if the whole tale is an elaboration of some less spectacular incident – or whether the entire narrative is nothing more than a shaggy dog story. On the other hand, if the story *is* true, it would certainly explain why, after half a century of searching by the police forces of many countries, including the FBI, Interpol, as well as a legion of private detectives, mercenaries and investigative journalists, Lord Lucan has still not been found. It has been assumed that someone, somewhere, knows where the missing aristocrat is hiding, but how would anyone keep a secret for half a century? When Osama Bin Laden went into hiding, he was found after ten years because American intelligence officials tracked one of his couriers, and they knew the name of the courier because someone gave them the information – there is always a weak link in the chain – and yet, a half century has gone by since Lucan's disappearance, and not one person has come forward, despite the huge financial rewards that are in place for anyone who knows even the littlest bit of information to indicate where he is and who is shielding him. He might have committed suicide, or perhaps, according to the time-travel claim, the 7th Earl of Lucan might have been executed on the guillotine in 1793, during the French Revolution's "Reign of Terror" – and some would say such a fate would be a case of poetic justice.

Here is another account of a person who allegedly sought asylum in the past, and like 'John' in the last story, this individual saw a bygone time as a place to make a new start, although in this case the new life involved the man going back in time to live with a woman he had fallen hopelessly in love with and having a family with her. I've changed a few names in this strange story for reasons of confidentiality. It all began on a sticky hot July afternoon in 1982, when 40-year-old PC Howard Poole was investigating reports of vandalism in the vicinity of Aigburth Cricket Club. There had recently been a spate of mindless attacks on several sporting grounds, including the Heron Eccles sports ground in Abbotshey Avenue, Mossley Hill, where the rampaging juvenile delinquents had started a fire which gutted the pavilion, and they had also destroyed the goal posts. When PC Poole arrived at the Aigburth cricket ground, he saw no gangs, just a serene, archetypal English scene under a cloudless Alice blue sky; drowsy spectators watching a game of cricket in progress, some sipping stout and smoking pipes, coupled with the sound of the leather ball on willow, and the sleepy drone of the occasional bee. The tranquil scene was an oasis of relaxation to the policeman, who had been under a lot of stress recently. Poole's wife no longer loved him, and the marital disharmony was playing havoc with his depression, and on top of that he had heedlessly lurched into heavy debt because of his gambling. Feeling there was nothing to go home to, Poole was spending an inordinate amount of time playing poker into the wee small hours on the nights when he was off work. The stress component of his current baffling illness - which included migraines with zigzag multicoloured shimmering lines and abdominal pains – was distracting him from something strange on this summer's day; he did not notice the anomaly at first, but his policeman's mind snapped him out the spell of self-pity. He noticed the dated, quaint attire of the people watching the cricket match: the men wore trilbies, wide trousers with turn-ups, their hair slicked with oil or Brylcreem – and the women wore floral print dresses and hats – and one stunning young lady in a red polka dot dress who was walking a toy poodle looked like a 1950s Hollywood starlet. She smiled at Poole, and he reflexively smiled back, and then he went to the bench where the spectators were sitting and saw a copy of the *Liverpool Echo* – and he squinted and did an on-the-spot eyesight test. He read the tiny print that gave the date of the newspaper – and he saw to his complete bafflement that the date read: Tuesday 12 July 1955. It was July alright, but 1982, the copper knew that – so had the *Echo* made a howler of a mistake and put the wrong year in? He asked the girl in the polka dot dress what year it was, and she gave a puzzled look, then said, 'Nineteen fifty-five.'

'You're kidding,' Poole replied, and he asked the gentleman holding the *Echo* if he could have a quick look at the newspaper. The man nodded in an unenthusiastic manner and handed the broadsheet *Echo* to Poole, and he looked at the headlines: "A Second Mersey Tunnel?" and adverts for the Liverpool Show, and being a policeman he was accustomed to memorising numbers; Poole looked at the edition number of the paper – 23,517. He used a simple mnemonic; he lived at Number 23 and his oldest brother was 51 – and 7 was his lucky number. 'Christ,' he said under his breath, as the beautiful young lady in the polka dot dress gazed at him with a curious expression. 'I've gone back in time, it's 1955,' he told the lady, and he handed the newspaper back to the bemused man sitting on the bench. Anyone else would normally be stunned at experiencing a timeslip, and perhaps a little uneasy, but PC Poole wanted to stay in 1955, where he could start a new life, and he silently prayed for 1982 to stay away. 'I could get used to this,' he said to the lovely lady, and she thinned her stunning eyes and said, 'Are you feeling alright, sir?'

'Oh yeah, I've never felt better,' PC Poole told her. He had never believed in love, never mind love at first sight, and yet he felt so drawn to this young woman. An exciting possibility struck him immediately; he could court this "looker" and settle down with her in 1955. If she was spoken for (but he couldn't see an engagement ring on her finger) he'd fight to have her. They would have kids and live in the suburbs, and he would no longer be a stressed out policeman; he'd become the landlord of a pub and he would never gamble. This time he'd make it work. He reached out and grabbed the young lady's hand, startling her, and an elderly man sitting in a candy-striped deckchair put his hand over his eyes to shield them from the blinding July sun and watched the strange behaviour of the policeman. The lady in the polka dot said to Poole, 'Oh, what are you doing?' and her poodle growled.

PC Poole then felt the small hand of the girl melt away into nothingness. He just knew it was all too good to be true; he was slipping back to his accursed time period. 'Don't go! No!' he protested, and the girl and her dog and the men on the bench and the lily white cricketers all rapidly faded away until 1982 had fully returned.

PC Poole found himself back in the soulless Hell of modern times. He was so choked up, and then the sorrow turned to anger, and he grunted and shouted, 'What harm would it have done for me to stay in 1955? Why am I needed back here in this shit-hole?'

He made an appointment to see his doctor because of the continual migraines and depression and stress and abdominal pains – and when he finally got to see the doctor, he mentioned the slip in time. He almost knew what the doctor would say, word for word.

'Stress can play some strange tricks on the mind, Mr Poole,' said Doctor Whitmore, 'anxiety can enforce a type of autosuggestion, and you seem to have created a way out of a life that was worthless in your estimation.'

'But I saw the cricket match, and what was strange was the newspaper with the exact date;' countered Poole, 'I mean, how could I dream up a cricket match and a newspaper and all that?'

The doctor gave a closed-mouth smile and then he sighed and answered: 'I'm not a psychiatrist, but I've had overstressed people come to me after seeing similar hallucinations. I'm not going to give you any tranquilizers at the moment – let's just see if you can get a good night's sleep, and try to adopt a positive attitude to life first.'

PC Poole visited the Central Library on William Brown Street, and to a librarian he asked if he could see the *Liverpool Echo* for Tuesday, 12 July, 1955 – and he was duly escorted to a seat in front of a screen that showed microfilmed copies of the old newspapers. He wound on the edition of the *Echo* he'd requested and received quite a shock, for it was the very same one he had read in paper form that sunny afternoon at the cricket ground. He recalled the mnemonic for the newspaper's edition number; he lived at Number 23, his oldest brother was 51, and his lucky number was 7 – and lo and behold, the edition number on this old newspaper was exactly that: 23,517 – so that doctor had been talking through his backside. It had *not* been some hallucination – PC Poole had somehow casually stepped into another decade. He read the rest of the newspaper and there in black and white he saw the details of the cricket match he had seen that day: it had been the 1955 County Championship between Lancashire and Middlesex at Aigburth. PC Poole felt all choked up again; that lady he had wanted for a wife was 27 years away from him now. Poole walked away from the microfilm viewer, head bowed. He often visited the cricket ground up in Aigburth, just in case time played a trick again, but the policeman never saw that beautiful lady in the polka dot dress again.

And finally, here we have a story which came my way some years ago via a letter to me care of the *Liverpool Echo*.

'This is the Zodiac club,' a smartly-dressed amicable pharmacist named Philip told the pretty petite blonde girl, pointing to the doorway of 98 Duke Street. She had asked him where the club was in the softest voice he'd ever heard. The girl, who looked as if she was about 25 years of age - and who later gave her name as Dianne - smiled at Philip that evening in 1962, and the chemist noticed something odd as she passed under the lamp at the entrance of the club: she had a tattoo of some symbol on her upper left arm – and tattooed ladies were a rarity in that day and age. Philip had been on his way to the quieter, more sophisticated establishment known as the Cabaret Club, further down Duke Street, frequented by the likes of mild-mannered businessman and Beatles manager Brian Epstein, but now curiosity about that silken-voiced girl Dianne had hooked Philip the pharmacist. He pushed the door of the club open for Dianne and gallantly stepped aside, and she thanked him and they went into a place where the Beatles and Cilla Black often appeared. Philip asked if he could get her a drink and assured her he was not 'being inappropriate' and she asked for a Pepsi. Philip asked Dianne what the tattooed symbol on her arm meant, and was told, 'It's the *Aum* symbol – written in Devanagari – it's the primeval sound of the universe.'

'Oh,' said a baffled Philip, none the wiser.

Dianne said she lived locally, but gave conflicting accounts of her job; saying she worked in the YMCA on Mount Pleasant as a cook, while she told someone else she was a secretary for the Prudential Insurance Company on Dale Street. Philip fell seriously in love with the evasive Dianne and asked her several times if he could take her out, and she finally agreed to a date; that date was in a week's time - but then a smartly dressed stranger turned up at the Zodiac Club that night, and he kept staring at Dianne. She seemed to know the man and appeared to be afraid of him.

'Is he bothering you?' Philip enquired, and clutched Dianne's hand at the bar, and she shook her head and said nothing, but seemed very on edge. 'Do you know him?' asked Philip, and again the girl shook her head.

On the third day this man made an appearance, he was heard to say to Dianne, 'You're going back; you don't belong here.' He grabbed Dianne by her wrist, pulled her into the corridor of the club with an enraged Philip close behind him, ready to throw a punch at the man who was roughly handling a lady he now regarded as his girlfriend, but when Philip hurried after the man dragging Dianne out of the club, he appeared to vanish into thin air, along with Dianne. Within a split second of Philip reaching the corridor which led to the Zodiac Club's exit, Dianne and the unknown man were nowhere to be seen. Brian and Chris, two friends of Philip, came into the club and said no one had passed them on the way out.

'Are you *sure?*' Philip asked the two men, and Chris said, 'Yes, unless they were invisible – no one passed us – why?'

Philip insisted that a man and a woman had just left the Zodiac Club and he stood at the entrance of the premises, looking up and down a rainy Duke Street. The street was deserted.

'No one came out of this club, Philip,' said Brian, brushing the raindrops from his face with his hand, and then he questioned whether the chemist had been drinking.

'I've had *one* drink – and I didn't imagine this,' said Philip, and he gave up the search for Dianne and that menacing stranger who had dragged the girl out of his life. Philip accompanied his friends and walked back into the club. The mystery of disappearing Dianne haunted Philip for many years, and it was his son who wrote to tell me of the uncanny incident which his father had often mentioned over the years. I have a feeling Dianne and that unknown man that she seemed to be afraid of were travellers from the future sampling 1960s culture; time tourists perhaps; maybe they were man and wife. The enigmatic man *had* been heard to say to Dianne: 'You're going back; you don't belong here,' and I wonder if 'going back' referred to going back to some future time.

THE INCA BAR

There are a few stories that come my way that are quite difficult to classify, and what follows is a story of that kind.

In July 1976, a 26-year-old small-time criminal named Rob moved in with a 20-year-old art student named Rose at her tiny flat over a shop on Renshaw Street. The heat was unbearable. This was during the 1976 British Isles Heat Wave when the temperatures peaked at 96.6 degrees Fahrenheit (35.9 degrees Centigrade) – and Parliament passed the Drought Act, with water rationing coming into being immediately. On this insufferably hot July evening at 9pm, Rose was visited by her 17-year-old sister Cathy, who decided to stay over. Rob wasn't expected to be there on this sweltering night, as he said he had to look after a sick auntie for the night, but he turned up at 9:20pm and admitted he was back early because a planned theft had gone wrong, and he stripped down to his y-fronts and got on the bed between a scantily-clad Rose and her under-clothed sister (who wore just a bra and shorts) even though Rose warned him not to lay a finger on her sister and she reminded him Cathy was just seventeen.

Rose said she needed ciggies and something sweet, and Rob insensitively said, 'Your time of the month then, eh?' And he gave a false chuckle and turned to look at young Cathy, as if he thought she'd think his remark was funny. Cathy returned an annoyed expression.

Rob put on a pair of shorts and a yellow vest with "Wild Thing" emblazoned in red upon it, then put on a pair of "Jesus sandals" as he called them. He left, and Rose said to her sister, 'What do you think of him?'

'He's a beast,' said Cathy and her lip curled at the thought of the repulsive Rob even thinking he had a chance with her.

Rob, meanwhile was outside, chatting to a girl of fifteen named Suzy, the daughter of a neighbour who was on her way to the bus stop on Renshaw Street. Rob's hooded eyes looked the girl up and down, and he asked Suzy if she was still with her boyfriend Paul. Suzy said she wasn't, and Rob asked the girl, 'Would you ever go with a fellah in his mid-twenties?' to which Suzy screwed up her face and said, 'Eee! No, why would I wanna go with an old man?'

'Twenty-five isn't old, ya cheeky get,' said Rob, trying so hard to smile.

'How old are you?' Suzy asked Rob, and then she gave a slight grin.

'Me? I'm twenty-four, like,' he said.

'You look well older,' Suzy told him, and she looked at his sandals and grinned.

'Why? How old do I look?' Rob wanted to know.

'Old,' said Suzy, then walked away saying, 'see ya!'

Rob went to a shop called Jack's on Mount Pleasant to get the cigarettes and 'something sweet' for Rose but it was shut. He then noticed a mobile shop on Benson Street, and he went over to it and bought the ciggies and then he asked the man in the mobile van for the cheapest chocolate bar he had because he was low on cash. The man handed Rob an "Inca Bar" - and said, 'eet free, no money,' in a foreign accent.

'Oh, ta mate,' said Rob, and he walked off, his eyes locking onto a friend of Rose named Babs.

'Hiya Rob, you alright?' Babs asked, and she swigged a bottle of Pepsi.

'Yeah,' said Rob, 'just on a message for Rose – she smokes like a 'chimlee.'

'Aw, are you still with her then, eh?' Babs asked, and offered rob the Pepsi bottle. He took a quick swig and nodded.

Rob thinned his eyes at the low sun and said, 'These young girls today are cases aren't 'thee? You know that girl who lives by me? What's her name? Suzy?'

'Oh yeah, Suzy,' said Babs, 'she's just a kid isn't she?'

'Yeah she is,' said Rob, nodding, 'but she turned round before and asked me to go with her.'

'Oh God,' said Babs, and she smiled and put her hand to her O-shaped mouth, 'you're kidding?'

'Honest-a-God, Babs,' said Rob, shaking his head, 'I was like, "beat it girl, I'm old enough to be your 'arl fellah!'

'You are as well, aren't you?' Babs said in all innocence, then asked, 'How old are you now, Rob?'

Rob looked as if he was in pain as he answered the question. 'I'm 26 – not old enough to be her dad yet, Babs, but still too old to go out with her, like.'

'Of course,' said Babs, 'still too old to go out with her. Isn't she a case, eh? Precocious, they call that.'

'You with anyone, Babs?' Rob asked, and added, 'I'm not sniffin' round or anything,' and burst out laughing.

She drank from the bottle of Pepsi and nodded. 'Yeah, I'm with Tony – you know Tony who works in the chippy on Lodgey [Lodge Lane]? I've just found out I'm in the club.'

'Is it his, like?' Rob asked.

'Hey you – course it is you cheeky thing!' and she looked at a tiny watch on her wrist and said, 'I better get a move on. The bus'll be here any minute. Tell Rose I was asking, Rob; see you lad!'

And she was gone.

Rob was just going to put the key in the ground-floor access door to the flat when a large hand landed hard on his bare shoulder and a gruff voice said, 'You're under arrest!'

Rob swung around and saw it was Des, an old friend he'd gone to school with many years ago, and the two men laughed. Des explained he was of no fixed address because his girlfriend Astrid had thrown him out because he was "work shy", and Rob said: 'I'm shacked up with two birds – you wanna meet them?'

'Two birds?' said Des, and laughed, 'How do you do it?'

'Always been gifted with the old bishop (Rob's slang for his favourite organ) mate,' he claimed, and opened the door and invited Des in with a tilt of the head, as if he was heading a football. On the way up the stairs he said, 'She's got a sister who's got the hots for me like, but she's too young.'

'How old?' asked Des with a seedy smile on his bearded face.

'Seventeen,' said Rob, and emitted a machine-gun laugh before saying, 'Stop sniffin' round Des!'

'He's with someone,' Cathy told Rose. She could hear the voices on the stairs.

The door opened, and in came Rob, followed by Des, a man who was six feet and five inches in height, plus he had on platform shoes, so he towered over Rob, who was five feet and four inches tall in his Jesus sandals.

'Rose, this is Des,' said Rob, throwing the pack of 20 cigarettes and the "Inca Bar" onto the bed, and then he turned to Des and said, 'Des, this is Rose and this is Cathy, her sister.'

'Don't tell me;' Des said to Cathy, 'let me guess; you're seventeen.'

Cathy rolled her eyes and looked at her sister and gave a toothy smile.

'Me and Des have had gotten into some scrapes over the years, haven't we mate?' Rob said to his friend, and they both grinned, and Des couldn't take his eyes off young Cathy. Rose was furious and told Des he'd better go, but Rob said Des was living on the streets, and so Rose reluctantly allowed him to spend the night sat in a chair in the corner of the room.

Rose tasted the "Inca" bar and contorted her face - it was sweet, and rich but it tasted hot and spicy – and seeing how the night was already tropical with the record heat wave, she had to drink a glass of orange juice in one go in an effort to stop her tongue burning. She gave the rest of the Inca Bar to Rob and he and Des ate it between them. Rob, forever trying to be the macho man, said, 'That wasn't hot, it was mild to me.'

Rose opened the windows fully now, but the fierce stifling heat made the four of them drowsy, and they had all dropped off by eleven.

Then something terrifying and bizarre took place; something that is still unexplained.

Des startled Rose and Cathy from their sleep with his screams. He was covered in blood, and the sight of it frightened Cathy. Then Rose saw that Rob, who was sleeping top-tail to her and Cathy, was moaning with his eyes closed and his face and bare chest were covered with both clotted and wet blood.

'Oh my God! Rob, what's happened to you?' cried Rose, and she shook Rob awake and he inhaled sharply and sat up – and spat out clots of congealed blood. Cathy screamed as a blood clot landed on her leg.

'Help!' shouted Des, and the girls saw his white tee shirt was soaked in blood, and the he also spat out vivid crimson blood as he stood up and stumbled against the wall. He looked about and seemed terrified of something. Rose tried to calm Rob down; he kept saying, 'They took my heart out! They're going to come back and kill us!'

Des closed the wide-open windows saying, 'They'll get in this way!'

'Des, will you leave those windows alone? It's like a furnace in here?' shouted Rose as she held Rob's trembling hand, then she asked, 'Where did all this blood come from?'

Both men eventually calmed down and it transpired that the two of them experienced very graphic dreams of 'Aztecs' cutting out their hearts, and both Rob and Des had wounds and deep scratch-marks on their chests that obviously required hospital treatment. Rob said he had heard the deep chanting voices in his nightmare and the music sounded as if it was produced by drums, flutes, ocarinas and something that made an unnerving rattling sound.

Cathy screamed and pointed to a shadowy figure of a man with a feathered head dress in the wall, but the apparition faded, although they all saw it. Rob gazed in horror with bulging eyes at the vanishing shadow and yelled, 'That's one of them! Let's get out of here! They want to sacrifice us!'

Rose wondered if there had been some hallucinogenic substance in the Inca Bar which had made Rob and Des imagine the Aztecs; perhaps the two men had attacked one another in a disoriented tripped-out state and inflicted those chest-wounds – and yet she and Cathy had seen the weird ghost with the headdress vanish into the wall.

Rose and Cathy got dressed and they took Rob and Des to the Royal Infirmary on Pembroke Place. The doctor who looked at the wounds said the cuts had been inflicted with a blade and were directly over the site of the heart.

On the following day, Rose and Rob went looking for the mobile van on Benson Street, as they both wanted to have words with the foreign vendor who had given Rob the Inca Bar for free – but that van was nowhere to be seen, and it was never seen again. Rose visited Jack's shop on Mount Pleasant and asked him if he had heard of an Inca Bar, and he said he hadn't. Rose went to so many shops, inquiring about that strange bar with its indigo wrapper and not one shopkeeper had heard of an Inca chocolate bar; some told Rose there *was* an Aztec bar, but it looked and tasted nothing like the Inca one. Chocolate was a holy sacrament and aphrodisiac to the Aztecs, and they made it spicy and even added red berries to foamy chocolate so it resembled blood - something they liked to drink, but why would an unknown chocolate bar conjure up long dead Aztecs? The name of the bar was

Inca, and the Incas probably never met the Aztecs because the Inca civilization was in Peru and the Aztec empire was in Mexico, which deepens the mystery. Rob said he felt the excruciating pain in his nightmare as the Aztec-like people carved a hole in his chest with a huge knife, and he had seen them take out his pulsating heart. For many years, Rob and Des had recurrent nightmares about the bizarre and terrifying incident.

THE MYSTERY OF
THE RETURNÉES

In the world of the occult there are intriguing solid-looking entities known as returnées - usually dearly departed celebrities or famous deceased historical people who seem to have been resurrected by an unknown agency. I first mentioned them in my book *Tales of the Weird 2* in 2016, and devoted a chapter to these inexplicably restored beings. There have been alleged returnées of people like Marie Antoinette, David Bowie, Vincent Van Gogh, and, if the following story is to believed - Roger Moore. On the Wednesday afternoon of 23 May 2018, a 34-year-old woman named Lyndsey was on her way to a second-hand bookshop in the Bluecoat Chambers in Liverpool city centre when she realised she was being followed by a man who had stalked her just over a year back, and this individual followed her towards the bookshop. Upon reaching the doorway of the shop, Lyndsey looked back, expecting the stalker to follow her onto the premises, and when she walked into the second-hand bookstore she was still looking back, waiting for the pest to enter the place when she bumped into a tall debonair, and tantalizingly familiar man who was browsing through the books. She apologised for stepping on his foot and the man, who was smartly dressed in a dark blue blazer and black pleated trousers, asked her if she was alright. When Lyndsey heard the deep, rich warm timbre of the man's voice she realised it was none other than Roger Moore, and she said, 'It's you,' as she couldn't recall his name because she was so star-struck.

The man smiled and calmly asked, 'Is he bothering you again?' as if he knew who the stalker was, and, stuck for words because she was so astonished at the bizarre situation, Lyndsey nodded, and 'Roger' said to her, 'I'll just have a word.' And he put the leather-bound book he'd been reading back on the shelf and walked casually and confidently to the stalker, who was in a dark corner of the bookshop, gazing at Lyndsey. Lyndsey could hear Roger threatening the stalker, who asked, 'Who are you?' to which the man replied, 'Her fiancé, that's who I am!' and he grabbed the stalker by the lapels, led him to the door and threw him out of the shop. The Roger Moore "lookalike" then took Lyndsey by the hand and walked with her to a taxi rank on Hanover Street, and he advised her to go to the police to report the stalker and just before she got in a hackney cab, she gasped, 'Roger Moore,' as she recalled his name at last, and the man smiled, and the cabby asked her, 'It isn't *him* is it?'

'Yes,' said Lyndsey, nodding to the driver of the taxi, and she thought the whole thing was so romantic and wacky. She wondered if Roger Moore was perhaps filming in the city, and then she realised he did not look as old as she had seen him in recent interviews; he had looked as if he was in his forties.

The cabby then told Lyndsey something which left her cold.

'It can't be the real Roger Moore – he died last year, didn't he?' the cabby recalled and Lyndsey froze, then said, 'He can't have; that was definitely him,' to which the taxi driver insisted, 'Nah, he died love – that fellah's been one of those impersonators, a James-Bondagram thingy or whatever.'

'You're wrong, it was him – no one could be *that* good impersonating Roger Moore,' said Lyndsey, and she watched as the cabby produced his iPhone. He opened the Google homepage on his phone and typed in Roger Moore, then thrust the iPhone through the gap in the window. 'Look, there in black and white,' the driver said. And Lyndsey narrowed her eyes and looked at the Wikipedia entry for Sir Roger George Moore – and in brackets it said 14 October 1927 to 23 May 2017.

'But – 'Lyndsey struggled for an explanation.

'That fellah was either a stand-in or a stuntman for Roger Moore in films or just a celebrity lookalike,' said the cabdriver – and Lyndsey looked into the crowd and saw Roger suddenly vanish among the crowds of Hanover Street, and she gasped, 'Or he was a ghost. He's just vanished.' Her baffling Good Samaritan had gone.

The taxi driver sat there and remarked, 'Where the hell did he just go?' And without asking Lyndsey where she wanted to go, he drove along Hanover Street to see where the man had gone too – but there was no sign of him anywhere.

Some returnées are possibly guardians, allowed back into the world of the living by some higher force, but no one's really sure; it's possible the man who helped Lyndsey that day *was* a mere lookalike, but Lyndsey said he literally vanished before her eyes that day, and even the cabby remarked on the sudden disappearance.

I wonder if the incident left her shaken - but not stirred.

For our next returnee case we fly 1,000 miles south of Liverpool to August 2002, to sunny Valldemossa, a beautiful historic hilltop town in West Mallorca, surrounded by the cobalt-blue Balearic Sea. Here, a 21-year-old blonde Liverpool girl named Amy was holidaying with her boyfriend, a Geordie bricklayer named Tony. Amy was a music student at Liverpool City College, and, out to impress his girlfriend, Tony had done his homework; he took Amy to the Carthusian monastery right in the centre of Valldemossa and he showed her a room at the monastery where her favourite composer – Chopin – had stayed with lover "George Sand" (the male pen name of female novelist Amantine Dupin). While returning from the monastery, Tony pushed his way through a crowd of other tourists to get Amy a banana caramel ice cream at a nearby Pizzeria, and, when he came back, his girlfriend told him something very strange. 'Tony, an old man came up to me before, and he was the spitting image of Hitler,' she said, and then her big blue eyes searched the crowd.

'What, pet?' laughed Tony, and Amy told him the old man had held her hand and remarked, 'Du bist so hübsch,' ["You're so pretty" in German], and then to a younger man he called "Odin", he'd said something else in German that Amy couldn't make out. The Liverpool student was convinced she had met Adolf Hitler, but Tony laughed, took her somewhere quiet and said, 'Amy, Hitler shot himself in the Berlin bunker in 1945, and he was in his late fifties then, girl.'

'Well, he looked dead old,' said Amy, 'and the fellah with him he called Odin looked like his son. It was so creepy; the two of them were like clones of each other, only one was much older than the other.'

Tony reassured her. 'Hitler died fifty-odd years ago, and if he was in his late fifties, he'd be a hundred and odd years old! Maybe they're shooting a film round here and he's just an actor who's been done up to look like him.'

'Oh my God! There he is!' Amy pointed to the old man, walking along a cobbled road, and Tony dragged her towards him, determined to get to the bottom of the mystery but found his way barred by twins who looked the image of a young Hitler, and Tony and Amy watched the old man and the man he had called Odin walk into the hazy distance, where a helicopter took off by a vineyard. All a case of mistaken identity, surely? I interviewed Amy and Tony at length and they were certain the old man and his son were identical to Hitler as he would have appeared both as a young and old man. This case differs from the typical returnée one in that the famous person was not a single entity, but an apparent father and son, plus twins who also looked like Hitler who acted as guards. If the whole affair is not some sophisticated hoax (perpetrated for what reason and by whom?) then it almost suggests a sinister cloning experiment, but whom on earth would want to genetically resurrect Hitler?

A very unexpected returnée came to the aid of a couple one rainy night in March 2013. The couple, Stuart and Jenna, both aged 39, had booked a private cab to take them from their Aintree home to the home of Jenna's uncle in Southport. The cab arrived at the home of the Aintree couple on Charterhouse Drive at 9pm, and the 16-mile journey would have taken about half an hour, but the driver of the private cab started asking the couple 'personal questions' of a very inappropriate nature, and so Jenna said, 'Will you just shut up and drive, please? You're creeping me out with your seedy questions.'

The driver pulled over and said, 'I don't like abuse like that from customers, and I tell you what, you two can get out of this cab right now! Got that? Get out!'

'I'll report you for this,' Stuart told the driver, and Jenna swore at the driver and said the same, and then the couple got out the cab, onto a rainy Scaffold Lane, literally in the middle of nowhere. As the cab moved away, Stuart fumbled in his pockets to find his phone – then recalled putting it down on the formica top in the kitchen before he had brought the cat in out the garden.

Jenna took out her iPhone – and saw to her horror that the battery was flat. And so the couple walked on, both of them fuming, hoping to see a public telephone box so they could give the private cab company a right earful because one of their nasty employees had dumped them on the A565. The rain became heavy, and so Jenna flipped her hood up, hoping it'd shield her from the rainfall and not make a mess of her foundation and mascara. She'd spent ages curling her hair and now it was all scrunched up in the hood of her coat. Stuart heard a beep behind him, and turned to see a car he had not seen for many years – a gleaming gold V8 BMW 530i SE – the car his late father used to drive back in the 1990s. The car had pulled over and the driver flashed his headlights at Stuart, who tugged on the hood of his girlfriend Jenna.

She swore and asked, 'What?'

'Someone's stopped for us here in an old BMW,' said Stuart, shouting over the wind, which was now howling, 'do you know who they are?'

'No,' replied Jenna, and she thinned her eyes against the knife-edged wind and cold rain as she looked at the car. 'Don't go over to them, they might be kidnappers or something,' Jenna told Stuart.

'Oh don't be daft,' Stuart replied and went over to the car, and the nearside window wound itself down and a spectacled man shouted from it: 'Hi there! Do you two need a lift?'

'What did he say?' Jenna asked Stuart.

'He asked if we wanted a lift,' he told his girlfriend and gave the thumbs up to the man in the car.

'He could be anyone,' said Jenna, and she grabbed the arm of her boyfriend as he headed towards the BMW.

'Oh, so we're gonna walk all the way to Southport from here?' asked Stuart, sarcastically, and Jenna reluctantly went with him. Already the front passenger door was opening. Stuart got in the front of the vehicle next to the driver and Jenna sat in the back, behind her boyfriend. It was then when Jenna realised she somehow knew the driver – but she couldn't put a name to his face at first. Stuart also felt as if he knew the bespectacled genial driver, who had short silvery hair combed in a side-part. He had on a finely-cut suit and his well-spoken voice was tantalizingly familiar.

'Now, where were you two headed on such an inclement night?' the driver asked, and Stuart said,

'Southport.'

The driver held his index finger up and said, 'Ah, then we go straight on, taking the Formby Bypass, and then – we turn left and take the Coastal Road. And then, I'm afraid, that's as far as I can take you – I only go as far as the Fishermens Rest public house.'

'That's boss,' said Stuart, 'Jenna's uncle lives right by there on Weld Road.'

'Oh really? That's fine then,' said the driver, and in a flash, Jenna realised who he was: Bob Holness, the presenter of the daily quiz show of the Eighties and Nineties - *Blockbusters*. She'd watched that show on the telly in her childhood with her mother (who had died a few years ago).

'Aren't you the fellah who used to be on that quiz show?' Jenna asked, and Stuart smiled as he finally recalled the name: 'Bob Holness,' he said to the grinning driver, who reacted by saying, 'Yes, guilty as charged.'

'I'll have a p Bob,' said Jenna, and she smirked and looked at Stuart and said, 'Of all the times for my phone to be flat; we could have taken some selfies with him.'

'Ah yeah, that would have been sound,' agreed Stuart.

The next twenty minutes seemed to fly over as Stuart and Jenna shared their memories of watching *Blockbusters*; they'd both been aged around 9 or 10 when the quiz show had started, and had always watched it around teatime with their parents. Bob dropped the couple off on Weld Road, and they waved, and then walked on to the house of Jenna's uncle – but then Stuart said, 'Hey – he's gone.'

'What?' Jenna turned back. The gold BMW had been outside the Fishermens Rest pub seconds ago, and now there was no sign of it. It hadn't passed the couple and if it had turned round to go in the opposite direction, it would still be visible. Jenna and Stuart thought it was odd. When Jenna's uncle opened the door, she said, 'You'll never guess who gave us a lift here?'

When she told her uncle about the gameshow presenter kindly stopping for her and Stuart on Scaffold Lane and driving them up to Southport, she received a bit of news she could not process.

'It can't have been him, he's dead,' said Jenna's uncle.

'Well obviously it *was* him,' Jenna retorted, 'he was very much alive.'

'I am almost certain he passed away recently,' Jenna's uncle replied.

'Nah, you're probably getting mixed up with someone else,' said Stuart, going into the kitchen to make a pot of coffee for him and Jenna.

'Look it up,' Jenna's uncle said, nodding to her pocket, suggesting she should Google Bob Holness on her phone, but she told him her phone was flat. Her uncle got out his old laptop, which took ages to come on because of the irritating Windows updates. But when he finally got the Google homepage on the laptop, he typed in the name Bob Holness, and the Wikipedia entry for him stated that the TV presenter and gameshow host had indeed died in 2012.

Jenna went cold inside, and she looked at the Wikipedia page for Holness and said, 'Sometimes hackers mess about with these pages and alter them so they look as if they're dead and that.'

'No, love, I vaguely recall it being announced on the telly,' said the girl's uncle, and he put on his glasses and read a little bit of the entry. 'He died aged 83.'

'Well the Bob Holness who gave us a lift looked as if he was only in his fifties,' said Jenna, and from the kitchen doorway, Stuart backed up the testimony of his girlfriend, saying, 'It was him – that Wikipedia's got it wrong. He looked about fifty odd.'

But Jenna's uncle researched Bob Holness a little further, and saw the many online obituaries – all of which mentioned him dying on 6 January 2012.

'Someone who looks like him has kidded you two,' said Jenna's uncle, 'that can be the only explanation. There's no such thing as ghosts so forget all that rubbish. Yeah, it's been someone who's had a look of him and he's gone along with it, yer daft things.'

'No, it was definitely him,' said Jenna, 'I'm not stupid, uncle.'

'It *was* him,' added Stuart, handing Jenna a coffee, 'but he did look as he was when he was on the box like, he didn't look 83.'

'There you go, then, softlad,' said Jenna's uncle, 'it's been someone with a sense of humour. Someone's told him he's a dead ringer for Bob Holness and he's played on it. Mystery solved. There's always an answer to these things when you just step back and think about them.'

'Wait a mo,' said Stuart, his eyes looked up at the ceiling; he seemed to be recalling something. He paused, then said, 'He was driving the exact type of BMW me dad used to have back in the 1990s; it was a gold V8 BMW 530i SE.'

Jenna's uncle smiled and said, 'What's that got to do with anything?'

'Now, I remember the registration of that car,' said Stuart, and he looked at Jenna and said, 'you know what I'm like remembering numbers?'

Jenna turned to her uncle and said, 'Yeah, Stu's got a photographic memory.'

'But he couldn't place Bob Holness, though,' chuckled Jenna's uncle.

'I'm talking about numbers and registrations,' replied Jenna, looking needled.

'I'll go and see Mick Johnson tomorrow,' said Stuart, 'he's got access to a massive vehicle registration database.'

'Oh, you two are just making a mystery out of nothing now,' said Jenna's uncle, and he looked a bit spooked, 'it wasn't the ghost of Bob Holness; for God's sake, what would Bob Holness be doing haunting a road up by Formby? It doesn't make sense.'

Mick Johnson looked up the registration he was given, and the result shocked Stuart. In 1994, Bob Holness had owned a gleaming gold BMW 530i SE. It *had* been his car the couple had travelled in, then.

'It goes against logic and common sense,' said Jenna's uncle when she told him how the car registration matched a car owned by Holness, and the elderly man added: 'it might have even been a relative of Bob Holness who inherited the car.'

'I think Stu said the car has been scrapped since, uncle,' said Jenna, 'so that's your theory out the window.'

'Look,' said the girl's uncle, 'do me a favour from now on, Jenna; don't ever mention this again. It's barmy.'

The question Jenna's uncle asked about Holness being on a road near Formby is hard to answer; as far as I know, Holness had no relatives, friends or business acquaintances in our neck of the woods, so what on earth would his ghost be doing up here? Maybe there is some higher intelligence which views famous individuals such as Holness as having some unique motivating power that can inspire others to carry out good deeds, and so these famous people are resurrected to harness the talents and humane nature of people who are themselves in distress with a view to achieving a greater good. Could the occasional cases of alleged reincarnation be something similar to the returnee phenomenon? This query brings us to the last two cases in this chapter.

In August 2004, a 25-year-old Fazakerley welder named Jon 'surprised' his girlfriend Helen, a 22-year-old West Derby hair stylist, by booking a week-long holiday in Paris – a city Jon had always wanted to visit – and Helen said she'd have preferred Ibiza, but went on the short holiday anyway. Jon said he'd love to give up welding and become a bohemian surrealist artist on the Left Bank, but Helen playfully blew in his ear and said, 'Reality to Jon, we lost you for a moment then.'

After the touristic visits to the Eifel Tower, Notre Dame Cathedral and the Arc de Triomphe, Jon and Helen visited the Musée du Louvre, and here something quite strange took place. Upon seeing a portrait of Marie Antoinette, Helen became dizzy and unsteady on her feet. Jon sat her down on a bench and Helen told him she felt as if she had just looked into a mirror when she gazed at Marie Antoinette's picture, and Jon realised the Queen in the painting was Helen's double. 'She's the spit of you;' remarked Jon, and he held his girlfriend's hand and asked, 'you okay, love?'

Helen nodded and squeezed Jon's hand in reply. Three impeccably-dressed Frenchmen then walked towards the couple and all three knelt before Helen as she sat there, and one of the men held Helen's sandalled foot and kissed her toes. Jon glared at him and retorted with, 'Aye-aye!'

The peculiar trio caused a scene, saying they were "Legitimists" - members of a controversial political party who wanted to bring the pre-Revolutionary monarchy back to France - and that they had long awaited "La réincarnation de Marie-Antoinette". A crowd formed around the Liverpool couple and a fierce argument then broke out between the three men and other tourists, both French and foreign. During this mêlée, Jon and Helen sneaked out of the Louvre, and went to a café, and there, Helen continued to receive peculiar looks from some people, and she was not imagining the uncalled for attention; Jon noticed the strange glances his girlfriend was receiving too. The hair stylist was only too glad to get home to Liverpool. Did Helen just facially resemble the doomed queen - or is she Marie reborn? There is still an obscure underground cult in France that is resorting to occultism to bring about a Third Bourbon Restoration, but in an age where monarchies are steadily being replaced with republics, the chances of a 21st Century France having a House of Bourbon is quite slim.

And finally, on the subject of returnées perhaps being explained by reincarnation, let me relate the following strange story which I obtained from several lengthy interviews with a lady in the summer of 2022; her name was Carmen, and she told me how, in 2010, she arranged to meet a friend named Amy at a bar in the Mathew Street area one evening at 7pm. The two ladies - both aged 21 at the time - would then go from Mathew Street to another pub, and then onto a club; that was their usual routine. Carmen got to the bar on Mathew Street, a little earlier than she anticipated, and she found it almost deserted - except for two bar staff (who were engrossed in their smart-phones), an old but modernly-attired man lost in thought in a corner seat - and two well-dressed men. One of these men was a dead ringer for Henry VIII in face and build, and at first, Carmen thought he was a bouncer. He kept looking at her and glancing at a smaller, slimmer man - and the two of them just didn't fit in; for some reason they looked like fishes out of water in the trendy Mathew Street bar. Carmen thought she had seen the smaller man before somewhere, but for the life of her, she just could not place him. She eavesdropped on the conversation between the two men, and heard a curious thing. The large and imposing man who looked like Henry VIII asked whether some person got along with another one and the smaller one said, 'After a fashion, Harry; they get on like Lancaster and York.' Carmen thought the comparison a strange one; she hadn't heard of Lancaster and York being referred to in that way since the days of her stuffy history lessons at school.

Carmen was so glad when she saw Amy arrive; the two of them sat in a snug corner of the pub, and Carmen told her about the two men. Now, Carmen believed Amy was psychic; she seemed to be able to read people and came out with some spooky predictions from time to time that came true, and when she looked at the two men, Amy suddenly said: 'They have really strange auras. That man who looks familiar to you is going to ask you out; he followed you here.'

Carmen's eyes widened and she said, 'Let's go, Ame, they're creeping me out.'

Sure enough the thin man Amy had talked about came over and said to Carmen: 'Is your surname Neville by any chance?' and Carmen shook her head and the man said 'You look like someone I knew,' and then he asked Carmen out. Carmen noticed him fidget with the silver cufflink of his left sleeve, and noticed the cufflink was inlaid with an image of a pair of scales in what looked like onyx.

'I'm sorry, I'm waiting for my boyfriend,' she told the peculiar out-of-place man.

He smiled and closed his eyes slowly then opened them again, looked at Carmen sideways and raised his eyebrows in a certain way, as if to convey disbelief in what Carmen had just said. 'Come with me,' he almost whispered.

Again, Carmen shook her head, and without a word of reply, she got up and left, dragging Amy with her. Several times that night, the thin-featured man turned up in the same pub as the girls; they went to the Vines public house – he arrived there; they went to a pub on Hanover Street – and he turned up there too, and so, fearing they were being stalked, the girls went to Amy's home on Lark Lane, and as Carmen made coffee and a snack, Amy went to a large illustrated volume of

British history that she spotted in her friend's bookcase. Amy flicked through the pages of the book, then stopped on one page and pointed to a picture of Richard III. Carmen saw the incredible resemblance, and she remarked on the man's friend, who had looked like Henry VIII.

'Just lookalikes,' said Carmen, but Amy slowly shook her head and said, 'No, it's them, but I don't know how; there are old souls where people have been here before, but those two men were physically from the past, and I can't work out how that would be possible; I'm not a physicist.'

At that moment there were three slow knocks on the front door, but the girls didn't answer. They stayed up most of the night. I've had so many reports of a bizarre double of Henry VIII knocking about in our neck of the woods before, and have written about the reports, but it's exceedingly difficult to explain. Are these historical doppelgangers mere doubles of people, or are they, as some have suggested, vampires or resurrected beings? Richard III's wife, by the way, was Anne Neville, and that man in the bar who had been a dead ringer for Richard Plantagenet had mentioned the surname Neville to Carmen. Maybe she reminded him of his wife – a wife who has been dead for over 500 years. Furthermore, Carmen mentioned the silver cufflinks with the inlaid images of the scales in onyx on them, and Amy said the scales were the symbol of Libra in the Zodiac – and Richard III, being born on 2 October 1452, would have been a Libran.

THE DARK BOX

In the 1990s there was a couple – Sally and George – both in their twenties, and George was left quite a few bob in the will of a relative and the couple moved from Norris Green to a semi on Menlove Avenue. Sally was a militant atheist – she needed to convert everyone she met into becoming a non-believer, whereas George was an agnostic – he was on the fence philosophically because he wasn't sure if there was or wasn't a God. Over a bottle or two of wine each evening after dinner, whether they had friends around or not, the couple would usually have a philosophical debate about something or other – usually that old chestnut, religion, and Sally knew her Sartre, Nietzsche and Camus, and George could rebuff her arguments with quotes from believers such as Kierkegaard, Plato and Kant.

On this otherwise pleasant evening, Sally was waving a paperback entitled *Seven Theories of Human Nature* under George's nose, and she was telling him how the philosophies of Plato, Marx, Freud, B. F. Skinner – and Jesus – were all detailed in the book, and how none of them really explained Human Nature. 'Exactly!' said George with a slow, elongated nod to his girlfriend, 'And that is why I'm an agnostic. An agnostic is – '

'I know what an agnostic is,' interrupted Sally.

'An agnostic is,' George continued anyway, 'someone who contends that there is not sufficient rational evidence to establish either the – '

'Jesus Christ!' yelled an annoyed Sally.

'It's ironic that,' said George, pointing at Sally's face, 'an atheist using Jesus to interrupt someone – why didn't you yell Karl Marx?'

'Karl Marx!' shouted Sally, thumping her fist on the coffee table.

'An agnostic, if I can get a word in edge-ways, is, as I was saying, someone who contends that there is not sufficient rational evidence to establish either the existence or the non existence of a Supreme Being!'

'I want to kill you when you talk over me like that you repetitive arsehole!' she told him, and poured another glass of wine for herself.

'It's because I'm right!' George retorted, shrieking the words as if he was trying to force himself to laugh, but he sounded hurt. 'There are billions and billions of suns and galaxies out there and we don't even know how life came about on this planet, so how can anyone be arrogant enough to say "Oh no, there can't be a Supreme Being"? You know nothing!'

'You know nothing, you're as thick as that wall George!' replied Sally, and she clinked down the wineglass on the coffee table and smiled, then said, 'Look, let me explain this so it gets through your thick caveman skull, alright?'

'Go on! Go on, but please, less of the insults,' said George, 'you're supposed to be a civilised philosopher!'

Sally put her hand across her forehead, gesturing that George was giving her a full blown headache. 'Alright, look, without insulting anyone, this is the answer to everything the philosophers were looking for – '

'Oh this should be good this,' said George, and emitted an attempt at a belly laugh, 'Nobel Prize stuff, this!'

'Listen, El stupido, the answer was found by the Existentialists, and they said this – now do try and concentrate with your Rice Crispie-sized brain, but here it comes: we are trapped in existence, living in a completely meaningless world! We can't get out of it so we have to make do with what we can. That is it!'

'Existentialism! What a cop out! That is an absolute load of horse manure!' George told her, and he fell back into the sofa holding his abdomen, miming a belly laugh. 'DNA and all of the atoms and electrons and quarks and gazillion subatomic particles are just meaningless!'

'I heard you were dropped on your head as a baby,' sniped Sally, 'I give up.'

George looked at the floor, slowly shaking his head, then said, 'Whenever I get you on the ropes with these discussions you always hit me below the belt.'

'It's not about philosophy with you, George,' Sally said through gritted teeth, 'it's about you wanting to be right – well you are wrong – and I'm glad I said what I said about you being dropped on your head!'

George gave a strange unhinged smile and looked at the wine bottle he'd picked up.

'You throw that and it's over, George!' she warned him.

He got up off the sofa and said, 'I'm off to bed.'

223

Sally got up and walked unsteadily after him. She was intoxicated, and choked up because of what she said.

She grabbed him from behind and apologised for what she'd said. He hugged her and said it was okay, and within minutes they were embracing in bed.

'George, I'm in the mood,' she whispered in the darkness.

George snored like a whale with Sleep apnoea.

Three days after this, it happened to be Sally's 27th birthday, and George, with his twisted sense of humour had a mahogany confession box (salvaged from a renovated church) installed at the house on Menlove Avenue, while Sally was over at her mother's home in Norris Green. It took two joiners less than an hour to assemble the confession box in the corner of the spacious lounge, and then George and the workmen toasted the completed job with a glass of sherry.

Sally came home and didn't recognise what the thing was at first, until George said, 'You need to go to confession Sally, and it's cheaper than seeing a psychiatrist.'

'That's what it is!' she gasped, and saw the funny side of George's bizarre gift. The odd thing was that the mahogany confessional had a lovely aroma within it that conveyed peace – perhaps all those penitents who had found peace of mind having their sins absolved had left some tracery of mental tranquillity behind.

'You can curl up in there with a lamp or a candle and some joss sticks and read your books,' said George, and he grabbed Sally's hand and lifted it. He kissed her knuckle. 'Or is it a daft idea?' he asked.

'No, it's a lovely idea, George,' she told him, 'there's

something quirky about an atheist using a confession box, but it could be worse, we could have used it as a lavatory.' She gave a long thoughtful look at George, and kissed him. 'Thanks,' she said, 'you're a one-off.'

Each evening, instead of arguing about metaphysical matters with George, Sally would grab a few books, a bottle of Moscato, and sit on a huge violet velvet designer cushion and read and sip, sometimes till midnight. But then one evening around 7:10pm Sally heard whispering voices as she sat reading in the confession box. She was reading *A History of Atheism in Britain* when she distinctly heard: 'Bless me Father, for I have sinned; it has been five weeks since my last confession.'

She was out of that box in a heartbeat. George said she'd heard the sound of the neighbour's TV set, and nothing more.

'That was *not* the neighbour's telly next door, George;' Sally maintained, with a nervous glance across the lounge at the confession box, 'it sounded like someone right next to me.'

George picked up a newspaper and flipped through the pages till he saw the listings for tonight's TV programmes. 'There we go - *Highway* with Harry Secombe. That's the religious programme you've heard; deaf-lugs next door has her telly on loud, and you've heard it. *Highway* started at 6:40pm and ended at 7:15pm – which fits the time period when you heard it.'

On the following evening, this time at 11:20pm, Sally was sitting in the confession box reading by three scented candles when she heard, 'Sally, this is Father Riley, you need to confess to me, child,' and she let out a yelp, but realised it was just George outside the confession box, messing about. She played along and said, 'Father Riley, I need to confess to so many dirty sins; this is Sally of Menlove Avenue.'

'Men love having you, more like,' answered George, laughing. He opened the door to the confession box and asked Sally if she was coming to bed. She nodded, and blew out the three candles.

Almost an entire week passed before something very strange took place in the confessional, and it would leave Sally with recurring nightmares for the rest of her life. The incident took place in broad daylight on a Saturday afternoon. Sally was sitting in the old confessional box when she heard a man say, 'Go ahead Sally, confess.' And she smiled and assumed it was George messing about again, this time from behind the little grille in the box's partition. She confessed to living "over the brush" – unmarried – with George – and the door of the box flew open and a stern-faced middle-aged nun lunged in and grabbed the petite Sally and dragged her to the sofa. A priest with bulging eyes came out the box with a lit candle and the nun grabbed Sally's index finger and held it over the flame until Sally screamed in agony.

'That hurt didn't it?' the nun asked, and yelled, 'Imagine that all over your body for an eternity in the fires of Hell! Do you know how long eternity is?'

The nun held Sally's finger over the flame again and Sally saw the blister appear at the tip of her index finger. She swore and struggled to break free of the nun but found the priest was also restraining her, and Sally let out a scream that brought the neighbours to the window of the lounge, but by then the ghosts of the priest and nun had gone.

Sally went to stay with the couple who lived next door until George came home. He could see Sally was in a terrible state, and he called the two joiners who had installed the confession box and had them dismantle the thing to take it away. George tried to rationalise what had happened but was simply unable to; Sally had been one of the biggest sceptics of the supernatural he had ever known, and she assured him the confession box had been haunted. For weeks, Sally would awake in the dead of night, trembling and believing she could hear the whispering voices of the kind that she had heard in that confession box.

Sally now truly believes in the unseen and is no longer an atheist.

IN THE WEE SMALL HOURS

Many ghosts walk by day, and in broad daylight they may be mistaken as members of the living, especially if they are wearing fairly modern clothes and look solid enough to cast shadows, but most people associate ghosts with the night – especially the dead of night; that period of the morning the Scots call the "wee small hours" – so called because the hour numbers of the clock (1am to 4am) are low during that period. It is during those early hours when a stillness descends – and I have experienced that deathly hush on many lone ghost vigils – when the sun is on the far side of the world and most people of sense are in their beds. Even in the so-called 24-hour society, a tangible silence enshrouds the streets and homes after the bustle of the living, breathing day has died. In the uneasy tranquillity of the wee small hours, the waking person may notice the little sounds that were swamped out by the hubbub in the daylight hours; the dripping tap in the kitchen, rustling trees outside the window, air bubbles in the radiator, the house 'settling down' as the temperature drops after the heat of day and floorboards contract, and so on. During this period, when the tick of the clock seems amplified, some strange things have happened, and this chapter is about just a few of these unnerving incidents from the middle of the night. Here's the first one, and it was never explained.

In 2016, a 24-year-old English Literature student named Rose moved into a studio apartment in a student accommodation complex on Caledonia Street, which runs alongside the Philharmonic Hall. Rose often had friends over, but was disciplined enough to only party occasionally, and always on Friday and Saturday nights, because she took her studying seriously, as she had once dropped out of university because of her excessive drinking. One warm Monday evening around 10:15pm, after her friends had left the apartment on Caledonia Street, Rose opened a window and sat in her favourite chair, a mustard yellow wingback chair from Habitat that her father had bought her. Rose settled down and opened a paperback copy of F. Scott Fitzgerald's *The Great Gatsby*, and as she started to read, the student dipped her left hand into the packet of Tesco's cheese savouries resting on a little side table, when a whispering voice at the window said, 'You greedy pig.'

Rose was startled by the voice. Although she was on the third floor of the four-storey building, she thought someone had somehow climbed up to her window because the voice had sounded so near. She crept over to the window and swiftly closed it, turned its aluminium handle, then peeped out. She could see no one about; no one on ladders or clinging to the brickwork – just an unusually empty Caledonia Street. She turned the light off in the flat then went to the window again – but no, Rose was certain that no one was about. She wondered if the voice had just been a case of sound playing tricks on her ears; she'd vaguely heard someone say that sound travelled further at night – so it might have been someone shouting in the distance, somewhere on Hope Street. Rose convinced herself this had been the case, and so she turned the light back on, opened the window again – but only by a few inches this time – and she sat down and read the four-line poem that prefaces *The Great Gatsby* - when again, she heard the elusive whisperer.

'Greedy guts.'

In the space of five seconds, Rose threw herself out of her Habitat chair, closed the window, peered out into the dark street, then picked up her mobile. She called her best friend Jess and got an answering service message. After hanging up on the automated reply, Jess called her back, and Rose told her what had happened. 'You've probably just heard a random bit of a conversation from someone walking by outside,' was Jess's explanation.

'No, this was definitely something spooky,' Rose insisted, glancing back at the window, 'it was a really creepy whispering voice and he was addressing me.'

'Do you want me to come over for a bit?' Jess asked, and Rose said she'd appreciate her company till she calmed down. Jess came over and she and Rose went into the kitchen area, which just occupied a corner of the studio apartment. Rose made a pot of coffee and then they both stood near the window where the voice had been heard. Jess sipped her coffee, then listened at the window and said, 'I can hear really faint voices from over on Myrtle Street; sound does act weird of a night.'

'I thought that but this sounded clear, and I got the

impression the person could see me, the way it said, "Greedy pig" as I was eating the cheese savouries. I've just got a shudder just talking about it.'

'Anyway, back to reality,' said Jess, and she started talking about the ups and downs of her relationship with her on-off boyfriend James, and the time flew over, and at 2:20am, Caledonia Street was bathed in the light of a full moon. Jess stood up and looked out the window and said, 'Well, I better be making tracks. Will you be alright now?'

'Yes, thanks for coming over,' said Rose, and she hugged Jess, and then walked with her to the communal entrance downstairs. Rose waved her off and watched her friend until she turned the corner of Sugnall Street onto Myrtle Street, where Jess lived near to the old Ear, Nose and Throat Hospital building. Rose then noticed the eerie atmosphere; not a sound of a passing car or taxi, which was unusual, and then the feeling of being watched. She cried out as something fluttered down through the night air; a small orange bag – it looked like the bag that the cheese savouries had been in up in the apartment. Rose ran into the communal area and the automatic door-closer creaked as the heavy front door swung ever so slowly till it closed with a muted thud. She felt too afraid to get in the claustrophobic elevator as she thought some unseen presence had followed her into the building, so Rose hurried up the stairs, and she thought she heard faint footsteps behind her. She got to her unlocked apartment door, shoved it open, then immediately closed the door and put on the safety chain and small bolt. When Rose looked about, she saw something very strange; the cheese savouries she'd

231

left in their bag next to *The Great Gatsby* paperback book were there in a pile on the little side table, but the orange bag they'd been in was nowhere to be seen. She thought of the bag that had floated down past her before in the street, and she felt her heart miss a beat. She looked at the window – it was still closed, so she wondered if the bag she had seen before had been the one that was missing. Rose stood there, looking at her bare arms. Goosebumps formed on them. It felt as if there was a high-tension electrical atmosphere in the studio flat now. The hairs on the nape of Rose's neck stood on end, and the girl just knew there was someone there. 'Greedy guts,' said a voice close to Rose's left ear, and the speaker of those two words was so close his breath was felt on her ear. Rose screamed and ran out of the flat. She ran down the stairs to the communal area and pulled open the door, but the automatic door-closer seemed to resist her for a moment. The girl almost threw herself onto Caledonia Street, and she tried to run but quickly discovered she was out of shape, and gasped for air and clutched at the stitch in her side. She ended up staying in Jess's flat on Myrtle Street.

'I think your imagination has gotten the better of you,' Jess told Rose, handing her a bottle of beer to calm her down.

'It wasn't imagination, Jess; there was someone there, a ghost, and they were right next to my ear,' said Rose, and she walked to her friend's window and looked out. She gazed up at the full moon then her gaze dropped to a solitary lit window in the distance. Rose thought she was looking at the wrong window in at first, but then she counted the windows in the apartment block where she lived about 240 feet away. The window was on the third floor and the sixth window from the right end of the building – that was *her* apartment – and there was a person there in her room doing what seemed to be a bizarre dance.

'Jess, come here – there's someone in my apartment – look!' Rose pointed to the only lit window. Jess smiled and said, 'Oh don't start,' but then she saw the figure too. She said it was wearing something red. It was definitely a man, but who was he?

'Did you just run out your place and leave your door open?' Jess asked.

Rose shook her head and said she had closed the door of the apartment behind her because she had known she had the door-keys in her pocket.

'That's no ghost,' decided Jess, 'that's some scally that's got into the place somehow, Rose, and he looks as if he's tripping out.'

Rose followed Jess from her apartment on Myrtle Street, and they lingered on a moonlit Sugnall Street, watching the demented dancer at the window at closer quarters now. Both girls could see the intruder had on what seemed to be a red jersey. 'We should call the police, Rose,' Jess suggested but her friend seemed reluctant and said, 'I think he's the ghost that was whispering to me. If we call the police out, he'll vanish.'

'Hello, hello, hello, hello, hello! What's all this then?' said a voice behind the girl which made them both yelp with fright. It was James, Jess's boyfriend. He said he'd just been to a party on Mulberry Street that had lasted almost two days and he just wanted to get his head down. He asked Jess if he could stay at her place,

233

and she excitedly told him about the weird intruder at Rose's apartment, and pointed him out.

'Just call the police,' James proposed, and seemed unsteady on his feet.

'James, can you go and sort him out?' Jess asked, and smirked as she looked at Rose, who was still gazing at the mysterious figure in her window.

'I can't even sort myself out,' James replied, then paused, and said, 'no – I'm not getting involved.' He looked up at the figure in the red jumper, who was still dancing and said, 'He looks as if he's enjoying himself. Probably just taken too many e's.'

'I'll have to stay with you Jess,' Rose declared, 'I'm not going home while he's there.'

'Oh, I don't believe this,' said James, and he hiccupped and started walking towards Rose's flat. 'If I end up being knifed or shot, it'll be on your head,' he said to Jess, who hurried after her boyfriend. Rose kept a few feet behind the couple, and continued to look at the man in the window as she neared her apartment.

Rose gave the key of her apartment to James and he went into the communal hallway with Jess, who halted at the doorway and turned to beckon Rose. 'Come on, we can't let him go up there on his own,' she said.

'No, I'm staying down here,' Rose said firmly, 'you go up with him.'

Jess accompanied James, who got the elevator up to the third floor, while Rose stood in the communal hallway, wondering what to do. In the six months Rose had lived at the flat she had never experienced anything remotely spooky, so why had all this started to happen now? She started to actually doubt herself; had she imagined the ghost, as Jess had suggested? No, she knew she hadn't. She heard Jess shout down to her, 'Rose! He's gone.'

'What?' Rose shouted up the stairs.

She heard movement behind the door of a ground floor flat in the hallway, and realised she was waking other students up, so she went upstairs to see what Jess was talking about. James had found the place empty, and he'd checked the bathroom too – no one was about.

'But we saw him,' Rose told Jess, 'we all saw him.'

'Well he's vanished into thin air,' said James, and he grabbed Jess by her hand and led her out of the flat saying, 'and we are about to vanish too. I am knackered.'

'I'm not staying here tonight,' said Rose, and James told her she'd have to sleep on a sofa in Jess's place because he was sleeping in the bed, and he added, 'three's a crowd; I'm not that type of guy.'

Rose stayed over at her friend's place, and when she looked out of her window, she once again saw the dancing figure in the window of her apartment, and Jess saw the figure too. That was enough. The next day, Rose visited the student accommodation office and told them about the supernatural goings-on at her apartment, and was given alternative accommodation. When I heard about this strange case, it rang a bell; I'd heard of something similar before and I went through my old files and discovered that a phantom whisperer had been heard at the flats that had stood on the site of the new student accommodation back in the 1980s. Those flats were demolished in 2014 and in their place the apartment built on the site was the one Rose moved into in 2023, but who is the whispering ghost

235

and why was it dancing at the window of the student's apartment in 2016? The entity remains a mystery, but perhaps if the haunting continues I may discover more about the baffling ghost in the red jumper.

Here is another story of a strange incident which unfolded with the deepening of the night. It was in the November of 2015 when a family of five moved into a house on Landford Avenue, Fazakerley. The house seemed pleasant enough at first, but then late one night in that first month at the property, the youngest member of the family, a 13-year-old girl named Amy, had difficulty sleeping. She'd had insomnia before and her mum had taken her to the family doctor, who deemed that the girl had been drinking too many caffeinated soft drinks. Amy was therefore given water and fruit juices with no stimulants, and she was soon back to normal – but now, after going through a bottle of caffeinated cola a day for a few weeks, the insomnia had returned, and this time it was acute. Amy sat up in bed, reading her older brother's GCSE Maths book, as mathematical formulae usually sent the girl off to sleep, but it didn't work on this night – or should I say morning? It was now 1:20am and so Amy was about to browse the Internet on her phone when she heard a voice. It sounded like someone singing, and whoever it was (and it sounded like a female voice) she was being accompanied by music.

Amy went to her bedroom door, turned the knob and opened the door slightly, and her right eye peered out at the cold dark landing. Now she could hear the singer a little more clearly – clearly enough to catch the words of a strange song:

Amy stood there, wondering who it was, singing at this unearthly hour, and she decided to step out of the bedroom. She turned on the landing light and tiptoed across the carpeted floor, to the door of the spare room where the singing was coming from. She knew that room was nicknamed the Pink Room because the previous occupiers of the house had painted its walls carnation pink. For some reason, Amy had felt uneasy in that room when she first stepped into it with her mum, days after they had moved into the house a week ago. Curiosity got the better of the girl, and she just had to know who was singing in the Pink Room, and so she took a deep breath and carefully turned the door handle to the room and looked in. This was something Amy later regretted, for it still gives her nightmares today. In the Pink Room, Amy saw the figure of a woman of about thirty years of age in a colourful mini dress with a flowery design, and this unknown woman had a gruesome red groove around her throat, and as she let out a shriek, blood sprayed out of her screaming mouth.

Amy slammed the door and ran in terror back to her bedroom, and within a few moments the girl's father came onto the landing, followed by Amy's mum. They went to their daughter's room, turned on the light, and found her crouching at the side of her bed.

'Amy! What the hell were you screaming for?' Her father asked.

'Dad, there's a woman with her throat all cut open in the Pink Room,' Amy replied in a distressed voice, getting up and hurrying towards her parents from the side of the bed.

'What?' the girl's mother looked at her husband, baffled, as Amy threw herself at her mum and hugged her.

'It was horrible mum!' Amy sobbed, her face pressed into her mother's chest.

The girl's father went to the Pink Room, opened the door, and saw no one about. The room looked exactly as he had left it, with cardboard boxes and a tea chest full of things he still hadn't unpacked from the old house. He switched the light off in the room and went back to his wife and daughter. He told Amy she must have had a nightmare and said there was nobody in the room.

A fortnight after this, Amy was again awake in the wee small hours, but this time her friend Alannah was staying over, and at precisely 3am, Amy was showing her friend a dress on eBay that she had her eye on when she heard that familiar song again – and she went cold inside.

'Oh my God can you hear that?' Amy asked Alannah, who listened, then nodded, and her huge eyes turned towards the bedroom door.

'Who is it?' Alannah asked, and right away, Amy went to the bedroom door as she replied, 'That's the ghost I was telling you about,' and she was going to open the door when Alannah shouted, 'Don't! Don't go out there. This is creepy.'

The singing stopped.

'It's a ghost of a woman with a cut throat, in the Pink Room,' Amy told her friend, with her hand on the doorknob of the bedroom door.

'Don't go out there, Amy,' said Alannah, 'I have a

really bad fear of ghosts. Turn the big light on!'

'I just need to hear if it's coming from the Pink Room again,' Amy insisted, and she switched on the bedroom light, then opened the door a few inches as Alannah gasped, 'Don't.'

Amy looked at the pitch-black landing, in the direction of the Pink Room, but this time she had no intention of going into that room. She was about to close the bedroom door over when the face of that woman with the cut throat popped around the corner of the door, inches away from a shocked Amy's face.

Amy screamed and almost fell backwards in shock as the woman with the cut throat came into the room. In the bright light of the bedroom, Amy could see the deep cut that went from ear to ear across the woman's throat, and the skin of the woman looked greyish-white and her eyes were bloodshot, which contrasted with the ghost's baby blue irises.

The apparition started to sing. *'Ha ha this-a way, ha ha that-a way!'*

Amy closed her eyes and screamed that hard, she felt salty blood on the back of her tongue. The ghost vanished into thin air, and Amy turned to see if Alannah was alright, but the girl was lying on the bed, her eyes rolled back, and she was shaking and making a choking noise. She had swallowed her tongue. Amy ran to her aid and saw her friend was urinating on the duvet, and as Amy tried to stop Alannah sliding off the bed onto the floor. The door burst open and Amy screamed again.

It was her father. 'What the hell's going on here?' he roared.

'Dad!' cried Amy, stooping over her unconscious

friend on the floor, 'Alannah's fainted!'

Alannah recovered from a seizure that had been triggered by the sight of the terrifying ghost, and needless to say, the girl never stayed over at Amy's house again. Amy's parents and the rest of her family – two older brothers – soon realised the place really was haunted, and that the haunter was coming from the Pink Room. Screams were often heard in the middle of the night throughout the house, as well as that peculiar song – 'Ha ha this-a way, ha ha that-a way' – and several priests were brought in to bless the house. The ghost remained active. A Church of England exorcist went into the Pink Room and detected an icy presence. The Rite of Exorcism was carried out – all to no avail – and so the family left the house. The new occupiers of the house on Landford Avenue had one spooky experience, not long after they moved in. Graham, the father of the family, entered the Pink Room and saw a flowery mini dress hanging motionless in mid-air in the centre of the room. Graham thought the dress was hanging from a thread but as he approached the garment it fell to the floor. There was no wire or any string attached to the dress, which dated back to the 1960s. The label bore the words "Peter Barron – London". Peter Barron was not a real person, but the name of a trendy clothing company – Peter Barron Fashions - that was based on Eastcastle Street in the Westminster district of London. Graham offered the dress to his 14-year-old daughter, but she felt there was something strange about the vintage mini dress that she just couldn't put her finger on, and so it was binned. The dress as described might have been the same one Amy saw the ghost wearing on the two traumatic occasions when she encountered the horrifying apparition. The second mystery concerning the ghost is that song it would sing – 'Ha ha this-a way' - is an old traditional English song from centuries ago that was adapted and reinterpreted by the American folk and blues singer "Lead Belly" (real name Huddie Ledbetter). The same song the ghost was heard to sing was used as the theme to *Wizbit*, a children's 1980s TV series. Why the ghost sings this old traditional song is unknown. Perhaps someone out there who lived in the house or nearby will know the tragic history of the Landford Avenue ghost.

From Fazakerley we next move to the ancient suburb of West Derby, and to Lewisham Road in particular. On the Thursday morning of 15 May, 1997, a 12-year-old girl named Marie told her 8-year-old brother Ben to go and get some packets of crisps, some Mr Kipling cakes and a few cans of Mountain Dew from the kitchen. Marie regularly sent her brother down to the kitchen in the wee small hours when she felt peckish, not just because she was lazy, but because a few weeks ago she had overheard her Mum telling her Nan that she felt as if there was a *presence* in the kitchen. The family had only lived at the house for three months. On this morning, less than a minute after Marie had sent Ben down to the kitchen, she heard him running up the stairs, excitedly shouting her name, and she went to the bedroom door, opened it and with gritted teeth she dragged him in and told him to be quiet. She wanted to know where the cakes, "lemmo" and crisps were.

'Some woman wouldn't let me in the kitchen,' answered Ben, wide-eyed, and he described the woman as looking, "scary". Marie thought he was just trying to spook her for some reason and so she went down the stairs - and there was the woman Ben had mentioned, standing in the doorway of the kitchen, which was all lit up, but it looked like an old-fashioned kitchen. The woman had her hair done up in a bun, and she wore a white apron and a black or dark brown shirt.

'Begone girl!' the stern-faced woman yelled at Marie - then vanished, and Marie screamed. Her father appeared at the top of the stairs and shouted, 'What are you doing up, making all this noise? I've got to get up at six for work!'

Marie told him about the woman but her dad yelled at her to get to bed, and then he chased Ben to his room as well.

On the following evening at 11pm, Marie lay on her bed, and she had on the main light in the bedroom, her bedside lamp, an old FM radio she had not switched on for years, and she kept thinking of the woman she had seen in the kitchen. Her parents had said she and Ben had imagined her, but that woman had been real, and Marie shuddered just recalling her harsh pale face and dark rimmed eyes. The bedroom door opened and Marie let out a squeal as she thought the ghost was visiting her. Marie's mum Linda popped her head around the door and said, 'Your nerves are gone; calm down will you? Do you want some supper?'

'Yeah,' replied Marie, ready to get out the bed, but her mum said, 'No, stay there; we're all getting in to bed now. I'll bring you a few slices of pizza up.'

Marie's mum closed the door and Marie could hear her slippers padding back down the stairs. She sat on the edge of the bed and wondered if she could go and stay with her Nan for a few nights. Marie's thoughts then turned to when she'd need to go the toilet. She'd be so scared of venturing out of her bedroom in the early hours of the morning. Marie then gazed at the brass knob on the bedroom door. She could have sworn it had turned. She took a deep breath and listened to her mum downstairs. She heard the clink of the plate on the formic top in the kitchen. Marie then wondered if she should ask Ben to come into her room when her mum and dad were asleep.

There was a scream downstairs which startled Marie. She heard the breaking of plates in the kitchen, and she heard her father asking, 'You alright love? Love? What happened?' Marie opened her bedroom door and looked down the lit stairs to the hallway, and she heard her mother saying something about a *ghost* - the word stood out and sent a shiver down Marie's spine. She went downstairs and asked her mum what had happened.

'I – I saw a woman standing over there by the fridge, dressed in an apron,' Marie's mum replied, the fingers of one hand covering her mouth and her other hand pointing a trembling finger at the corner of the kitchen.

'Linda, stop filling her head with nonsense,' Marie's father said to his wife, noticing his daughter standing in the doorway of the kitchen wide-eyed and scared.

'I'm not filling her head with nonsense! It was a bleedin' ghost!' Linda retorted, and she stepped unaware on a shard of the plate and a slice of pizza that had been destined for Marie before the heart-stopping appearance of the figure.

'It's been your own shadow or something,' said

Marie's dad, and he seemed on edge, as if he didn't believe his own explanation.

'Oh my God, that ghost has been the thing Marie and Ben saw and we said they were imagining things!' Linda realised, and she continued to gaze at the corner of the kitchen, close to the fridge, where the woman had appeared and glared at her.

Ben came down the stairs in his pyjamas and his father said to him, 'Your mum just dropped a plate, that's all,' but the boy wasn't convinced, and Marie held his hand.

'He's in his bare feet,' said Linda, glancing at Ben before her eyes scanned the fragments of plate on the kitchen floor, 'don't let him come in here.'

The family ended up sitting on the sofa eating what was left of the pizza, as well as crisps, and they watched a film called *The Dirty Dozen: The Fatal Mission* with the volume turned down to almost a whisper. Linda kept talking in hushed tones to her husband and he kept telling her to 'give it a rest' – and Marie and Ben knew their mum was talking about the ghost. The father was definitely in denial, and seemed reluctant to visit the kitchen, even thought the light had been left on in there. When the film ended at 1:10am, Marie and Ben were allowed to sleep between their parents in the king size bed, and Marie kept waking up as she imagined she could hear footsteps on the stairs.

A week after this, when the ghost was a dim memory, Marie was in her bedroom one night around eleven when there were three taps on her bedroom door. The girl imagined her mother had brought some pizza supper up, but was holding the plate with both hands and using her foot to tap on the door, and so an excited Marie yanked open the door – only to see that it was not her mother standing there, but the old fashioned lady in the apron. The ghost stood there with a tray with something on it, and Marie screamed, slammed the door, and ran into her bedroom, where she hid in the gap between her wardrobe and the wall. Moments later she heard the footfalls of her mum and dad as they hurried to her up the stairs, and when they came into her room she told them how the tray-carrying ghost had knocked on her door.

The ghost was seen by both of Marie's parents not long after. They had just returned from the pub, and as they entered the hallway, they saw the woman in her dark dress and white apron move sideways as if she was on wheels, going from the bottom of the stairs to the back parlour. At the time, Ben and Marie were staying at their Nan's house. Enough was enough, Marie's parent's found another house to live in, and they moved to Sedgemoor Road, Norris Green not long after the hallway encounter with the ghost. I hear the ghostly woman is still occasionally seem haunting the kitchen of the house on Lewisham Road, but why - and who she is for that matter - is not known.

From West Derby we move now to Wavertree, and to a semi on leafy Abbeystead Road. In 1997, an old lady named Gloria died at a house on this road, and she left her home to a 44-year-old niece named Elsie. In July of that year, Elsie and her long-term partner Bryan moved into the house (along with their ginger cat Wotsit) from their maisonette in Edge Hill and started to do the place up. Bryan was a perfectionist and when he started a job there was no cutting corners or anything slapdash about his work, and that Elsie admired, but what she didn't like was the way Bryan would often work into the night, and this was precisely what he was doing on this hot July night in 1997. Elsie finally convinced him to put his tools and paintbrushes away for the night and put his feet up. Elsie bought a couple of bottles of wine (for herself) and a few packs of lager for Bryan, and they sat watching the TV until around 2:20am, when Elsie started to yawn. Because it was such a prickly hot night, Elsie and Bryan couldn't sleep, and they ended up sitting on a sofa in the living room, talking about the old days. All the old anecdotes came up, and a few new ones as Bryan remembered some old adventures from his youth. During these reminiscences in the dead of night, the couple's ginger cat Wotsit, who had been curled up asleep in a ball under the coffee table, suddenly awoke, looked at the living room doorway as if he had heard or seen something, then ran into the hallway. The couple then heard the rustle of cloth and the faint tread of feet going up the stairs from the hallway. 'Who's that?' murmured Elsie, looking at Bryan, who was already getting up from the sofa. He went into the hallway and said, 'Someone's just gone up the stairs – it was a woman.'

'What!' Elsie hared out of the living room and into the hallway, which was in darkness. The only illumination in the hallway was coming by way of the light shining down the flight of stairs from the landing upstairs.

'I saw the bottom of a woman's dress, and a boot – like an ankle boot, going up the stairs through the balusters,' said Bryan, and he seemed reluctant to go up the stairs to see where the stranger had gone, but he did go, and Elsie went up the stairs behind him saying, 'Be careful Bryan, they might have a knife!'

But Bryan and Elsie found no one upstairs. They searched all the rooms, and then Bryan searched downstairs, even though Elsie told him no one could have passed them to go down the stairs; Bryan looked anyway, and found not a trace of the woman he had seen ascending the stairs.

'Are you sure you actually saw someone going up those stairs, Bry?' asked Elsie as they walked back into the living room, and Bryan nodded slowly and said, 'Of course I saw her; I'm not in the habit of seeing things; she was going pretty fast up those stairs.'

'That's all we need – a ghost,' said Elsie, and she went to the bottle of wine on the coffee table and drained it into her glass. 'It couldn't have been Auntie Gloria's ghost – she had a stick and she took ages getting up those stairs. She should have had a stair-lift put in.'

'If it was a ghost, it was a pretty solid-looking one,' remarked Bryan.

'The light can play some very strange tricks on the eyes at night,' Elsie told her partner, 'I remember seeing a shadow of a man with a hook nose on the wall of the lobby in our old house, and it was just the shadow of me dad's coat hanging on the newel post.'

'This was no trick of the light, Elsie,' said Bryan, firmly, 'even the cat saw it the way he ran out there if you remember.'

'He could have been chasing one of those little flies – ' Elsie started to say, trying to rationalise the incident, but Bryan said, 'Baloney! Elsie, someone went up those stairs, and I don't even believe in ghosts but I know what I saw.'

'We'd better be getting up those stairs ourselves, look at the time,' said Elsie, and she nodded at the clock over the fireplace, and then she swigged the last of the wine from the glass and saw Wotsit curled up under the coffee table again. She decided not to put him out. She needed all the company she could get on this spooky morning.

On the following evening at 11pm, Bryan was still artexing the kitchen wall when Elsie said, 'Alright Bryan, leave it for tonight – ' and Bryan turned and smiled and said, 'I don't know when to stop. I love artexing – ' And the smile vanished from his face and his eyes widened as he looked at something over Elsie's shoulder – at something in the hall.

Elsie turned in time to catch the sight of a woman in a long dark brown dress crossing the hallway, walking towards the bottom of the stairs, and the unidentified woman kept her face turned away from Elsie and Bryan, and then, upon reaching the stairs, she ran up them but there was no sound of her boots (which Elsie clearly saw through the balusters) as they went up those stairs.

'Believe me now, do you? Eh?' Bryan asked Elsie, who stood there in the kitchen with her hands to her shocked face.

Bryan ran after the ghost, and upon reaching the stairs he looked up and saw the woman turn right, and he would have seen her face in profile if she hadn't turned her head to the left – again hiding her face. All Bryan saw was the back of her head and the bun of her dark hair.

'Bryan, don't go after her!' shouted Elsie from the

hallway, 'Leave her! It's unlucky to confront them.'

But Bryan was already at the top of the stairs and he saw the figure turn right at the end of the landing and go into a room. When Bryan reached the room he saw the door was closed; the ghost had gone straight through it. Bryan bravely went into the room and switched the light on, but there was nobody there.

'I don't fancy living in here with a ghost,' Elsie told Bryan.

'The Church has people who can get rid of these troubled spirits,' Bryan replied, 'I'm not leaving here after all the work we've been putting in trying to renovate the place.'

The couple told no one about the ghostly woman. Elsie was tempted to ask the old neighbour who lived opposite the house but Bryan told her not to say a word or soon the whole of Liverpool would know. Elsie's best friend Audrey visited a few days later, and said the house had a welcoming atmosphere. Audrey and Elsie sat in the kitchen, catching up on each other's lives, and Elsie was aching to tell her friend about the haunting, but said nothing. She went to put the kettle on, and Audrey followed her to the sink, talking about her forthcoming holiday in Spain in August, when she suddenly said to Elsie, 'Who's she?'

'Who?' Elsie asked, switching the kettle on.

Audrey was looking out the kitchen window at the back garden. 'Her, in the antwacky clothes.'

Elsie looked through the window. It was the ghost, standing in the garden in broad daylight with her back to her and Audrey. Elsie turned to Audrey, stuck for words for a moment, and then Audrey said, 'She vanished!'

Elsie had no choice but to let Audrey in on the secret, and she told her about the ghost. Audrey said she wouldn't tell a soul but later asked an old neighbour on Abbeystead Road about the ghost, and the old woman said she had heard of the apparition back in the 1960s in her younger days, and no one seemed to know who she was. A window cleaner had seen the ghost one morning as he cleaned the windows of the back bedroom at the haunted house, and he had almost fallen off his ladder in shock, because her face looked ghastly; it was described as being as white as chalk with black sockets for eyes.

The renovation work on the Abbeystead Road house continued, even though Bryan could not get a priest to visit the house to give it a thorough blessing. Elsie tried a vicar, and he said he didn't believe in ghosts (even though they are mentioned many times in The Bible).

On what was to be the final night at the house, Bryan stopped painting the ceiling in the living room at 11:50pm and went into the kitchen to have a few cans of lager and something to eat. He sat at the table with Elsie and said, 'I wonder why your Auntie Gloria never mentioned the ghost?'

'She probably would have done if I'd stayed around her long enough but I was always paying a flying visit,' said Elsie. 'I should have stayed with her longer, she was a very lonely woman.'

The couple talked until 1am, and then Bryan yawned. He looked up at the kitchen clock and at that precise moment it stopped. The last tick of the clock heralded what could only be described as a solid silence which fell upon the kitchen. Elsie noticed the strange stillness and Bryan remarked upon it too, saying, 'It's just gone awfully quiet, hasn't it?'

'Ooh!' Elsie shuddered and said, 'Just went all shivery then.'

Bryan went up to the toilet with drinking all of that lager, and then as he was leaving the loo, he heard Elsie scream downstairs. He rushed along the landing and was about to run down the stairs to her when he saw the ghost running up those stairs – and when it saw Bryan it turned to face the wall but kept on running up the stairs, heading towards him. He had downed a lot of cans of lager earlier, and was full of Dutch courage, and so he blocked the path of the ghost – and she turned to face him near the top step – and her face was an abomination. The eyes were black sockets with something red burning in them and the face was skeletal. The mouth opened twice as wide as a normal human mouth and the woman let out a deafening scream. Bryan threw his hands up to his face to shield his eyes from the most disturbing thing he had ever seen, and the ghost went *through* him. Elsie screamed as she saw Bryan trip and fall down the stairs. He landed at the bottom of the stairs in an unconscious state, and there was a piece of skin hanging from the palm of his hand where he had tried to stop himself falling but the friction of his palm against the wall had almost taken the skin off. Bryan regained consciousness but Elsie called an ambulance and Bryan was kept in for observation, as he was suffering from concussion. The couple decided to leave the haunted house, and it was later sold. Whether the unidentified ghost with the ghastly face still haunts the premises I do not know.

And finally, a rather uncanny spectacle was glimpsed in the wee small hours by an insomniac, and it led to a very scary outcome.

On the Sunday morning of 13 October, 2019, a 55-year-old lady named Gwen, who lived on the twelfth floor of York House - a tower-block on Croxteth Road, overlooking Sefton Park, was finding it hard to get to sleep. She lay there in her bedroom, with the diffused light from the street lamps far below casting a faint orange luminescence on the walls of the bedroom. The stillness invited introspection on this limbo of a Sunday morning. Gwen thought over the events of her life, from the days when she was a child in the Kensington area of Liverpool, right through to her marriage and divorce from Roy. She pulled her mind back to the present, and noticing what she perceived to be an eerie lull hanging in the air, she had a strange, unaccounted-for urge to look out the window. It was around 6:20 am, and yet it didn't feel like a morning at all – it was still dark out, and being Sunday the traffic noise was almost nonexistent. Gwen found herself getting up, placing her bare feet on the carpeted floor, and walking in 'sleep inertia' – that state of grogginess and drowsy cognitive impairment we often find ourselves in after rising from our beds of a morning. She lifted the net curtains and saw that the full moon was ready to set. It looked like a luminous ping-pong ball resting on some Welsh hill.

But what was that?

Gwen saw the tiny silhouettes of three figures against the glowing face of the moon. They seemed to be female and they were performing a mesmerising dance; the dancing reminded Gwen of the way Pan's

People (an all-female dance troupe) used to dance on *Top of the Pops* way back in the Seventies. The shadowy dancers were throwing their arms up in the air, kicking their legs up and jumping about. Gwen was useless at estimating distances and she could not tell where the silhouetted trio where; all she knew was that they were somewhere in the west of the city, or perhaps even over the water, as the moon might have been magnifying the images of the women. Within a few minutes the moon had sunk into a dark cloud on the horizon and when its light faded as the dawn began, the trinity of pitch black silhouettes also vanished. Gwen then went back to bed and slept till around 10:30am, and her friend Christina (who lived two floors below) called Gwen on her mobile. Christina said she was going to 'the Asda' and asked Gwen if she wanted anything at the supermarket. Gwen said she needed nothing, and then Christina said something that really woke Gwen up.

'Hey, I forgot to tell you,' said Christina, 'this morning around half-six, I was looking out the window of my bedroom, and Bobby [Christina's husband] said, "What are you looking at?" – I think I gave him a start because he woke up and saw me leaning out the open window. Anyway, as the moon was setting, I saw these three women dancing – '

'I saw them as well,' Gwen interrupted, and she went on to explain how she had been suffering from a bout of insomnia and had somehow felt drawn to the window.

'Wonder what they were?' Christina asked.

Gwen said, 'Well, I know it's silly thinking this in this day and age, but I had the feeling they were witches;

253

just the way they were dancing, it was like some pagan ritual. Or, more likely, it was just three girls miles away having a good time from the Saturday night before, and that moon might have made them stand out.'

'No, I think you were right, Gwen,' said Christina, 'there was just something a bit eerie about the whole thing – I think they might have been witches as well.'

On the following morning, around a quarter to eight, it was getting light, and the moon was almost in the same position it had been on the Sunday morning; it was almost setting, and looked as if it was disappearing quickly behind a distant hill. Like last time, Gwen was suffering from insomnia and was standing at her window, gazing at the moon – and she was shocked to see the three silhouettes of the women, but this time they were not dancing; the three of them were standing in a row, and as Gwen thinned her eyes and opened the window to get a better look (as there was condensation forming on the pane) she clearly saw the middle figure wave. This gave Gwen quite a start, as she had the unsettling feeling the woman was waving at her, as if she *knew* Gwen was observing her, which should be impossible, because the three mysterious women must have been too far away to notice Gwen, who was watching from a darkened room. The three silhouetted figures were only noticeable to Gwen because they were contrasted by the glowing disc of the setting moon; otherwise she would not have been able to see them. Gwen closed the window and adjusted the net curtains. She then saw the moon slowly sink into an opaque cloud, or possibly below the horizon.

Later that day, Christina told Gwen she had seen the

three women again, silhouetted against the face of the setting moon, and she had seen the middle woman wave.

'Yes, I saw that too,' said Gwen, 'it really gave me the creeps. I felt she was waving at me. I won't be watching out for them tomorrow.'

'I won't be looking out for them either,' seconded Christina, and then she smiled and said, 'She hasn't been waving to us, that figure – she wouldn't be able to see us from that distance, she'd have to have bionic vision. It was sinister though, and with Halloween being near now, the whole thing's just creeped me out.'

Both women were tempted to see if the figures were there against the moon's disc on the next occasion, but they stayed in their beds, and the morning was cloudy and rainy anyway. That morning, Gwen and Christina each received identical manila envelopes which came through their letterboxes. There was nothing written on the envelopes and no stamp, so the envelopes must have been hand delivered. Inside each of the envelopes was a piece of paper bearing the question, 'Would you like to join us?' and it was signed with the symbol of a crescent moon. Gwen thought Christina had posted the envelope through her letterbox as a practical joke, and Christina thought the same thing about Gwen, but the two women assured the other that she had not sent the envelope. The mystery then deepened when a woman who lived next door to Gwen said she had seen a strange-looking woman with long dark brown hair down below her waist, posting something in Gwen's door at 5am on Tuesday morning – the morning Gwen and Christina had received their enigmatic letters. The woman had worn a long green satin-like robe which went down to the floor. She had been there one moment, and then she seemed to have disappeared a moment later, Gwen's neighbour told her. Gwen and Christina were so scared of meeting the witches, they refused to go out at Halloween, which was just a few weeks after the weird letters had been received, and the two friends never cast more than a cursory glance at the moon when it was in the skies beyond their windows.

DID THAT REALLY HAPPEN?

Sometimes when we get a little time to ourselves we sit down and delve into our memories, and sometimes we may recall a bizarre occurrence from our far memory and think, 'I'd forgotten about that; did that really happen?'

Memory is a strange thing; it's choosy what it remembers; it forgets the imposing spectacle of a grand cathedral yet indelibly imprints the image of your first love blowing a chewing gum bubble which bursts and gets stuck to his or her nose. Memory can hold on to the worthless mud of your life and let the gold dust fall through like a prospector's worn out sieve. A psychologist would probably say that the nastiest experiences tend to stick, whereas others believe we repress them from our memory.

'Cast your mind back,' is a common phrase we hear when we attempt to plumb the depths of our memory – as if the mind can be launched across decades of spacetime into the past like a stone, whereas it's often difficult to focus on a particular time in our past, but sometimes a memory that has lain unrecalled since it was formed will suddenly spring forth into the conscious mind of its own volition, or something will jog that memory, and that was the case with the woman who suddenly remembered something very strange from her childhood.

Erin was 34 when she suddenly remembered a bizarre memory from when she was a little girl. The memory was jogged by someone on a local radio station mentioning Cavern Walks, the boutique shopping centre off Mathew Street which opened in 1984. Upon hearing the name "Cavern Walks" by the radio DJ, Erin had a flashback to 1994, when her mother took her to the shopping centre. Erin was five at the time, and she recalled her mother taking her down a long alleyway from Lord Street; this would have been Dorans Lane, a narrow 165-feet-long narrow passageway which leads to Cavern Walks. Instead of reaching the trendy shopping centre, Erin and her mum entered what looked like a hall of mirrors, and it proved to be a labyrinth of looking glasses. The mother and daughter soon became hopelessly lost in the strange mirrored maze, and Erin remembered her mother panicking and remarking, 'Where the hell are we?'

The mirrors reflected back multicoloured, kaleidoscopic shapes which made Erin and her mother disoriented. Little children of five can only walk so far until their legs get tired, and Erin was soon crying to be carried by her mum. With the child in her arms, the mother ended up turning around, going back the way she had come and eventually ended up on Lord Street. When she and Erin looked back down Dorans Lane, the tunnel of mirrors was nowhere to be seen. The grown-up 34-year-old Erin told her mother about the hazy weird recollection and her mum nodded and gave her version of what had happened that day in 1994, and the details dovetailed perfectly with Erin's recollections. Her mum said it had been an afternoon in September of 1994 when they had become lost in a maze of corridors with mirrored walls, and when she got out, she discovered the maze didn't exist. She told her husband about the incident and he flippantly told her she'd probably just got lost and entered some empty shop down at Cavern Walks. The incident was never explained. Perhaps the mother and daughter entered some dimensional aberration; it really is hard to speculate further on what happened that September afternoon in 1994.

I would say that forgotten odd incidents of this sort exist in most people's minds, and that they lie buried beneath the layers of years and decades of countless experiences until something gently prods the dormant memory and it replays its strange recollection. Here's an example of a hibernating horror story that was awakened in the back garden of a house during a barbeque. It was on a scorching August afternoon in 2017 when a 50-year-old joiner named Paul visited a friend named Gerry at his new home on Huyton's Pilch Lane. Paul, Gerry and the latter's girlfriend Rosie, sat in the back garden of the house, when Paul experienced the intriguing but baffling phenomenon of déjà vu – that feeling that you are currently doing something that you have done before in some vague past period of time, and you get the overwhelming feeling that might move you to say, 'This has all happened before.' That's how it felt to Paul. He looked at the greenhouse, the beech tree in the neighbour's garden, and the whole sunny suburban scene looked familiar – and then, in an instant, he recalled a very creepy memory that had lain forgotten for over forty years in the vast labyrinthine corridors of his mind.

'You alright, Paul?' Rosie asked the joiner, noticing the peculiar expression of subdued astonishment on his face as he gazed across the garden. She'd been holding out the plate to Paul with a barbequed burger in a bun upon it.

'What?' Paul turned to the lady, startled, as she brought him back from his childhood, 'Yeah, sorry. Just remembered something very strange,' he said, and took the plate from Rosie. He turned to Gerry and nodding to the house next door he asked, 'Isn't that where Mrs Marshall lived?'

Gerry looked at the garden next door with the beech tree and nodded. 'Yeah, that's right; she used to live there.'

'Do you remember what happened in her garden?' said Paul.

'No,' answered Gerry, 'what happened? I can just about remember what Mrs Marshall looked like. She used to wear an apron and we were always doing jobs for her, painting her fence and that.'

'Why, what happened Paul?' asked Rosie, sitting down at the table. She handed a paper napkin to Paul and grabbed a bottle of beer.

'I've only just remembered it now, and it was really creepy,' said Paul, and he told them the story as he could remember it from the eyes and mind of the eight-year-old person he had been when the incident had taken place, back in the summer of 1975. That year, Paul and his family had lived on Woolfall Crescent, Huyton, but each Saturday, Paul would visit his auntie on Pilch Lane half a mile away, and she always bought him a comic – usually *The Topper* - as well as some sweets and lemonade, and sometimes Paul's best mate, Gerry would accompany him to his aunt's in the hope of receiving a treat. A widowed woman in her seventies named Mrs Marshall lived across the road from Paul's auntie, and she would often ask him to go on errands to the shops for 50p and sometimes Mrs Marshall would give Paul 50p for brushing up the leaves outside her house or for helping her to put washing on her clothes line in the back garden. One Saturday morning in 1975, Paul called at Mrs Marshall's house hoping she'd have a job or two for him. Around this time, Gerry was also on his way to Mrs Marshall's house because he'd called at Paul's home and Paul's mother, Rita, had told the lad that Paul had gone 'on the cadge' to Mrs Marshall's house.

Anyway, Mrs Marshall answered the door to Paul on this fine summer's day, and she stood aside in the hallway (which she called the lobby) and said, 'Oh Paul, something strange is going on in the back garden!'

Paul returned a puzzled look and walked into the house. Mrs Marshall closed the door and nodded to the kitchen, gesturing for the boy to go through that room to get to the back garden. She pointed to what looked like a bunch of light brown wires that were coiled around a drainpipe. Those wires were tendrils that stretched from the lawn of the garden to the drainpipe. One of the tendrils was thicker than the others and could almost be classed as a vine. The odd thing was that these tendrils were all moving independently of one another. They were shaking, and yet it was a calm, windless say with not a cloud in the blue sky.

'See them moving?' Mrs Marshall asked Paul, and he nodded as he looked at the tendrils, and then glanced back at the old woman as if he was expecting her to explain what was going on.

'Is someone pulling them?' Paul asked Mrs Marshall, and the widow smiled and shrugged and said, 'I can't explain it. I hadn't even noticed them before today. I think I shall ask my neighbour Walter to get to the bottom of this mystery.'

Paul went next door with Mrs Marshall. The door was wide open at the neighbour's house and the widow just walked in and shouted, 'Walter? Are you about?'

Walter appeared at the top of the stairs in his string vest with shaving foam on his face. 'I'll be down in a jiffy Mrs M! Just getting a shave! Make yourself a cuppa!'

Mrs Marshall beckoned for Paul to come in the house. After about five minutes Walter came down the stairs and he went into the living room, where he tore tiny bits of paper from a page of the *Daily Mirror*, and he applied these bits of paper to the red dots of his face where the razor had nicked him. Mrs Marshall told him about the shaking tendrils and asked if he'd heard of that before.

Walter nodded and said, 'Could be rats.'

'Rats!' Mrs Marshall threw her hands to her face; dark pink hands veined and twisted by arthritis, Paul noticed.

'Yeah,' said Walter, 'when they tunnel they sometimes get caught up in weeds and that, and start to try and free themselves like, so you might have a rat problem Mrs M.'

'Oh, can you come and have a look?' Mrs Marshall asked in a trembling voice.

'Yeah, I'll be round in a minute,' said Walter, and he picked up a pen and said, 'I've just got to write a note for the missus, telling her what I want for the tea. I just feel like scallops; how do you spell scallops though.'

Paul spelled the word and Walter patted him on the head.

Mrs Marshall and Paul returned to the back garden and now the tendrils had stopped shaking. 'They're still now;' the widow told Paul, 'I hope Walter doesn't think we're pulling his leg.'

There was a knock at the door, and Mrs Marshall shouted from the kitchen, 'It's open, Walter!' but then she saw it was Paul's friend, Gerry, standing there with his hands behind his back, looking all innocent and angelic.

'Oh, it's your friend, Gerald,' Mrs Marshall told Paul, who grimaced; he didn't feel like splitting any money from Mrs Marshall with Gerry. Mrs Marshall told the boy to come in but to leave the door ajar. Paul told Gerry there were rats under the back garden and showed him the sinister tendrils stretching from the grass to the cast iron drainpipe.

Walter arrived a few minutes later and the tendrils shook violently. He looked at them and smiled. 'That is definitely rats Mrs M,' he said confidently. 'You'd be amazed where rats get,' he continued as he grabbed at the tendrils leading from the drainpipe, 'you see they have no backbone, and if a rat can get its snout in a crack or a hole, its whole body can squeeze through it as well.'

Paul went cold as he looked at the grass below his feet. He pictured that 'nest of rats' the neighbour had mentioned.

'What are you going to do?' asked Mrs Marshall, 'put down poison?'

Walter scratched his head. 'What I'll do first is just do a bit of digging to see where these thingies – '

'Tendrils,' said Paul.

'Yeah, them,' said Walter, 'I'll see where they are going and how far down they go. I'll go and get me spade. I might need me air pistol too.'

'Are you going to shoot them?' asked Paul, shocked at the thought of the rats being shot.

'If they're big sewer rats, yeah;' said Walter, 'because if they're sewer rats they'll be the size of a Jack Russell, and when they jump at you they go for your eyes.'

Paul let out a yelp as a daddy bunchy – the floating bristly seed of a dandelion – brushed against his left eye. He thought it might be one of the super-rats Walter was talking about.

Walter returned, placed the large air pistol on the grass, and then he cut the tendrils from the black metal drainpipe with a penknife. He then whistled as he tried to yank the cheese-wire hard strands from the grass but they cut his finger. He used his spade to excavate a few square feet of the badly-kept lawn and he and Mrs Marshall and Paul saw the eerie tendrils writhe about like long worms. It was as if those tendrils were alive.

Gerry and Paul kept glancing at the air pistol on the

grass, aching to hold it and to fire it. He could almost feel his index finger curling around the trigger.

Walter dug away around the tendrils and kept pulling at them, and every ten minutes or so, Walter would scrape away more soil, until he uncovered a mass of the tendrils in a bizarre shape: it looked like a human body, but this body was made from weeds that were wound and interwoven into each other. At first, Mrs Marshall thought Walter had unearthed a statue that had become covered in tendrils, but unlike the brown filaments strung from the drainpipe, these ones forming the 'body' were milky white.

'I have never seen anything like this in all my life,' said Walter, wiping the sweat from his forehead. 'Doesn't that look just like a man made from weeds?'

'Eee!' emitted a disgusted Gerry, leaning forward, hands on his bare knees as he took in the grotesque sight of the weird simulacrum of coiled strands.

Then the dull grey blade of Walter's spade gently scraped another layer of dark soil away from the effigy of growths to reveal the hideous *horned* head of the thing – and it's long curved aquiline nose, black socket eyes, and a dark crescent of a mouth. It looked like some Devil made from the windings of a mile-long worm. Paul giggled and whispered something to Gerry out of earshot of Mrs Marshall about the thing's 'willy'; its genitalia were prominent but Mrs Marshall and Walter pretended not to notice them.

'Oh! It'll have to be taken away!' said Mrs Marshall, almost yelping the words. She backed away into Gerry and said to Walter, 'I don't know what it is but it's not staying! Take it away, Walter!'

'I'll burn it,' Walter told the widow.

'Take it away to burn it,' Mrs Marshall said sternly, and she grabbed Gerry's upper arm to steady herself, for she felt a weakness in her legs and her knees threatened to buckle beneath her.

'It might be difficult to remove it Mrs M,' said Walter, unwilling to touch the thing in order to uproot it, 'those weeds that it's made out of probably go down six feet or more.'

'It's evil,' said Mrs Marshall, and as she trembled she shook poor Gerry. 'That's why those tendrils were moving; that thing's *alive*.'

Walter looked at Paul and raised his eyebrows (which were joined in the middle), smiled, and whispered to the boy, 'It's not; it's not alive – just looks like a person.'

But Mrs Marshall insisted on the removal of the uncanny figure of intertwined fibres, filaments and caked soil, and Walter tried his utmost to wrench the unearthly form from the excavated hole, and when something snapped in the ground, they all heard what sounded like a faint squeal, and the boys backed away and the widow screamed, and Walter stumbled towards his air pistol, because he thought for a moment that some subterranean creature was about to emerge from the disturbed soil – but nothing showed – only his fear of something in the ground that he could not comprehend. Walter handed the air pistol to Paul and said, 'The safety catch is off; if you see anything moving in that soil, pull that trigger, but mind you don't shoot me, alright? Don't get trigger-happy.'

Paul was overwhelmed with excitement and he needed both hands to hold that heavy black metal gun.

Walter dragged the devil of weeds to the end of the

garden, and dumped it there, and then he went to Paul, took the air pistol from him, and to Mrs Marshall he said, 'I'll go and get some paraffin and burn that thing.'

'No, not here,' said Mrs Marshall, looking at the figure at the end of the garden. It lay there in the shade of a beech tree, its smile clearly visible.

'I can't burn it in our garden, the missus has got asthma Mrs M,' replied Walter, already walking away through the kitchen. He returned with a lime-coloured rectangular can emblazoned with the yellow logo initials of BP, and he unscrewed the cap of the can, and after warning Paul and Gerry to stand back, the unearthed weed man was doused with paraffin and set alight. Mrs Marshall, the two boys, Walter, and the 15-year-old daughter of a neighbour who was watching the strange proceedings over a fence all heard a scream – the distinctive sound a of an agonized shriek – which came from the burning horned facsimile of that body of plant fibre. Walter made the sign of the cross, and walked away. On the following day he inspected the carbonized outline of that nameless thing at the bottom of Mrs Marshall's back garden, then smashed the blade of the spade down on the charred remains until they were powder. He filled in the hole he'd excavated, and Mrs Marshall offered him two pound notes but Walter refused and he kissed the knuckles of the widow's hand and went home. About a week after this, Paul's mother took him aside one day and said, 'Listen you, from now on, you are not to go near that woman Mrs Marshall, have you got that?'

'Why?' Paul asked, immediately thinking of the lucrative jobs he did for the kind old woman.

'She's lost her marbles, that's why,' the lad's mother

told him.

'What does that mean?' said Paul; he'd heard the phrase before about people losing their marbles and had gathered it was something to do with going mad.

'She's seeing ghosts looking through her window at night,' said Paul's mum, 'she's away with the mixer.'

Paul later heard that Mrs Marshall had told her neighbours, her postman, her milkman, and the local priest that a glowing figure with horns had been looking through the kitchen window and had also climbed the drainpipe and looked through her bedroom window. Paul immediately remembered the horned figure sculpted from the musty vegetation. Weeks after this, Mrs Marshall suffered a nervous breakdown and was put in a mental hospital. Rumours circulated about her being attacked by her "imaginary" horned phantom, and no one heard of the old woman again.

In 2017 in the back garden of Gerry's house, Paul saw the goosebumps on his arm as he wound up his terrifying recollection of that inexplicable incident from 1975. To this day, he does not know what that thing from Mrs Marshall's garden was. Paul thinks he may have repressed the incident because he remembered having nightmares about the bizarre assemblage of intertwined tendrils that formed that ghastly image of a horned man. Gerry remembered the incident and he was surprised he had only just recalled the "weed man". The whole episode remains a mystery to this day.

In 1987, a 55-year-old woman named Maureen was sitting on the sofa in her flat on Belvidere Road, relaxing as she watched motes of dust drifting about in the sunlight, when the memory of a very unusual incident suddenly resurfaced in her mind from thirty years before. In June 1957, Maureen had been doing a spot of gardening in the back garden of her home on Townsend Lane in Anfield when her dog Sandy whined and ran into the house. Then Maureen saw a glint of something out the corner of her eye and turned to see what she later described as two spacemen in silver suits and huge helmets in the wild, overgrown garden of a reclusive neighbour. One of the figures was picking purple and yellow flowers while the other entity walked with a strange gait through the knee-high weeds and grass. Maureen ran indoors, shouted to her husband (who was on the toilet) and by the time he came down the "spacemen" had gone. Maureen's husband said she had been seeing things and believe it or not he took her to her doctor, thinking his wife was "going round the bend". The doctor was very open-minded for a 1957 GP; he told Maureen's husband the figures might have been 'men from another planet' collecting botanical samples, and that it was not beyond the bounds of possibility for the visitors to have come off one of the many 'flying saucers' that were being reported across the world. The doctor asked Maureen to describe the silver-suited men in detail, and she did, and she recalled that the visors of the unearthly men had been silvered too, and for that reason she could not see their faces. What the helmeted visitants were remains a mystery; they might have been from one of the many worlds of space, or they might have been from the future; it really is hard to say. Maureen smiled after she recalled the extraordinary memory. She had forgotten all about the spacemen and for some reason they had sprung out of her memory three decades later.

About four months after that strange encounter in the back garden in 1957, the Space Race began in earnest when Russia launched Sputnik I - and literally overnight, travelling into space was no longer seen as a far-fetched science fiction fantasy.

The next case of a recovered memory of something spectacularly strange came about through the sense of smell. The senses of taste and smell can be doors to memories reaching way back into childhood. In the following case, the mere whiff of candy floss evoked an astonishing memory in the mind of a woman named Sandra, and it transpired that the recollection had not been a false one (technically called pseudomnesia), because so many other people recollected the event, and it was left to me to contact all of these people in an effort to piece together an extraordinary event. In 2020, whilst recovering from a bout of Covid, Sandra realised she had regained her sense of smell when she sniffed candy floss she'd bought online. Before this, Sandra had found coffee to taste awful and even the spiciest food tasted drab – a classic symptom of the dreaded Covid virus, with the lack of taste and smell persisting in some people for well over a year. Sandra was relieved to detect the sweet smell of the candy floss, and an unexpected side-effect of the distinctive scent was that it took her back to the mid-1990s. Sandra ate a piece of the pink candy floss, and as it melted on her tongue, she instantly recalled something that had somehow lain forgotten in her memory. Sandra was transported in her mind back to July 1996, to her university days, and she recalled the picnic in a park; it had been Wavertree Playground (also known to the locals as "The Mystery", as the philanthropist who gave the park to the public was a mystery for years). People started to picnic in the park in recent weeks that month in 1996 – picnicking had become a fad for some reason, with some people from the streets close to the park bringing trestle tables to Wavertree Playground, and upon these tables they would throw a tablecloth and put on a spread of white paper plates with sandwiches, blocks of ice cream, cakes and some even brought bottles of wine, so that the picnics were more like alfresco banquets. Sandra sat on the grass that day with her six friends from Uni and she reclined on her elbows, taking sips now and then of Bacardi and Coke as she watched the gormandizers at their tables and some less adventurous picnickers sitting on red and white gingham tablecloths sipping lemonade and eating crisps. The whole optimistic atmosphere of that time in history came flooding back as Sandra almost felt the blistering sun upon that long-vanished scorching blue-sky afternoon, and she even recalled someone's far-off radio emanating the dreamy hypnagogic lapping waves that introduced *Champagne Supernova* by Oasis. Such peace. And then something took place; something so utterly moving, Sandra could not understand how she ever came to forget it.

A girl in her late teens who had been sitting about twenty feet from Sandra with a circle of friends, got to her feet and said, 'What is *that?*' and her friends said, 'What? What are you talking about?' And the girl pointed to a sparkly light in the clear blue sky, somewhere in the direction of Smithdown Road and the bowling greens. Sandra sat up and placed her hand horizontally at her eyebrow to shield her vision from the blinding sun, and she saw something – it looked like a cloud at treetop level to her, but to others in her circle the smudge of mist took on the resemblance of figures of people, and the amorphous object came down onto the grass of the park about 600 yards away, and then, according to everyone else, there were phantoms of people – ethereal figures – strolling north, towards the picnickers – including Sandra. There was a strange, almost hallucinatory aspect to the vision of the advancing crowd; the figures were mostly in white, and it was a radiant white, but whether this was because of the intensity of the sunlight, or whether it was some spiritual radiance is unknown, but as they drew nearer, Sandra could see them as distinct people. The teenaged girl who had first noticed the phantom multitude, cried out, 'It's Pixie!' and ran toward the multitude of phantom-like people. She later explained that Pixie had been a dog she had owned which had passed away three years ago. Sandra saw a little Yorkshire Terrier that ran to the girl, whining, and another person in another picnic group – a student – saw his mother, who had died five years ago, and he said that he went over and spoke to her, and she hugged him and told him that he was seeing part of the "Next World" – and the student was so emotional at the reunion, he started crying and clung on to his mother. He kept saying 'I don't want to wake up,' to which his smiling mum replied, 'You're not asleep, you're awake'.

Other people saw folk they believed to be deceased, but they looked alive and well, and the people in the park mingled with them, and they all later reported some type of emotion I'd describe as a spiritual high. There was no religious talk from the people in white; no mention of any Heaven or any references to resurrections, and this aspect lent a secular aspect to the proceedings. Some said they came away from the experience realising that the dead are just like us, they are alive but in some other place – a true "secret society" I suppose you could call it, where everyone who is born must go to one day. About fifteen minutes after the arrival of the mystical multitude, a hazy mist came over the crowds 'from beyond' and they were gone. Some people continued their picnics but a majority of those who had encountered the otherworldly people left the park in tears because they'd said goodbye to loved ones they had thought they would never see again. Of course, when I interviewed some of the witnesses on air, some callers (not many) phoned in and said it had probably all been the result of someone spiking the picnic food and drink with LSD. Anyone who knows anything about LSD will tell you that it would not produce effects such as those reported then stop dead; the hallucinations would go on for many hours. I can't explain what happened that day, but I have a feeling something allowed this world and the world to come to overlap for a short while, perhaps to bring some comfort to those who had lost someone. The girl who saw her little dog Pixie was in tears for days, so I am certain she experienced *something*, but what, I do not know with any certainty. Through the power of radio (a cliché I know, but true nevertheless) I managed to trace many of the people who said they had been in

273

the park that day, and lots of them talked of a strange change in their consciousness and a feeling of immense optimism which a few likened to arriving at a far-flung holiday destination when you step off the plane. And when the figures all said goodbye, and some of them laughed and waved before vanishing into the mist, a lot of people present felt as if they now knew that death was not the end, and that some great mystery of the ages had been solved at last. It is strange how Sandra came to forget the epic incident of that July day in 1996 – it had been something that, on a personal level, was more awe-inspiring than the Moon Landings. I have a feeling that something – some higher intelligence – censored the full memory of the phenomenal incident from her memory, but for some reason, perhaps because of the trivial recollection of the sweet aroma of candy floss of all things, Sandra was able to retrieve the suppressed memory. The odd thing is that many of the witnesses who heard her account on the radio also started to slowly recall their own experiences – as if some amnesic bloc was being removed which had prevented them from remembering the event. The whole incident is one of the most fascinating ones I have ever looked into.

Remaining on the subject of loved ones who have returned from the mysterious world that seems to exist beyond the grave – and the crematorium furnace – we next come to an incident which might seem minor, compared to the previous story, but it was an incident that provided a Dovecot man named Kevin with a great comfort regarding the painful loss of his much-loved and much-missed father. Kevin had been dozing off in bed one night in 2002 when the memory of a remarkable occurrence suddenly popped into his mind.

In late May 1994, Kevin – then aged 34 - was in the kitchen of his home on Campbell Drive one morning, filling a kettle to make himself a cuppa when he glanced through the window and noticed his father in the back garden - three days after his dad had been buried. Kevin unlocked the kitchen door which gave access to the back garden and went out to talk to the ghost but the apparition had gone. Thinking the ghost had been some form of hallucination brought on by the depression Kevin had been experiencing since the death of his dad, he said nothing to anyone about the ghost, but three days later the same ghost was seen by a neighbour who was looking out of his bedroom window of a morning, just after he'd risen from his bed. The neighbour saw Kevin's father in the garden, inspecting a rose bush. The neighbour rang Kevin, who was still in bed, and told him what he had seen. Kevin rushed to the window of his bedroom and looked out, but the ghost had gone by then. A week after this, two cousins of Kevin were in the kitchen one afternoon when they were both shocked to see their uncle (Kevin's dad) in the greenhouse in the back garden. The two nephews of the deceased man were a bit reluctant to go and investigate but they eventually ventured outside and found the greenhouse locked – and empty. In a broken voice, Kevin told me his father's life had revolved around the garden when he was alive and he had the feeling it was still the case after his death.

And now our final story of a long-buried memory that came to light one day and filled a lady with fascination and wonder. Her name was Gemma, and she was 44 when she accidentally recovered a memory of something very unusual. Gemma had been doing the dishes in the sink in July 2022 when she glanced at the bottle of Fairy washing-up liquid, and seeing the name "fairy", she suddenly recalled a very strange incident from her younger days. The following is what Gemma remembered.

In 1998, Gemma was a 20-year-old living with her parents and two older brothers at her home on Almond's Green, West Derby. One day in the summer of that year, Gemma went shopping in Clayton Square, and she bought Smoke and Mirrors lipstick at Boots, then wandered over to Wax Lyrical, a candle store (and this was in the days before Yankee Candles were popular in this country) and here, Gemma bought a box of long matches and "Fairy Oil" to put in her oil burner in her bedroom. She had a drink at The Swan on Wood Street then got a lift to her home in West Derby from a biker she knew from college. She arrived home just in time for tea. Sitting at the dining table during teatime, Gemma's dad asked her what she had bought in town, and she casually answered, 'Fairy oil,' and her father returned a blank expression. Gemma explained further: 'It's for me oil burner, and it actually smells magical. It gets rid of me stress.'

'You? Stressed?' her dad asked with a look of puzzlement, 'Gemma, you don't *do* anything; ask me and your mam what stress is.'

Gemma ignored him and said to her mother, 'Do you believe in fairies mum? I do; I've always felt connected to them, ever since I was a kid – '

'Gemma, can we drop the subject – just have your

tea, instead of all this table talk,' her mother suddenly said, and seemed a bit 'narky'.

'God, who got out of bed the wrong side today?' Gemma said, thinking her mum was ignorant at the blunt way she had told her in no few words to shut up.

Gemma's mum looked at her husband and said, 'Don't like talking about *them*, it brings something out the woodwork.'

'Oh don't start with your superstitions and all that crap,' he told his wife with a dismissive sneer, then turned to Gemma and said, 'Your mother thinks talking about fairies and spirits conjures them up.'

'What?' Gemma looked dumbfounded at her mum, who was gazing at her husband with gritted teeth.

'Cos she's Irish,' laughed Gemma's dad, and he gazed at the TV, smiling.

'Irish descent,' said Gemma's mum, and she looked over to Gemma and said, 'you've heard of that saying: talk of the Devil and he'll appear – well they're the same.'

'Who is?' Gemma was baffled. Her querying eyes looked at her father, and he never looked at his wife but the words were addressed to her. He said: 'You're the one who's going on about them – shut up then – God, there are saner people walking around in mental hospitals.'

The couple started arguing and Gemma left her tea and went upstairs.

'Gem!' her mum shouted to her back as Gemma reached the top of the stairs, 'Come and finish this tea! You're too thin-skinned! Gemma!'

'Shut up!' Gemma whispered and went into her bedroom and slammed the door shut. She wanted to desperately get her own place. Tonight her parents were arguing, but the night before it was her two older brothers. All Gemma wanted was peace. She poured the fairy oil in the burner, lit the tealight candle, and sat on the mini-sofa in her room. She realised her bedroom was like a miniature living room with a bijou sofa, armchair, portable TV and a mini fridge. She thought of her mum's comments about how talking about fairies supposedly brought them out of the woodwork, and so Gemma looked at the ceiling and with anger in her voice she solemnly said, 'If any fairies are listening, please spirit me off to my own place!'

No sooner had she said this when one half of her room changed before her eyes. The pastel-coloured walls were replaced by what looked like dark brown oak panelled walls, and for a few seconds, Gemma saw a figure of a red-haired woman in a green and gold outfit, and she was kneeling before a small table upon which she was writing something. This woman looked beautiful – more beautiful than anyone Gemma had ever set eyes on, and so, despite being a bit afraid of the apparition, Gemma was also transfixed by her loveliness. She smiled at Gemma, winked, then vanished, and that half of the room where the apparition had appeared reverted back to the pastel-coloured walls. Gemma recalled there had been old-fashioned cabinets behind the strange woman, framed paintings on the wall and a carpet on the floor with an ornate design woven into it. The next thing Gemma knew, she was running down the stairs to tell her mother what she had just witnessed. Gemma's mum was furious at her asking the fairies to spirit her away, and sounding as if she was going to burst into tears, she told her daughter to stop mentioning them and to get rid of the fairy oil. Gemma unquestioningly did this. The woman who Gemma had seen had been no tiny cute Tinker Bell fairy, but a realistic full-sized woman. The Fay – as we call the collective people of the faeries – can range in size from a few inches to a life-size person, and yes, it's true, if you have but a drop of Celtic blood in your veins, merely talking about the Fay can bring them into your life, and they are renowned for mischief-making. People refer to them as the *Good People* to avoid mentioning their name for fear of invoking them. You have been warned.

Gemma told me that she felt as if something had concealed that memory of the 'fairy woman' from her because she had only recalled the astonishing incident in 2022 – twenty four years after it had taken place.

When you get time, sit down and relax, and cast your mind back – let it wander if it must, and you may find that when your mind is able to roam the back roads of your memory, it might just unearth some recollection of something wonderful or mysterious that you'd completely forgotten about.

TWO TALES OF
TWO COINS

As digital payment methods continue to become the norm across the world, it is obvious that in the not-too-distant future, coins and paper money will be phased out. I often wondered, when I was a child, how many people had held the ten-pence piece I was now holding; how many hands had it passed through? And when I was lucky enough to hold a five or ten-pound note, I'd sometimes see numbers written upon it – the total of someone's wages, a phone number, and sometimes the odd name. When I got older, I collected old coins as a hobby, and sometimes wondered if the double florin in my palm could have once been held by Jack the Ripper. Of course, one day, when we are all gone, some future archaeologist may ponder the history of any of today's coins he or she has unearthed; they will wonder what we bought with those one pound and two pound coins. The money stays and we go, and there's an irony in that. Greed has driven people to murder for money, for gold, for diamonds, and the gold rings and jewellery remain in circulation long after we have been buried or cremated, and they continue to draw a new generation of people to kill for their ownership. This chapter concerns two little tales, each about a coin, and its dark history.

I've changed a few names in this first story for legal reasons. It was around 3pm on the Thursday afternoon of 11 March 1971 when a debonair Lancashire gigolo named Howard Beecroft was gliding aimlessly along the B-roads of Worcestershire in a Rolls Royce Silver Shadow he'd conned off a rich but sick old lady in Telford that he'd recently 'dated'. Howard loved these long drives through the country, for they relaxed his mind and induced a very pleasant altered state of consciousness that often gave birth to ideas for new confidence tricks. Here he was cruising in luxury in a Rolls Royce, winding his way through meadows and hop fields, cider apple orchards, accompanied by one of the most beautiful rivers in the land, the sinuous Teme, and Howard was just going to switch on the car radio, which was tuned to BBC Radio 3, when he saw an elderly hitch-hiker come from a secluded footpath, and with a smug grin, Howard observed the old man's beseeching thumb before he pulled over.

'Are you going near Kidderminster?' the old man asked in a Scouse accent, and Howard Beecroft grimaced and said, 'Bit out of my way, actually.'

The man took out an old wallet and emptied a single silver coin onto his palm. 'I'll pay you with this; it's antique, very old.' He said, and he handed it to Howard's leather gloved hand.

'What is that? Look's Roman,' Howard queried, thinning his eyes.

'Real silver it is;' said the old hitcher, 'real silver draws black lines; if you scratch that across a piece of paper it'll score a black mark.'

'Hmm, doesn't look real silver, looks more like tin, and feels as light as tin,' Howard told the man as he lifted his palm up and down as if he was weighing the coin.

'Stop palavering and take me down to Kidderminster, pronto,' said the aged Liverpudlian, reaching for the door handle to the Rolls Royce.

'Your attitude stinks, you old goat,' said Howard – and drove off in almost total silence - with the silver antique coin, and he smiled at the shrinking figure of the Liverpool man in the rear-view mirror.

Days after this, Howard's mature fiancée passed away and so he made himself scarce before her family found out about the Rolls Royce she'd bought him, and he hid in London. He visited the much respected Pavilion Jewellers in Piccadilly to have that Scouser's so-called silver antique coin valued, thinking it was probably just silver-plated, but the jeweller recoiled in horror and dropped his loupe when he examined the coin.

'One of the Blessed Coins – although that's a bit of a misnomer;' he gasped, and quickly placed it back in Howard's palm, and then the appraiser continued his explanation, 'a Tyrian Shekel, over two thousand years old, but like the other twenty-nine specimens it belongs to, you'll get no takers.'

'What on earth are you babbling about, man?' asked Howard, and the valuer stammered: 'They all have a certain mark on them; that coin is one of the thirty pieces of silver that Judas Iscariot received. They're cursed coins, and once you receive one of them you can't give it away; they have to be stolen from you.'

'I've never heard anything as ridiculous as this in all of my life!' Howard told the jeweller, and then he gave an uneasy smile and said, 'This is 1971, not 1571 – superstitious mumbo jumbo! I demand to see your senior!'

'Very well, sir,' said the jeweller, and he walked away into a back room, and Howard could hear the superstitious valuer talking excitedly to someone. A corpulent urbane gentleman dressed in a pin striped suit came out of the back room fidgeting with his bowtie. The second man smiled, but he told the same story as the other man, almost word for word.

'I shall write to *The Times* about this nonsense,' Howard promised, and he left the jewellers in a right state. It was the same result at every jewellers – they would recoil upon seeing the little silver coin and quickly hand it back to Howard. Howard even tried a pawnshop in the East End of London, and the gentleman who looked at the coin made the sign of the cross and asked Howard, 'Do you *know* what you've got there?'

Howard snatched the coin back and said, 'Yes! One of the bloody Blessed Coins! I've heard it all before – it belonged to Judas and all that claptrap; I might just melt it down!'

Howard had solid bad luck for seven years, and ended up penniless, and he slowly came to accept that the Judas coin was responsible for his descent into poverty, and he just wanted to throw it away, but he had been told over and over that giving the coin away or throwing it away could lead to even worse bad luck or even death. Then one day, as Howard sat in a park swigging a cheap bottle of wine, he was mugged, and that accursed coin was taken along with his wallet. The police found him on the floor, bruised and cut – and laughing hysterically. His luck then started to steadily improve.

And now we move back in time to the Swinging Sixties for our next tale of a haunted coin. In 1964, a 22-year-old West Derby man Jason P Moon was left £50 in the will of his grandmother, along with four very old coins from the 18th century as well as a fifth one of an unknown denomination, and they all had holes in them, as if to be worn on a chain as good luck charms perhaps. Those holes in the coins rendered them practically worthless. Jason wore one of the lucky coins on a gold chain around his neck; it was the one with no date on, just the face of some un-Royal-looking lady. In June 1964, after going to the Cavern Club to see The Yardbirds, Freddie Starr and the Flamingos and the Five Dimensions, Jason came out of the venue with a little red-haired Lulu lookalike named Patsy and asked her if she wanted to go to a coffee bar. She screamed at something behind Jason, and he turned to see a lad of about his age charging at him with a butcher's meat cleaver that was about 12 inches long and 4 inches wide. Jason froze, his bulging eyes fixed in terror at the glinting cleaver blade, and just when it looked as if the cleaver would end up embedded in Jason's head, a stunningly beautiful blonde woman came out of nowhere and gripped the assailant's wrist and shook the meat cleaver from his hand. A crowd gathered and watched the woman punch the would-be attacker, knocking him clean out.

The blonde then vanished into the night as the crowd enclosed the KO'd cleaver man lying prostrate on the floor; he was Patsy's ex boyfriend by the way.

Jason wondered who the blonde saviour was who had saved his life, and he was to meet her, and a beautiful statuesque brunette, on a few more occasions that year, always when his life was in danger. In July, Jason was swimming at Crosby beach when the tide came in with unusual ferocity and he was slammed by a pummelling wave into a rock which stunned him and left him with a bleeding nose. He recalled an athletic brunette woman who came from behind him in the raging sea and put her arms under his armpits before calming him down by kissing his face. She told him to kick his legs and within a few minutes he was lying on his back on the shore, and the dark-haired lady who had saved his life was nowhere to be seen. Three weeks after this, Jason lost control of an old banger of a car he had bought for £25, and the brakes failed on a steep road in Everton. People dived out of the way as the car hurtled down the slope, heading for a sandstone wall. The blonde woman who had prevented the cleaver attack was suddenly in the front passenger seat; she had literally appeared out of nowhere like a ghost. She shoved Jason aside, gripped the steering wheel and changed the gears to slow the car, finally making an emergency stop which almost resulted in the car tipping over – and then she was gone. Jason sat there in shock, realising that the blonde woman had once again save him from what would have been a fatal crash into a sandstone wall. The ghostly women appeared on the scene on a few more occasions when Jason's life was in danger, and he realised who these women were: the faces of his saviours were on each side of the 'lucky coin' he had been wearing. Jason was determined to find out who these women were on the coin, and he showed it to his cousin Clement, an amateur numismatist who said there were worn letters and symbols around the edges of the coin on both sides that seemed to resemble Runes, but he could not decipher them. Alas, Jason had the mysterious coin stolen when his wallet and satchel were taken by an opportunistic thief as he swam in Woolton Baths one day in 1967. Just who those saviours of the coin were will probably never be known.

THE HIGHWAYMAN

On the morning of Monday 20 June 2016 at around 2:15am, a 22-year-old girl named Abi, who lived on Penny Lane, was making tracks home from the city centre, where she had just experienced one of the worst nights out in living memory. The night had been a total disaster because her best friend had an allergic reaction to shellfish food in a chippie and ended up going home after being monitored in an ambulance for ages. Abi's two friends took the girl home to Formby and Abi, living in the opposite direction, made her own way home, and was currently trying her utmost to find a hackney cab. She had tried the private cabs firms and they were all unusually busy. On Slater Street, Abi thought she was seeing things - there was a man all dressed in black with a three-pointed tricorn hat, of the type we associate with the highwaymen of old, and he was on a horse, and he and the horse were peeping out of an alleyway in the street, and while some clubbers thought the man was either an eccentric or even part of some ghost tour, Abi just had the weird feeling the horseman was looking at her; she could barely see his shadowed face under that three-pointed hat, but he seemed to be looking at her.

The girl hurried to Bold Street, and as Abi looked stunning on this morning, she got quite a few wolf whistles, and yet she was glad of the company, even of the lecherous drunks, because she noticed that the "highwayman" was following her on his horse. She got to the top of Bold Street and here, Abi could not believe her luck – a hackney cruised past and she waved frantically to the cabby. The hackney swung 180 degrees and came to a perfect halt at the kerb. 'Where to love?' said the cabby, and then he added: 'And I must say you look like a Hollywood star – you look a million dollars babe, but no fellah with you eh? How come?'

Abi ignored the question and breathlessly told him: 'Penny Lane, please!' and she lunged into the back of the taxi and looked back as she slammed the door. She couldn't see the highwayman and his steed. But as the taxi was travelling along Upper Duke Street minutes later, the cabby said, 'I don't believe it! There's a fellah galloping behind us and he looks like Ned Turpin [meaning *Dick* Turpin] – what friggin' planet do these people come from?'

Abi went cold when she heard the cabby's words, and she slowly turned and saw he was right – the highwayman was closing in, and she could see sparks flying off the shoes of his horse. Could it just be all coincidence though? Abi hoped it could, but she knew somehow that the man on that horse *was* following her.

The taxi just made the lights – but the strangely-attired horseman raced through a red light and just missed a BMW - and its furious driver beeped the vehicle's horn in anger at the horseman three times.

'That plantpot shouldn't have beeped his horn,' said the cabby, 'could have scared the horse.' The taxi driver then swore under his breath as he eyed the oddball on horseback in the rear view mirror, and he turned the hackney right, from Canning Street onto Catharine Street. The horseman accelerated after the cab, getting too near for the driver's liking. 'He's got to be on drugs, this fellah,' said the taxi driver, 'if I had to stop now he'd ride into the back of us! And I bet that dickhead's not insured either.'

'Be careful then,' said Abi, her huge eyes full of anxiety – and she put on her seatbelt.

'Thingio used to play him, didn't he?' the driver asked Abi, 'Oh, what's his name now? Richard O'Sullivan – you won't know him, you're too young. Yeah, he used to play Turpin. It was a cracker series.'

'Is he still following us?' Abi asked, a tremor in her voice. What a dreadful night out this had been.

'Yeah,' said the cabby, and he grinned and chuckled, 'I just hope he doesn't hold us up – stand and deliver. That was a song years ago.' The driver's face became serious. 'Bleedin' hell he's coming alongside us! What's he playing at?'

Abi froze in terror as the outdated horseman rode parallel to the hackney carriage. She could see his pallid face looking down at her, and he was bent forward in the saddle as if he was trying to see Abi. The cabby wound down the side window and yelled, 'Hey bollocks! This isn't the Grand National! Get off the road or I'll report you! Dickhead!'

'The lights!' Abi cried, and the taxi driver saw they had changed to red, but he was going too fast and had no alternative but to continue and jump them onto Princes Road, and he turned the air blue, blaming the nut on horseback, but that rider did not even react, he just kept looking at the female passenger of the taxi with an expression of fascination. As the cab swerved left onto Princes Avenue the horseman vanished down Selborne Street, and the cabby gave him the two fingered salute. 'This city is getting worse; you alright girl?' he asked his fare.

Abi was shaking and she kept looking out the window, expecting the weird rider to return. She wanted to call her father but knew he'd be fast asleep in bed by now and she didn't want to wake him up.

'I think I might start giving the nights a miss from now on,' said the taxi driver, talking to Abi via his rear view mirror. On Croxteth Road the driver swore and said, 'What the f - he's back again. I'll have to tell the bizzies if he starts tailgating us again. I never grass anyone up me but I'll have to get him arrested! He's gonna cause a fatal accident!'

Abi turned with great difficulty because of the way the seatbelt was restraining her, and she saw the horse and its rider as silhouettes, about a hundred yards away.

'Maybe I should pull over and have a word with him...' muttered the cabby and Abi cried, 'No! Just get me home please!'

'If I lose me rag with him there'll be nothing down for him!' growled the driver.

'Just calm down please, I'm scared!' said Abi, sounding as if she was going to cry, 'I have anxiety problems.'

'Sorry girl,' apologised the cabby, 'just makes me so mad when you get divvies like him on the road.'

The menacing horseman followed the cab down Ullet Road and Smithdown Road but then it sped up at one point and disappeared onto a poorly lit Grant Avenue near Wavertree Playground. Abi was glad to reach her home, and she went upstairs and was so on edge she just had to wake her father to tell him about the highwayman and he said it had probably just been someone in fancy dress playing a practical joke. Seeing how scared his beloved daughter looked, he came downstairs with her to make her a strong coffee. 'It's been a stupid student dressed up as Dick Turpin,' said the girl's dad, 'didn't you say there was a fellah who went to college with you who was into that dressing up thing? That Stuart fellah?'

'Stuart was into cosplay, but he's younger than me;' said Abi, 'that fellah on the horse looked as if he was about thirty-odd. It wasn't Stuart.'

'It wasn't a ghost, Abi – ghosts don't exist,' her father stated all matter-of-fact.

'I don't know dad,' said Abi, standing in the kitchen, gazing out the window at the full moon, 'I think it really was a highwayman – ' and she couldn't finish the sentence. Now she was unsure of just what that stalker had been; a living flesh and blood weirdo or a ghost.

Her dad smirked as he poured water into the coffee maker, 'Abi, there are no highwaymen around now, believe me, they all died out in the eighteen-hundreds.'

On the following evening at 10pm, Abi was on Allerton Road, going to get a pizza before calling at her boyfriend's place – when she saw the horseman again. It was like a repeat of the first time when she had seen him in the alleyway on Slater Street. He was on the horse and he was peeping out from Plattsville Road. Abi was in two minds as to whether she should turn around and hurry home or go to the pizza parlour, but before she could make up her mind, she heard the clatter of iron-shod hooves and the horse came galloping towards Abi. She screamed and ran into a pizza parlour, and the owner of the pizza joint, a man named Jon, saw the highwayman outside on horseback, gazing through the plate-glass window at the frightened girl – and he bravely went outside and asked, 'What are you playing at?'

The horseman took no notice of Jon and he continued to look through the window at Abi before he pulled at the reigns of the huge horse and rode off, and the pizza parlour owner came back into his premises and looked shocked. He said the man and his horse had seemed to melt away into the night as it travelled down Allerton Road. Abi returned home in a dreadful state, accompanied by the pizza parlour owner Jon, who told the girl's father what had happened. Jon urged Abi to report the matter to the police, but she thought no one would believe her account, and so she simply stayed in for over a week, afraid to venture outside. A few nights after this, Abi and her father heard the clip clop of horse's hooves passing the house – and then that was it; the highwayman made no further appearances. Abi has not seen that stalker on horseback since that night on Allerton Road and she hopes she'll never set eyes on him again. Who he is remains a mystery. I have heard of a similar ghostly Highwayman who roams parts of Huyton and Roby, but whether that ghost is the one who was fixated on Abi is unknown.

TRULY PECULIAR

A majority of the stories in my books and newspaper columns are unusual, sometimes scary, and often inexplicable. This chapter is about a handful of stories that are, in my opinion, *truly peculiar* - downright odd. Most of the accounts are hard to explain and some defy any serious attempts to expound upon them with a plausible theory. To give you an idea of the type of peculiarity I am talking about, here's the first story of this kind.

One furnace of a June afternoon in the legendary droughty summer of 1976, a 33-year-old lady named Jasmine returned from the wedding reception of a neighbour with her friend Iris. They went to Jasmine's home in Fulwood Park, Aigburth, kicked off their high-heeled platforms and intended to have a quick drink in the back garden before changing out of their outfits into something more light and comfy. The two friends talked of the wedding of Jasmine's neighbour, and Iris said the wedding dress had looked too tight and they both giggled as they recalled the way the bridegroom had started crying during the service; Jasmine and Iris – and the rest of the wedding guests – had not been able to work out who or what the bridegroom's tears had been shed for; the end of his bachelor days or had they been tears of joy at becoming a husband?

Jasmine grabbed a bottle of 'proper wine' (as opposed to the cheap supermarket wine of the wedding reception) from the kitchen, and she found the corkscrew in the cutlery drawer. Iris collected two glasses from a cupboard. Out of the kitchen they did go, with Iris impersonating the bridegroom saying, 'I do' as he sobbed.

Entering the large back garden, Jasmine noticed something which gave her a start; there, next to the greenhouse, among the palms and some potted flowery plants, was a full size white marble statue of a woman in a type of toga. Jasmine pointed it out to Iris, who said it looked 'a bit ostentatious for a garden in Fulwood Park.' Jasmine recalled her boyfriend Adam - currently still at the wedding reception - saying he had a surprise for her, and she shook her head and said, 'What on earth possessed him to buy this for me?' to which Iris quipped, 'Maybe he sees you as the Greek Goddess type – statuesque and unattainable.'

The two ladies went to look at the statue, and Jasmine remarked on its smile, which she found unsettling.

The bottle of wine was uncorked and the two good friends enjoyed a few glasses, and the sun was shining fiercely in the clear ice-blue sky, and it should have been a great afternoon, but for Jasmine, that statue was casting a shadow over the tropical afternoon, and she didn't know why; she couldn't put it into words – she just felt the sculpture had a dark aura of misfortune around it. Jasmine was not at all superstitious and in the past she had laughed when she had accidentally broken mirrors and been told of the seven year curse a shattered looking glass was supposed to bring, and she never shied away from walking under the ladders of window cleaners and workmen when she was in town – but this was different; this statue seemed to be radiating something malevolent.

When Jasmine's boyfriend Adam came home about an hour later, Iris had gone and Jasmine caught up with him in the living room, sitting with the curtains closed. Adam said he felt a migraine coming on.

'The statue looks daft – it's got to go,' Jasmine informed him.

'What statue? What are you talking about?' Adam asked, and Jasmine led him outside - the statue of the woman was nowhere to be seen.

'It was here;' Jasmine nodded to the space next to the greenhouse, 'someone must have taken it. I hope to God someone *has* stolen it; it looked ridiculous.'

Adam said he had not bought any statue for her, and she said, 'The surprise you mentioned.' Adam said he'd bought her a Bang & Olufsen record player. That night, Jasmine's favourite uncle dropped dead of a heart attack. She saw the grinning statue of the woman on three further occasions in the back garden, and each time, a relative died within 24 hours. Jasmine was so convinced the white marble figure was some harbinger of doom, she eventually talked Adam out of moving from the Fulwood Park house, and she never saw that creepy statue again.

The following peculiar tale could probably have been included in an earlier chapter in this book entitled, *Rhea and Her Sisters*, as it seems to hint at witchcraft, but the trouble is that this is an assumption on my behalf. The story came my way many years ago from several people who lived in the Everton district of the city during the infamous City Council slum clearances of the 1960s when entire communities were forcibly broken up by the municipal authorities and scattered everywhere. Hi-rise blocks were built on the sites of the swept-away streets, and these tower blocks became dystopian disasters. One sunny Sunday afternoon, a group of children were playing in the half-demolished ruins of a row of streets up in Everton when one young lad named Alan, who was playing hide and seek, went into the shell of a house (known in those days as a "bombdy"), looking for his hidden friends, when he saw a hole in the corner of what had once been someone's living room, and from this hole, emerged a single file of six women, most of them all dressed in black, and some of them were wearing the pointed archetypal "witch hats" (as Alan described them). Most of the women were about fifty-something, Alan recalled, and they chased the boy out into the daylight and then they all started letting out the most disturbing cacophony of disharmonious screams - and Alan saw what looked like a Roman Catholic Monsignor with a cross and a book, standing on a mound of rubble, and he was spouting Latin and holding a crucifix out at the women, and then, from another direction came a long-haired man with a thin beard and slight moustache who looked like the orthodox stereotypical image of Jesus, and he was reciting some prayer (not in Latin) in a scouse accent. The boy burst into tears when he saw the women screaming in fear. The lad said the face of one woman seemed to shrivel up. Alan turned and ran home. His mother heard her son's strange story and casually told him with a dismissive smile that the "fellah who looked like Our Lord is one of those hippies" – so she must have seen him before in the area somewhere. A few of Alan's friends had also witnessed the screaming 'witches' incident that day from the places where they had secreted themselves during the game of hide and seek. Alan felt he had witnessed some witch culling rite and had nightmares about the events of that Sunday for years. I've since found out an awful lot more about the two "witchfinders" and they seem to have been extremists to put it mildly. The one who looked like a modern-day Jesus was a man from Kirkdale with religious mania, and the man in the robes who Alan compared to a Roman Catholic Monsignor was a self-appointed "Bishop" who waged a war against demons, witches, vampires and ghosts, often accusing ladies who were looked upon as 'loose' as possessed nymphomaniacs. What became of the self-ordained exorcists and witchfinders is unknown.

Remaining on a religious theme, we next come to a very peculiar personage – a nun who appears to know people's darkest secrets. She seems to have started doing her rounds in June 1996; that month, she called at many houses which, when joined up on a map, seemed to form an almost perfect equilateral triangle. The first call at a house on West Derby's Storrington Avenue at 9pm involved the nun telling the young lady who answered the door that she had been "forgiven" for having an abortion after 'falling pregnant' to a man she was seeing while her husband was in prison – and, well the husband didn't know about this but he overheard the nun at the front door. The nun handed the angered husband a small violet tea-light-sized candle and told him to light it at 10pm and leave it burning "to cleanse the house of sins". There was later a huge argument between the couple at the house that night which required police attendance. The nun in the know then cold-called at Whitefield Drive, Kirkby later that same night and gave a small scented cerise candle to the woman who answered the door, telling her to light it and that she would be forgiven of 'the act of adultery' she had carried out in the 1980s. The woman said she would report the nun to the church but her husband came to the door and asked the visiting holy woman for details of the so-called infidelity his wife was alleged to have carried out and the nun casually provided him with names and dates, then made the sign of the cross and told the couple to be at peace and to forgive. Over the next few days the nun called at addresses in Aintree, Bootle, and Tuebrook, and during one after-dark visit, a priest just so happened to be at the house where the nun turned up to address the sins of the householders. The priest had been discussing funeral arrangements with the family regarding their grandfather and he confidently confronted the nun and asked her what convent she belonged to and she said, "Conchobair Convent, Green Lane" and spelled out the name of the convent to the suspicious priest. 'Which Green Lane? There're Green Lanes all over this city!'

The nun gazed into the eyes of the priest and said, 'The Green Lane where you nearly got into serious trouble that time – with those young lads in the Boy Scouts.' And as she said this, the nun gave a knowing smile, and the priest seemed to abreact with a look of horror and stammered, 'Well, Sister, maybe you shouldn't be paying visits to people's houses unannounced at such a late hour; you could be mugged – or worse.'

And then the priest made an excuse to leave and almost ran out of the house. I talked to many people

298

over the years who said they answered the door to the strange nun with her "candles of atonement" as she called them, and I also interviewed people who had heard stories about her from witnesses, and some of the accounts are quite eerie, like the time the nun visited a family at a house in Old Swan one night, blessed them, gave them a little blue candle, and as she was leaving, the youngest member of the family, a 7-year-old girl, pointed out what looked like a *tail* of some sort protruding from under the nun's pleated habit. This tail curled and slowly withdrew under the habit. And what of the "Conchobair Convent, Green Lane" which the unknown nun mentioned to the shamefaced priest? It has yet to be found. One man told me how he followed the nun after she had called at his home on Carr Lane East, near the Church of the Good Shepherd, West Derby. He tailed the nun to the corner which leads onto Dwerryhouse Lane, and he saw her actually turn into an eerie shadowy shape which then faded away. Except for this latter report of the nun, she was not regarded as a ghost and those I spoke to who talked to her told me she looked solid enough, although she seemed to make herself scarce soon after leaving a house. Her true nature may never be known, unless someone can confront her if she starts paying house visits again on her mission to save sinners. The nun reminds me of another strange cold caller - a lady who made headlines in May 2017. This was a blonde woman who was heard to sob and ask for help through letterboxes at Liverpool and Knowsley houses in the wee small hours. In late May of that year, a lady named Pat on Bentham Drive, Childwall heard a woman crying "I have nowhere to go! Help me!" at 3:20am and when she looked out her window she saw a blonde woman, in her twenties or possibly early thirties standing outside the house. The woman walked off and seemed to vanish. There were more cases in that area of Childwall, and then the mysterious caller moved to Knotty Ash, where she woke up a family at a house on Thingwall Lane at 3am. No one opened the door to the sobbing girl because they suspected she had accomplices hiding, and that the whole thing was a ploy to get into the house to perpetrate a robbery – or even a sexual assault. Again a blonde woman was seen but went to ground exceedingly fast when the police arrived. What seems to have been the same blonde was then heard crying through the letterboxes of houses in West Derby, Huyton, Kirkby and parts of North Liverpool, where one woman found her back garden gate wide open. The theory was that the woman was working with several men who were ready to waylay any Good Samaritan answering the door in the dead of night. This was probably the case, but many said the woman's cries were very creepy.

Another creepy entity features in our next tale of the truly peculiar, and it's been difficult for me to get to the bottom of this one. One fine July afternoon in 1997, two sisters, Hilary, aged 19, and Kate aged 21, decided to clean their palatial home on Ullet Road near Sefton Park, as their father Nigel – a bank manager - would be home in less than an hour and the girls wanted to borrow money from him so they could go out later in the evening. Their father loved having a clean house with everything spick and span and so the girls set about tidying the place up. Hilary started by picking up her young brother's toys which were scattered around the living room, while Kate made a half-hearted attempt to polish the floor in the hallway, but their work was interrupted by the sounds of someone coming into the house via the front door, and the girls assumed it was their dad arriving home early for some reason - but instead of their father entering the hallway, the sisters were startled to see a towering stranger all in black - a giant of a man who must been about seven feet or more in height. He was smartly dressed in a dark blue blazer and mustard-coloured polo-neck sweater but his attire seemed a bit dated, as he had on a pair of flared trousers and two-tone men's platforms (which were all the rage back in the 1970s). He had sandy-blondish hair combed over his head and a pair of hooded emotionless pale blue eyes. The lanky stranger called the girls names I couldn't possibly print here without contravening the Obscene Publications Act; they really were disgustingly offensive names, and he grabbed Hilary and Kate by their long hair and dragged them as they screamed into their father's bedroom. The girls were thrown onto the bed and the giant of a man told them - in a very well spoken voice (a way of speaking that is known as Received Pronunciation) what he was going to do to them and how, after he had been satisfied, he'd break their necks. 'Remove all of your clothes! Come on!' he roared at the girls, and he undid his belt and walked around the bed and warned the girls if they tried to escape he'd kill them without compunction, adding, 'I've topped quite a few women before – it's just like wringing the neck of a chicken to me.' He pulled down his trouser zipper and said, 'I'm big all over,' and the way he delivered this distasteful innuendo, with a leering smirk, scared Hilary and she ran screaming to the bedroom door, opened it, and urged Kate to follow her – which she did, but she seemed unsteady on her feet, perhaps feeling weak in her legs with fear. The huge man laughed deeply as Hilary and Kate fled from the room, down the hallway, and out of the house. The neighbours saw the girls in tears, and went to their aid, listened to their shocking story and went to confront the would-be rapist and murderer - but they found the house empty. Hilary and Kate went back into the house, going from room to room with the neighbours, and when they all reached the hall, the girls screamed as the front door opened; but it was their father Nigel and their younger brother Tim who had been picked up from his grandmother's house by his dad.

'What on earth is going on?' Nigel asked, looking at his hysterical daughters and the neighbours in the hallway.

'Oh Daddy something terrible happened!' cried Hilary and ran into his arms, and she tried to tell him what had happened, but was mindful of the fact that Tim, who was 13, would hear some things that were only suitable for adult ears, so his father persuaded the boy to go into the kitchen and have some sweets and cola.

The place had no history of hauntings, and the girls could not make up their minds as to whether the giant assailant was a ghost or simply someone who had let himself in with a key or perhaps a skeleton key. Hilary said the man's hands had been very pale and ice cold. At the time of the shocking incident, a group of workmen were renovating a dwelling opposite the house on Ullet Road, and the father of the girls went to see if any of the men had witnessed a man of very tall stature coming into the house that afternoon; the workmen said they had seen no such person at that time, and funnily enough, the road had been unusually quiet that afternoon. Two of the workmen had seen Hilary and Kate run out of the house, but had not seen anyone else near the house before or after that point in time. The father of the girls said he had heard the heavy footsteps of someone coming into the house a few evenings before the attack, but had seen no one in the hallway when he heard the unexplained sounds. A New Age relative of the family visited and said she sensed something very unsavoury at the house and she left a large white candle in the hallway on the parcel shelf, supposedly to ward off evil spirits, and said it must not be moved until the candle wick had burnt itself out. The attacker was thankfully never seen or heard from again. Just who the lascivious goliath was remains a mystery to this day.

Compared to the last story, the following little tale is but a minor paranormal peculiarity, but nevertheless one aspect of the account is an oddity. Here's what I could glean from the main witness to this incident.

One night in November 1988 at Dillons bookshop which was then at 52 Bold Street, a security guard investigating a troublesome alarm that had been going off all night saw a woman sitting at a desk at the back of the bookstore. She was pretty, aged about 25 perhaps, with long curly platinum blonde hair (which had some type of tiara in it), and she was dressed in old fashioned - possibly Victorian - clothes. She had a brass lamp of some sort to her right and a candle in front of her and by these light sources she was writing in a book. The guard did not think she was a ghost as she was using a modern green plastic pen, and he asked her how she had got into the bookshop.

No answer came. She did not even look at him to acknowledge that he was there.

'Who *are* you love?' the guard asked, and glanced about, thinking she might have accomplices with her and could be serving to distract him from them. Then, in an instant that woman was gone, along with the book she had been writing in, and the lamp and candle, but the modern Ball Pentel pen she had used fell to the desk. The guard remembered the month and year because footballer Emlyn Hughes had done a book-signing at the store around that time; he had written a book called *My Great Britons* in which Hughes interviewed sixteen sporting champions. The guard checked the place, top to bottom, and told no one for many years about the ghost, then one day he was having a drink in The Newsham Park pub on West Derby Road, when he met a friend named Terry who had until recently been a security guard himself. Terry was reminiscing about the places he had worked when he said that when he was a security guard in the early 1980s, he was once called to investigate an alarm that went off in the Comet store – at 52 Bold Street; this was later the premises of Dillons, the book store where the Terry's friend saw the woman sitting at the back of the shop, writing at a desk. Terry remarked how he had gone into Comet to see what had tripped the alarm, only to encounter the solid-looking ghost of a blonde woman in Victorian clothes with a glittering tiara on her head, and she was standing there at the back of the shop, wringing her hands as she belted out some song in a powerful operatic voice. When Terry shone his torch at the woman she vanished, and only then did he realise she was a ghost. Her identity remains unknown. That building on Bold Street where Dillons had its book business and Comet had earlier sold its hardware and white goods had been a music hall in the Victorian and Edwardian eras, and it has since been the Reflex – a 1980s bar, as well as the Coyote Ugly saloon. I personally know that the building on Bold Street has quite a few ghosts besides that unknown lady. I am still curious to know what that female ghost was writing about at that desk with a modern pen that night in 1988.

We remain on Bold Street, the scene of the last peculiarity, and travel back two decades to the Saturday morning of 6 May 1967. Upon that morning around 11am, a pretty but immature 16-year-old Wavertree girl named Alice appeared on the Bold Street thoroughfare after she'd had a row with her parents because they had stopped her from seeing Tony, a lad who they deemed to be a juvenile delinquent. As a result of her parent's "restraining order" (as Alice saw it), the teenager, without much aforethought, had decided to leave home. She got on the first bus to town and visited Bold Street, intending to go and have a coffee at the trendy El Cabala café, when she noticed a tall debonair man in the reflection of the window, and he was taking a photograph of Alice. Alice later described this man as being the double of the actor Francis Matthews, famous for playing TV detective Paul Temple and voicing Captain

Scarlet, the Gerry and Sylvia Anderson puppet creation. Alice turned to look at the handsome man taking snaps of her and he said, 'Perfect – just hold that pose – you're a natural.'

Alice was impressionable and the man, who said his name was James, soft-soaped her into letting him get her a coffee in the El Cabala. James asked the girl where she was from and she told him she had run away because her parents were squares who wouldn't let her go with a Mod named Tony, and James said, 'Tell you what, Alice, you can stay at my pad if you like; you'll have your own room of course, and, let's see – it's Saturday now, isn't it? Yeah, there's a party on Sunday night at my place.'

'Don't you be going to his parties love, they end up as orgies,' said a man on the next table in the café, and James countered the claim, saying, 'Alright, they're not vicarage tea parties but they're not bloody orgies!' and Alice smiled. James took Alice round the shops, bought her a necklace, an orange mini dress, and said he'd introduce her to "Charlie Boyd" – a very hip young man who was rich and owned a recording studio. James had persuaded Alice to sing when she'd had a drink in the pub, and had assured her she was destined for pop stardom. He took Alice to his flat on Wood Street at 10pm, and said he'd introduce her to Charlie Boyd – but left her locked in a second floor room which was illuminated by a solitary low-wattage bulb. Alice didn't know the door was locked at first, but when James hadn't returned to the room after a quarter of an hour, the girl decided to leave – and found that the handle of the door wouldn't even turn. She slammed her hand on the door and cried, 'Help!

Let me out!'

Alice then heard a hissing sound behind her, and she slowly turned and from a dark corner of the dimly-lit room she saw something roughly cylindrical; it resembled the trunk of a tree minus any branches with a flat top, and was about six feet in height and 3 feet in width. Set into the top of this bizarre and unfamiliar-looking entity was a single cyclopean eye ringed with something blood red, and veins ran from this scarlet ring to the grey iris of the eyeball. A huge mouth, about two feet below the single ghastly eye opened, showing a top and bottom row of discoloured sharp teeth, and Alice screamed and was so scared she wet herself. She distinctly heard the creature say, 'I am Charlie Boyd.'

Alice picked up an old ladderback chair, and although it was heavy, the adrenalin being pumped into the terrified girl's bloodstream enabled her to swing the chair at the entity, and she saw one of the legs of the chair strike its top row of teeth, but the leg of the chair splintered. Upon being struck, the thing made a buzzing and humming sound like that of some giant wasp, and it lunged at Alice and snapped its teeth at her then moved backwards, and the girl screamed as the weird being kept going to and fro. Alice somehow ran around the alien-looking creature, grabbed the old-fashioned monkey-tail handles of a window and turned both of them and to the girl's surprise, and then relief, the two windows swung open – but there was a drop of about 20 feet to the pavement below. Fear drove Alice onto the window ledge, where she screamed for help. Three young men in the street gazed up at the screaming girl and one of them asked what was wrong.

'Something's trying to kill me!' Alice yelled, and she saw the tubular form of the freakish entity shuffling towards her, making a hissing sound again, and the girl thought she felt some liquid being sprayed onto her legs.

'Jump! We'll catch you!' shouted one of the young men in the street, and he took off his coat and his two friends held different sides of the coat the way firemen hold a life net to catch jumpers from burning buildings. Alice screamed, and seemed to fall backwards, and by sheer luck, she was caught by the three lads in the street and never suffered a scratch. When Alice told the men what had been attacking her, they thought she was either lying or on drugs, but one of the young men walked to the other side of Wood Street and gazed into the room – and he thought he saw the scary single eye of the creature Alice had described. That eye was rolling about, and then the dim light in the room went out. The lad saw that the thing was still there in the darkness, watching him. His friends said he – and Alice – had been seeing things. The police visited the Wood Street flat after Alice reported the attempted abduction and found it empty, and James – and that weird creature – "Charlie Boyd" was never heard from again. Just what that thing was, and who its procurer James was for that matter, are mysteries that will probably never be solved.

A very peculiar incident was reported to me at Radio Merseyside in 2002, and the subject of the report puts this story squarely in this chapter, as I cannot explain it; it really does defy any rational explanation. Two 22-year-old students, Cheryl and Debi, were walking from their friend's flat on North Sudley Road in the district of Mossley Hill and decided to cut through Sefton Park at around 10pm to get to their flat on Ullet Road. People were walking dogs about in the park at this hour so the girls felt relatively safe, and as they strolled along, Cheryl saw what looked like a green luminous man in the distance, and she pointed it out to Debi, who laughed and said it was the Green Man sign on the pelican crossing, but Cheryl said, 'You need your eyes testing, Debi, that thing is *not* the Green Man,' and Debi insisted, 'It's the pelican crossing man over by Aigburth Drive,' and she marched in the direction of the green light to prove her point – but when the girls got nearer to the light, they saw it really was a green glowing figure floating about 3 feet off the ground, and the two women turned and ran. They heard a very deep bass echoing voice shout after them, 'Don't be afraid, ladies!'

Debi swore at the figure without turning around which shocked Cheryl because she had never once heard her well-to-do friend use a four-letter word.

The thing floated after the women for about twenty seconds (but it seemed much longer to Cheryl and Debi) and as Debi stopped a man walking his dog and pointed the figure out, it vanished like a light being switched off. The man with the dog said, 'What on earth was that?' He had seen that the green light was shaped like a figure. Cheryl and Debi never took a short cut through that part of Sefton Park again, even during the daytime. If the Green Man incident had been an isolated one, I'd be able to explain the episode away as an overactive imagination and the possible misidentification of the Green Man on the Pelican Crossing in the area – but weeks before Cheryl and

Debi reported the incident to me, a young couple in their late teens were in Sefton Park one moonlit evening, and they got a bit romantic as they embraced near to the so-called Fairy Glen, an enchanting spot that in times past was a meeting place for courting couples. As the teens kissed and perhaps whispered sweet nothings in one another's ears, they heard a faint noise which sounded like someone giggling. The girl then screamed upon seeing the green luminous Mephistophelian face of a 7ft-tall figure watching her from behind a nearby tree. Her boyfriend turned and he saw it too, and the couple instantly put all thoughts of romance aside and fled in terror. I mentioned the previous two encounters with the Green Man in my *Liverpool Echo* column and received quite a response from readers regarding the enigmatic luminous park entity. A lady in her eighties named Rita contacted me to say how, in the 1970s, she had been driving her car along Livingston Drive North one night at around 11pm when she saw a giant green luminous figure step over the gates of a mansion on the corner of Aigburth Drive and walk with a strange gait - swaying side to side – towards Sefton Park. Rita was naturally unnerved by the sight of the weird towering figure, and she turned right from Livingston Drive North onto Aigburth Drive, and was so nervous she cut a corner and actually mounted the kerb – but then Rita looked in her rear view mirror and saw to her horror that the green giant was giving chase, and it was so tall it was stooping to avoid hitting its head on the branches of the sycamores lining Aigburth Drive. Rita stepped on the accelerator and got out of the area as fast as possible, and when she reached her home on

Menlove Avenue, her mother and father thought she had been taking drugs when they heard her excited account of the glowing green figure. Another *Echo* reader named John wrote to me to tell me how, in January 1972, he had just become a doctor, and had been working late at his surgery in the Sefton Park area. John got in his car on this bitterly cold January night around 7:30pm and drove home. His route meant that he would have to drive along the North West stretch of Aigburth Drive, which curves around Sefton Park, and then John would drive up Lark Lane to reach his home. He was looking forward to his wife's shepherd pie, and also the luxury of a glass of wine after a hard day's slog at the surgery. Before John reached the junction of Aigburth Drive and Lark Lane he saw a tall – well over seven feet in his estimation – glowing greenish figure which stepped out from behind a sandstone gatepost to his left. John was distracted by the unnatural being, and sensing there was something evil about the entity, he quickly turned right onto Lark Lane, and noticed three men standing on the corner of Livingston Avenue, and they appeared to be looking at the tall glowing figure. John then slowed down as he went over black ice, and drove carefully home. When he told his wife what he had seen she looked at him with a concerned expression and warned him to stop overworking at the surgery. John assured his wife the thing he had seen had not been the product of overwork or fatigue; it had really existed but the doctor was at a loss to explain just what the entity was, and he kept a lookout for the baffling figure each time he drove along the same route home, but he never saw it again. The aforementioned accounts are just two of dozens of similar reports I received from the readers of my column. Some witnesses saw the luminous green humanoid floating along, but it was mostly seen to move about by plain old walking. What the Green Man is, I do not know. It's easy to say it could be extraterrestrial in origin or a being from another dimension, but such speculation really gets us nowhere. I have a feeling we haven't heard the last of Sefton Park's green man.

The following story is another example of a bona fide phenomenon of a most peculiar kind, although I do offer a possible explanation at the end of the strange story, but I think the proffered possibility I offer is neither here nor there.

In early August 2002, a 43-year-old woman named Deborah, who lived on Eaton Road North, West Derby, had just split with her husband, and she started drinking to ease the pain of separation. Some people can cope with the trials of life and others turn to drink or even drugs in an attempt to soften the blows life sometimes throws at us, and in Deborah's case it was vodka. She had really loved her husband and she found life almost unbearable without him, and the only person who kept her going was her 14-year-old daughter Suzy. One afternoon Deborah had a little too much vodka and in a slurred manically optimistic voice she announced to Suzy that she was going to "pick all the apples off the tree" in the back garden. Suzy said she'd go and look for a ladder and that she'd do the picking, as her mother was obviously in no fit state to climb a ladder. Suzy had to put her make up on first, she said, and wear something decent, and her mother yelled, 'You are so vain, Suzy! You put your make up on and get all dolled up even when you're only going to the shop round the corner,' and Deborah stormed out after swearing at her daughter. Unabashed by the drunken insult, Suzy put her make up on and changed her clothes and looked out her bedroom window - and could not believe her eyes. Her mother was floating off the ground as she picked the apples from the tree, and weirder still, a few of the apples she had already picked were floating about like balloons. The window was partly open with it being such a hot August day and Suzy could hear her mother giggling and saying, 'Put me down!'

From her bedroom window, Suzy also noticed the neighbour peeping at the weird scene through a gap in the garden fence. He was always at that gap, 'perving' at Suzy and her mother. The girl ran down into the garden and found her mother stretched out on the grass on her back, giggling with an apple in her hand. The apples Suzy had seen defying gravity were scattered everywhere on the path and lawn. The girl knelt by her mum and gently patted her face with her hand and asked, 'Are you alight? Mam? Mam what happened?'

Deborah opened her eyes and said, 'Someone picked me up; I felt like Jayne Torvill when Dean lifts her into the air. He had big hands.' And then Deborah started chuckling again. Suzy helped her to her feet and they made their way to the kitchen. Again, Deborah told her daughter Suzy that someone had lifted her up to the tree; it had frightened her at first but then for some reason she felt ecstatic. There had never been any ghostly goings-on in the house or garden before, so this scared Suzy, but her mum thought it was a scream; it had been a welcome distraction to the depression she had been going through because of the break-up with her husband.

Days after this, Suzy was playing with her little Yorkshire Terrier Sky in the back garden and she was throwing a beach ball at him and laughing at the way the tiny dog was trying to jump on the ball. The girl's mother was out at the time and Suzy had made herself a Mojito cocktail. The nosy neighbour was peeping through the gap in the fence again and Suzy shouted to him, 'Stop spying on me you freak!'

Then suddenly, Suzy felt something lift her about 7 feet into the air; she felt as if the world had turned upside down and that she was 'falling' upwards into the clear blue sky. The dog whined and ran into the house and then came the sound of a howling wind which knocked over the garden furniture. Suzy experienced a feeling in her solar plexus area which she later compared to the feeling when she had been on the big dipper at Blackpool Pleasure Beach. The neighbour next door came sailing through the air - over the fence - as if he had jumped off a hidden trampoline. He landed in slow motion. Suzy then fell just as slowly onto her back and lay there shocked. She got up and saw the neighbour standing over her. He said, 'I was thrown over the fence; I didn't jump over it, honest.'

'Get away from me you perv,' she told the man, and she added that he was always spying on her and her mum.

'That's not true,' said the man, timidly, and he turned and ran at the fence. He tried - unsuccessfully - to climb over that fence, but was unable to do so and he resorted to using a chair.

Suzy's mum returned not long after this and Suzy told her what had happened. What seems to have been poltergeist activity then broke out in the kitchen with drawers opening and closing as if some invisible hand was yanking and shoving at the drawer handles. There were a few other incidents in the garden, but then, when Deborah's husband returned to her three days later the weird incidents came to an abrupt end. It's possible some emotional turmoil being experienced by Deborah, or by Suzy, or by both of them, triggered the bizarre events, but Deborah had been through traumatic times before and nothing paranormal happened, so the whole thing remains a complete mystery.

Here's a rather peculiar story that only came my way in 2022; in the summer of 2014, two girls in their twenties named Gayle and Heather came out of a club in town near Slater Street at around 2:30am, both quite drunk, and Heather said, 'Oh my God, look at that!' and pointed to a little silvery figure – and to her eyes it looked like a toy spaceman with a helmet on and spacesuit and it was about 10-12 inches in height, maybe less. Gayle's eyesight was terrible and she said it was a rat, but Heather ran towards the tiny humanoid, and it ran off but Heather, obviously having a bigger stride than the pint-sized entity, soon caught up and told Gayle, who was walking along unsteadily behind her, that she thought the "spaceman" was a robotic toy, and that she'd take it home to her kid brother, Callum. Gayle narrowed her eyes as she tried to focus on the strange gleaming figure, and she said, 'Heather, leave it alone, I have a bad feeling about it! Heather! Will you leave it the f**k alone?'

But Heather, high as a kite on all of the cocktails and beer she'd consumed for the past six hours, stooped down and said, 'What are you eh?' And Gayle walked up to her and looked down at the little oddity and was just going to once again say, 'Leave it alone,' when the two girls were momentarily blinded by a flash of light from the visor of the tiny entity. The whole of the alleyway was bathed in rainbow light, and the little doll-sized man was gone. The usual explanations were put forward by the sceptical friends of the girls; they'd obviously had their drinks spiked with LSD, and one of their friends said he knew this was the case because he had taken a tab of LSD once and whilst tripping he had gone into a pub and everyone had looked about 2 feet tall and he could not stop laughing. Heather was certain she had seen the little figure in the spacesuit, and Gayle said she had also seen it, but no one believed the girls. If the thing was not some drug-induced hallucination, what on earth was it?

One strange case which definitely belongs in this chapter because of its extreme peculiarity is alleged to have taken place one evening in July 2011 at around 11:30pm: two cars, one with three Liverpool women in it, which was returning from Ashton-in-Makerfield, and a vehicle with three men in it, returning from Manchester. Both Liverpool-bound cars were travelling along the East Lancs, and there is a stretch of this motorway which seems to start near the Game Bird pub, which has a very high incidence of strange goings-on; people have seen angels here, UFOs, experienced phantom passengers in their vehicles, lost time - all kinds of weird things. On this night, the three men were listening to Pink Floyd's *Dark Side of the Moon* on a radio station when suddenly, they saw everything in front of the vehicle - the road, the lamp posts, other cars - all fade away and there appeared a bright light with colours streaming from it, and these colours and streams of light were very hypnotic, and the driver, a man named Rob, swore and said, 'What's that?' and at this same time, the three females in a car that was travelling parallel to the vehicle with the men in it - also saw this same weird mesmerising sight. They had been overtaking the men's car at the time. All psychological time suddenly seemed to have no meaning for all six people; the English language fails us sometimes when we try to explain these inner feelings but according to the six witnesses, time just seemed like an illusion, as if it had been a clock which had now stopped. All of the witnesses to this intriguing occurrence felt completely at peace, a feeling they had never had before, except perhaps when they were babies. There were stars and nebulous shapes visible through the windscreen, and the man in the back of the all-male car, a 30-year-old named Ken, had his window down a few inches because of the July heat, and he could smell some type of sweet perfume coming into the vehicle; to him it just had a scent that said it was feminine - it was hard for him to say why but that's what he personally gleaned from the smell.

Both groups of people in both cars then saw the face of a woman with long swirling (possibly blonde or silvery) hair appear in the middle of the light play, and she had her eyes closed and the way her hair was undulating, in slow motion, as if it was being blown by some wind, was making the witnesses even more mesmerised. Rob, the driver of the car with the trio of males in it, said, 'She's the mother of all,' over and over like a mantra, and he could not say why he was saying this phrase. The women in the car also had this overwhelming impression that the female was somehow their mother - almost like Eve in the Bible - or some personification of Mother Nature perhaps - but they all felt some connection with her, and when she started to fade, Rob said, 'Don't go, take me with you.'

The female driver in the other car saw the face start to vanish and felt very sad to see her go, and then the lamps of the motorway reappeared and the red tail lamps of cars some distance off down the East Lancs could be seen. Both cars pulled over, their drivers feeling so emotional with the weird encounter. Rob got out the vehicle in a depressed state to have a cigarette, and saw a woman get out of her car on the hard shoulder about twenty yards away, and he chatted with her and they realised that they had seen the very same thing. They all became friends that night. None of them had been drinking or smoking weed or taking tablets, they had all just wanted to get home to Liverpool. Just what they all experienced and who that woman was with the cascading hair remains a mystery.

And finally, what must rank as a stellar example of the truly peculiar is the strange case of the man who read stones. I am still delving into this fascinating affair, but here is the basic outline of the strange story as related to me by several people who saw some bizarre and inexplicable things with their own eyes. In the mid-1980s a Danish man in his fifties named

Søren, who professed to be a self-taught geologist, visited parts of Wales and then Liverpool to collect particular samples of stones; slate from North Wales and Triassic Sandstone and various rocks taken from material excavated at Liverpool building sites to accommodate footings. Søren even risked his life taking small samples of Triassic sandstone from a railway tunnel at Edge Hill. And why was he obtaining samples? The Dane claimed he had uncovered strange images and encoded information in some stones from North Wales and Merseyside that could not be explained, and the images hinted that they had been encoded hundreds of millions of years ago. Søren said that by treating the stones with certain chemicals and applying electrolysis to them, he had 'brought out' some bizarre images on the surface of the stones and slate - figures depicting crowds, battles, and several clear images of smiling women's faces. He had a collection of female faces where they were winking, perhaps, as Søren suggested, as some ritual gesture. The images on the stones - some of slate, belonging to the Lower Palaeozoic era (417 to 545 million years ago) could not be explained. Geologists at the university were dumbfounded and said they could not explain the figures and female faces but they could not accept them, as it would make a mockery of the orthodox version of history and accepted dating methods. Modern humans are thought to have originated in Africa about 200,000 years ago and supposedly evolved from *Homo Erectus*, (Latin for upright man) – an extinct form of human that existed on earth between 1.9 million and 135,000 years ago – but the images of humans in the stones, when dated, put the artists as being active many millions of years before *Homo Erectus* walked the planet. What's more, cave paintings only date back to about 45,000 years – not millions of years – hence the geologists would be joined by the archaeologists at rebuffing the claims of the Dane. Søren then stretched credibility by saying that sometimes, when crayons, charcoal or graphite was rubbed over paper that had been laid over a stone, the resulting rubbing produced patterns in which faces and figures could be seen. The faces and forms were naturally explained away as the mind joining up the dots – or pareidolia as it is officially known. The self-taught Danish geologist said some stones were like books with information encoded into them only to be read by the initiated. Rocks can provide valuable information about the Earth's history through the study of their composition, texture, and formation, and can even tell us about the orientation of the world's magnetic field as the rock was formed - but Søren's claims were something else. Those who saw the images Søren *developed* from the Welsh and Liverpudlian rocks said they were not vague images of the type the mind sees in clouds, and the faces were not like the 'face' of the man in the Moon we perceive through the illusions of pareidolia – the images seen in Søren's rocks were clearly defined and the faces of the mysterious winking women looked almost photographic in quality. If the images are indeed somehow encoded into the stones, who are these women and the various figures? We can store feature films on tiny silicon chips today and, God forbid, if our civilization was wiped out by a virus or a nuclear war, would any primitive descendants be able to read those silicon chips and extract the moving images on those tiny chips of silicon? Likewise, Søren's images might be someone's archive, stored in stone millions of years ago. I'm still delving into this intriguing case. In the meantime, perhaps you should try a crayon or graphite rubbing of any old stones you can find - even an old sandstone wall - you never know.

If there is something to be gleaned from all of these cases of the truly peculiar detailed within this chapter, it is this: that we humans cling like frightened children to what I term the 'comfortable known' – a thing we cling to called 'reality', but our knowledge of the things which make a mockery of our reality remains very scant. We have technological marvels like the James Webb Space Telescope which can see how the Universe looked a quarter of a billion years after the Big Bang (which, at present estimates, happened around 13.8 billion years ago), and that telescope can see billions of galaxies, and at the other end of the scale, more and more powerful electron microscopes and particle accelerators are showing us the strange world of subatomic particles, the bizarre and unfathomable antics of photons and neutrons, and somewhere in between the ends of the Universe and the almost unimaginably small world of quarks and neutrinos lies *our* level of existence - our reality – and that reality is a very thin and delicate one, easily shattered by unexplained things big and small. Hiding our heads in the sand won't make the unexplained things go away. When the strange virus known as Covid19 first started to spread around the globe, one world leader called it "fake news" and I personally knew someone who said the virus did not even exist -

it was a PsyOp – a psychological operation; something designed and put into circulation to induce or reinforce behaviour perceived to be favourable to the mysterious powers that be. In other words, a PsyOp is a devious way to manipulate the public. The person who told me Covid19 wasn't real later died from the virus. We live in our own little bubble of reality and when something threatens that reality we either ignore or deny it is real or we acknowledge it and study it. There really is so much more to learn about this Universe we are living in, and we need to be more open-minded.

MATILDA AND
THE CAVEMAN

In the oppressive heat of the early summer of 1994, a 25-year-old blind lady named Matilda sat at a table in the back garden of her Heswall home, listening to Mozart on BBC Radio 3. As the sonorous strains of classical music graced her ears, an unexpected intrusion disrupted the harmony of Matilda's secluded green haven. An earthy aroma had interrupted her reverie, and then she felt someone's breath – the breath of a stranger - almost caress the nape of her neck. Her voice, laced with a blend of caution and curiosity, pierced the silence, 'Who's there? Who's that?'

The young lady knew from the masculine odour hanging in the air that the presence was not her older sister Pru (short for Prudence), who of late wore the Clinique Happy fragrance – this was a strong, almost overpowering masculine smell – similar to the aroma given off when rain falls on dry earth, and of acrid BO and also, bizarrely, a musky odour of fish. With measured resolve, Matilda extended her hand, seeking the familiar buttons of the radio on the table, and she switched off the music. Now, she could hear the usual faint hum of a passing wasp, the zephyr whispering through the leaves of the yew tree in the garden, and what almost sounded like a grunt. The low gruff noise reminded Matilda of the funny grunting sound her 5-

year-old niece made to express displeasure whenever she was reprimanded by her mum for bad behaviour. Who *was* this?

And now someone was putting a flower under Matilda's nose – she could tell it was inches from her face because she could detect the sweet smell – a scent like honey on warm toast – and the flower touched her nose tip, startling her.

'Pru!' Matilda cried, and she heard the heavy tread on the lawn as the visitor hurried away. Then came the squeak of the kitchen door and Pru was on the scene in seconds.

'Matilda, what's wrong?' Pru asked, reading the frightened expression on her sister's face.

'Someone was here,' gasped Matilda, 'a man, and he was teasing me, poking flowers at my nose.'

'What flowers?' Pru asked, but then she noticed the sprig of Sweet Alyssum on the white marble-topped table. Her eyes then travelled over to the ornamental 'cloud' of Sweet Alyssum she had grown in a border at the end of the garden. 'You sure you never plucked them? There's a little sprig of Sweet Alyssum on the table.'

'No I never plucked it! Someone was here in the garden,' said Matilda, rising from her chair. 'He might be hiding in the bushes!'

Pru glanced around and held Matilda's hand. 'There's no one hiding in any bushes here unless he's a tiny leprechaun.' And she took Matilda into the kitchen and sat her down and made her a cup of coffee. Matilda said the culprit might have been the young window cleaner, Damon, but Pru said he wasn't due to clean the windows for four days, and said it would be out of character for him to scare anybody, and on top of that, Damon always wore a strong overpowering aftershave.

Matilda exhaled and shook her head. 'Pru, someone was standing by me; they breathed down my neck and they touched my nose with a flower. I didn't imagine it, and they had this horrible body odour.'

'Matilda, look,' Pru sat down next to her at the kitchen table and held her hand, and squeezed it slightly. 'There are no doors to the back garden; you can only get into the garden through this door here in the kitchen, and unless it was the invisible man, no one passed me. I was in here washing strawberries and cleaning up.'

'Someone got into the garden,' asserted Matilda, 'why would I lie?'

'I know you're not lying,' said Pru, 'you're just mistaken, that's all. There is no way anyone could have got into the back garden without me seeing them, and no one passed me in the kitchen and I never saw or heard anything, so I'm just going on logic, Matilda – you must have either dreamt the whole thing or maybe a cat sniffed your face. But no person could have got into the garden.'

'He could have gotten over the fence,' Matilda suggested.

'On three sides we have neighbours here who are in their seventies, eighties and nineties,' Pru reminded her sister tracing a plan of the garden on the table top with her index finger, 'Mrs Greaves is seventy-five and not in the habit of pole-vaulting over the fence, and on the other side we've got Ted, who's just celebrated hitting ninety, so I think we can safely discount him, and at the end of the garden on the other side of a fence that's covered in ivy, we have 82-year-old Mr Hargreaves, who has just had his hip replaced with a plastic one.'

'Yes, but these old people have visitors,' reasoned Matilda, 'and they might have a nephew or grandson who decided to climb over the fence.'

'Matilda, you shouted me and I was out of this kitchen in a flash,' said Pru, 'so whoever this phantom joker was, he must have flew off like a bird.'

'Yes but...' Matilda went on, and advanced more unworkable theories as to who the mysterious visitor was until Pru said, 'Matilda, I can see my glowing zigzag migraine lines in front of me. Just let it go, please. I need some paracetamol and a lie-down in a dark room.'

'I wish mum and dad were back,' Matilda said, as Pru opened the kitchen drawers, searching for the box of painkillers. The parents of the sisters were in Spain for a fortnight and Pru was wishing they were back too. She really did think her sister had imagined the man in the garden. The two sisters had only come to live at the house in Heswall five years ago. They had been born across the Mersey in Childwall, and from the age of five, Pru had loved having a younger sister, and had dutifully looked after Matilda, who had been born blind. She hated arguing with Matilda, but today, Pru believed her sister really had imagined the intruder to the garden, and put it down to her sister's occasional anxiety problem.

Two days later, Pru finally persuaded Matilda to sit in the back garden again, and assured her no foul-smelling man was going to visit her and poke flowers up her nose. 'I'll be at the kitchen window watching you soak up the sun and vitamin d. Alright?'

Matilda nodded, and sat at the table with a Braille book. Pru switched on the radio on the table but Matilda switched it off again. 'I prefer silence when I'm reading,' she told Pru, who kissed her hand then went to the kitchen to do some washing up. About twenty minutes had elapsed when Pru was looking for two ice cream Magnum lollies in the freezer when she heard Matilda scream. She slammed the freezer door and ran into the garden – and she saw a tall, extremely stocky long haired man with a beard, and he was wearing only some animal skin that only partially covered his crotch, and his body looked hairy from his neck down to his shins. The immediate impression Pru got was that the stranger was some cave man. Matilda was backing away from the bizarre-looking stranger, and she had flowers in her hair, as did the savage-looking oddball. Pru grabbed a rake that was leaning against the wall of the house and ran to Matilda brandishing the gardening tool. The 'wild man' looked bewildered, and Pru grabbed her hysterical sister's hand and slowly retreated with her into the house.

The 'cave man' made a loud moaning sound as he saw Matilda being pulled away from him, and he reached out to her and walked slowly forwards to Pru and Matilda as they backed into the house. As the sisters entered the kitchen, Pru looked at the weird Stone Age interloper – and she saw him turn and run to the bottom of the garden, where he literally vanished into the wall's tapestry of ivy. Pru drove Matilda to their Aunt Freda's house in Pensby. Freda heard the strange account of the "cave man" from her nieces and said that years ago, she and others had heard a drumming noise and chants coming from the end of the back garden of the house in Heswall on a few occasions, and the source of the sounds could never be traced. When Pru returned to the back garden on the following day, she examined the ivy that the hairy brute had vanished into, wondering if there was some gap in the fence there, but there was just solid wood there. Pru went back into the house and sat next to Matilda on the sofa in the living room, and she told her how there was no way the visitor could have walked through that ivy-covered fence. 'He put flowers in my hair, and he did it so tenderly;' Matilda told her sister, 'I know I'm being a silly romantic, but I think he loved me.'

It would seem that some male from our remote past – possibly Palaeolithic times – was somehow able to visit 1994, where he developed a crush on a 20th Century girl, courting her nonverbally with flowers – but was he a ghost, or was he a living, breathing early human who reached Matilda via some timeslip?

SOME UNEXPLAINED
HAUNTINGS

Few things bother me more than a ghost that cannot be explained; part of the enjoyment (if you could call it that) of ghost hunting is the research carried out which explains the whys and wherefores of a haunting – the back story of the ghost – but sometimes no such historical information can be found to throw any light on the ghost, and the following case is a prime example of an unexplained haunting.

On Saturday 26 June 2010 at around 9pm, a 17-year-old girl from Huyton named Emma went to see her Auntie Deb at her ground floor flat on Arundel Avenue (off Smithdown Road). The visit was partly out of boredom for Emma, who was skint, and her Auntie usually gave her a tenner when she went to see her. Emma had been nagged by her mum to tidy up her room on this Saturday evening and so getting out of the house was a sure fire way of dodging that chore.

About ten minutes after Emma had arrived at Auntie Deb's flat, the girl was in the kitchen mooching about for a snack when she found a packet of Jacob's Clubs – chocolate covered biscuits – but as Emma picked them up, someone rang her auntie's bell and Deb, who was in the toilet, shouted to her niece and asked her to answer the door. Deb thought the caller might be her friend Audrey. Emma went down the hallway to answer the street door - and found herself looking at a very familiar face; it was a girl who looked just like

Emma - same shade of red hair and blue eyes - only whereas Emma had long hair, the caller's hair was in a bob.

'Ha! You look like me,' said the caller, and then she walked past Emma and went along the hallway and walked up the flight of stairs to the flat above. Emma went back into her aunt's flat and Deb came out of the toilet and asked Emma if the caller was Audrey.

Emma shook her head and told her about the girl, and mentioned how she looked like a double of hesrself.

Emma's Auntie Deb acted oddly - she made the sign of the cross and told Emma: 'She's a ghost.'

'What?' Emma's eyes widened, and then she smiled nervously and said: 'She wasn't, she was a solid person.'

'Since I moved in here last September, I've seen her four times,' said Deb, 'and the first time I saw her I thought it was you. I pulled the curtains back and nodded to her head, thinking you'd had your hair cut, and when I opened the door she walked past me, went upstairs, and vanished on the landing.'

'Oh my God is this a wind-up?' Emma asked, her anxious eyes turning towards the living room door as if she thought the ghost might come through it.

Aunt Deb held her niece's hand. 'I am not blagging or anything, Emma; why would I want to scare you? I didn't want to tell you in case it put you off coming to see me. My brother doesn't visit because of *her*.'

Emma gulped. 'She said "Ha! You look like me" and she looked so real.'

'I know, she's the spit of you,' said Deb, 'that's why I'm not as scared as I would normally be if I knew there was a ghost haunting the building where I live.'

'All the little hairs on the back of my neck have just gone up;' said Emma, 'I wonder who she was?'

'I was going to ask the neighbour upstairs who lived here before I moved in, but I think she's only been here for two years. I felt a sort of warm welcoming atmosphere when I first entered this place; I didn't have any spooky feelings about the flat at all.'

'She had on sort of fleece dark jumper and high-waisted jeans, like they wore in the Eighties,' Emma recalled.

The lights flickered, and there was a commotion in the flat above - and a female scream. Deb and Emma went into the communal hallway and saw a woman in her fifties - the upstairs neighbour Mrs Edwards - come running down the stairs in her slippers. She was in such a hurry she almost fell, and grabbed the handrail to steady herself.

'You alright Mrs Edwards?' Deb asked, and her neighbour held her hand to her chest and seemed out of breath. 'I've just seen a girl in my bath, and she was being electrocuted! There were wires in the bath - I don't know how - and she was shaking and oh! It was horrible!'

Deb and Emma took hold of the distressed woman and brought her into the ground floor flat and sat her down and Deb poured a small amount of neat vodka in a glass and Mrs Edwards grabbed the glass with both of her trembling hands and gulped the drink down in one go, then coughed. She started to cry, and Deb rubbed her back and Emma went to fill the glass with vodka again but Debbi shook her head.

Mrs Edwards wiped the tears from her eyes with the back of her hand and said she had seen the lights flicker and had heard splashing in the bathroom. She went in and saw a red-haired girl she had never seen before shaking in the bath water with her eyes rolling back. She was naked and her body seemed white as snow. Mrs Edwards then looked at Emma and gasped, 'She was the double of you!'

Deb and Emma told Mrs Edwards to stay put and they went into the flat upstairs and heard the TV. *Match of the Day* was on, Emma recalled. She and her aunt gingerly entered the bathroom. There was no one there and the bathtub was bone-dry. Aunt and niece then looked in every other room – and not a soul was about, and they could hear the sobs of Mrs Edwards downstairs.

Mrs Edwards had lived at the flat for just over two years and had never seen a ghost on the premises - but she said that on some evening she had heard footsteps coming up the stairs and the sound of someone walking along the landing, and the footfalls always stopped dead outside her door. Within a fortnight, both Mrs Edwards and Emma's auntie had moved from that house on Arundel Avenue. I still haven't found any case of accidental electrocution at that address - or was it perhaps a case of *deliberate* electrocution? What would wires be doing leading into a bath? People have accidentally dropped charging smartphones in the bath and electric heaters and they have been fatally electrocuted as a result, but Mrs Edwards just saw wires. The mystery of the red-headed girl remains unsolved.

Here's another case of an unexplained haunting.

On June 21, 2003, Sue, a Belle Vale woman, told her daughter Lucy that she had just seen a stranger - a woman - in the back garden of their home, walking away from the end of the garden, and when she had gone outside she had found what looked like vintage and "antwacky-looking" dresses, knickers, candy-striped pillow cases and matching sheets on the washing line. Lucy went outside and saw the washing items on the line and was going to remove them but her mum told her to leave the clothes there and to see if the person came back for them. On the following day at around 1pm, the same stranger was seen in the back garden and this time Lucy saw the unknown woman walking away from the washing line, and she said, 'Excuse me, love - why are you putting your stuff on our washing line?' and the woman returned a perplexed look and said, 'That's *my* washing line.'

Sue, Lucy's mum, came out and said, 'No, that's our washing line, and take all those daggy clothes with you, you cheeky get.'

'Look, there's my house, and this is my back garden,' the woman said, raising her voice and pointing to a lovely home beyond the fence - a house that had not been there before. Sue noticed the woman had the Farrah Fawcett feathered hairstyle - a popular hairstyle that dated way back to the Seventies, and as Lucy was baffled by the appearance of the woman's house, Sue said to her daughter, 'Ooer, I think she might be a ghost, Luce.'

Lucy asked her mum, 'Hey, what's happened to the fence at the end of the garden?' Now one side of it had gone and there was a path running through the place where the fence had stood - a path that went to that unknown house.

The woman said something unintelligible then

turned and walked away. As soon as she walked up the path to her home, the fence reappeared. Lucy staggered backwards, standing on her mum's toe.

'Didn't I tell you she was a ghost?' Sue said to her stunned daughter. They looked at the washing line; the clothes had gone.

On the following day at sunset, the fence at the bottom of the garden faded away and that house reappeared again as Sue was in the back garden having a ciggie. Sue whispered to herself, 'Bleedin' hell,' and then she shouted to her daughter Lucy, who came running out to her mum.

'It's back, again, look!' Sue nodded at the phantom house, and this time a long-haired man with a moustache who wore green flared trousers walked from the ethereal house and headed for Sue and Lucy, and mother daughter swore with nerves and tried to decide whether they should stay put or 'leg it' to their house and lock the door behind them. Mother and daughter decided they had to face the ghost in the hope it could explain what was going on, and they bravely stood their ground. The man stopped about 20 feet away and in a well-to-do accent he said, 'Hello. You must be wondering what's going on. My name is Maurice...'

And he vanished in mid-sentence, and so did the house he had walked from.

Mother and daughter looked at one another, then hurried to their house and went into their kitchen in a right state. They closed the door and both had a beer out the fridge. They never saw "Maurice" or the unidentified woman again and no more vintage clothes appeared on the washing line. The couple had appeared to belong to the 1970s, and Sue was later told by her neighbour, a man in his late seventies, that a house had never stood where she had seen the phantom residence – there had always been fields there. If the couple and their ghost house had been from the future, via some timeslip, then why would the couple have hairstyles and clothes that date them to the 1970s? Unless of course, Seventies fashions do return at some point in the future. The case remains another example of an unexplained haunting.

Not all unexplained hauntings involve a ghost – there have been baffling hauntings concerning inanimate objects too, such as in the following case.

On the morning of Saturday 24 June 1978, at around 3:20am, a number of clubbers returning home in taxis and on foot saw an eerie and baffling sight on Duke Street - some type of illuminated hearse with a long coffin, estimated to be about 7 feet in length, inside of it. An old-fashioned lit oil lantern with a hook had also been left in front of a nearby house. A night watchman across the road who had been looking after a house undergoing renovation had seen three abnormally tall men in top hats bring the hearse to its location via two horses and the hearse was unhitched and left there. A fog rolled up Duke Street from the Mersey at 4am that morning and the hearse seemed to melt away into nothingness as the mist covered it. The significance of the hearse is not known. The 7-foot-long coffin in that enigmatic hearse reminds me of the mysterious and equally baffling apparition of a long bed that has been seen on the cobbles of Wolstenholme Square, close to the modern art sculpture "Penelope" (see more of this bizarre mystery in *Haunted Liverpool 26*). The bed that is seen on Wolstenholme Square – always in the wee small hours of the morning - is estimated to be about 12 feet in length. Wolstenholme Square is about 70 yards from the site on Duke Street where the elongated coffin was seen. Alas, no 7-foot-tall ghost has been seen in the vicinity of these unusual hauntings to link them.

For some years, possibly since Victorian times, a ghostly girl has been heard laughing, crying and shouting in Sefton Park, particularly near the caves in the park's grotto, which is located on the wooded parkland between Croxteth Drive and Mossley Hill Drive. I took a medium named Billy to Sefton Park grotto once and he told me he was tuning into a little Victorian girl who had been murdered in the caves there, but, to date, I have found no record of a child murder in those caves. Billy told me there was something evil lurking there in the caves that had been there when the caves had been inhabited by Neolithic tribes. I didn't have the heart to tell Billy that the caves were in fact man-made and had only been created in the early 1870s by a French craftsman named Monsieur Combaz. A body *was* found not too far from the caves in Sefton Park by two newsboys, but this was not in Victorian times; the sad discovery was made on the Saturday morning of 12 April 1930. The body was that of a newly born girl, wrapped in pages from newspapers dated January 8 and December 29, 1929, and the dead child had a cord coiled around its neck. Who disposed of the baby remains unknown.

The ghostly girl of Sefton Park, whatever her origin, is apparently still being heard, and that brings us to the following story.

In the summer of 2010 a lady in her forties went in search of love, although she wouldn't admit it to herself or to anyone, really. Her name was Becky, and she needed an excuse to look for love in Sefton Park in the clear light of the sun, because when she had gone to clubs and looked at various prospects through the haze of alcohol and coloured lights, she had seen nothing but illusions of love and sometimes fleeting glimpses of *the one* (oh how she hated that phrase). Her excuse to linger and loiter in the park was the grey-muzzled dog of Rose, her neighbour. On this day, Rose's dog, Daisy, was led around the park and Becky was on the lookout for *him* and thought this might be the day. For some reason a memory from so long ago – back when she was thirteen – surfaced in her mind; a bittersweet recollection of being in the kitchen and telling her mum (who was putting a knob of lard in a frying pan) that a boy at school named Michael had said he loved her. Her mum had pointed to the tealeaves strainer on the draining board and quipped, 'A boy's love is like water in that sieve.'

And she'd been right. Michael was soon gawping at Becky's best friend Patricia.

Becky stopped looking for *him* after a while, and she came to a halt with her head bowed, feeling so down, and Daisy looked up at her with her tongue hanging out and seemed to ask, 'What next?' because Becky had unknowingly done two circuits of the park. She was just about to go home when she heard a voice – it sounded like a little girl's voice - which said, 'Someone loves Becky.'

Becky looked around, and so did Daisy, but there was no one there. The nearest people were hundreds of yards away. Becky thought the quality of the voice was dreamlike, and it reminded her of the hallucinatory voices she sometimes heard when she was sitting up in bed, reading a book as she was about to drop off – but she knew it could not be imaginary because Daisy had heard the voice too. Becky heard the voice again in the same part of the park on the following day, and it clearly said, 'Someone loves Becky,' and this time she thought she also heard a giggle.

'Who is this?' Becky asked out loud, her eyes searching the trees – no child was hidden up in the branches – so could this actually be a ghost? Becky had never believed in ghosts or life after death because she had never seen or heard from her mum once she had passed away – even in her dreams.

Becky tried to persuade her neighbour Rose to go to Sefton Park with her on the following day, but the old lady said ghosts frightened her and she didn't want to hear the disembodied ghost – she believed Becky's claim and had no reason to doubt her.

The voice was heard a third time, and then, on the fourth day, Becky went to the spot, determined to confront the ghost – but instead, she saw a man step out from behind a tree. He looked about fifty-something, but Becky was useless at estimating age. She thought he had a look of the comedian Ricky Gervais. He seemed startled by Becky's presence. He remarked how hot it was and then he paused, and seemed stuck for words for a moment, and Becky had the feeling he was trying to think of an explanation to account for him being in this wooded part of the park.

'I wasn't up to no good or anything behind that tree,' he said.

Becky returned a blank stare.

The man then puffed up his cheeks as he blew air in a measured way, and then he asked Becky a question that caused a cold shudder throughout her nervous system on such a steaming day. He asked, 'Do you believe in ghosts?' and his eyes swivelled from side to side. 'I mean, I don't, but I'm not so sure now,' he added.

Becky answered the strange question with a question: 'Are you talking about the voice of the little girl?'

The man, who later told Becky his name was Darren, seemed shocked, and he asked, 'Have you heard her as well?'

'Three times so far,' said Becky, and she had to yank Daisy away from Darren because the dog liked him and lunged at him.

They talked of the voices they had both heard over the same amount of days, and Darren said, 'Everyone said I was hearing things. I clearly heard her say "Someone loves Darren" and I was convinced it was someone playing a joke.'

'I thought the same,' said Becky.

'I was going to lay in wait and hope to catch the joker,' said Darren, 'but I get the feeling it's a real genuine ghost.'

And the couple got talking and Darren met Becky again at the park on the following day, this time without Daisy, and they listened at the spot where they had heard the ghost or whatever it was, but heard nothing. The couple talked of their lives and explained to each other why they were single, as if they *had* to do that – and that day, at some magical point, they – well,

I'm not going to say *fell* – why use that word? It's not a fall, it's a decision made by two hearts to share the universe in a lovely way. They walked down a path from that spot in the park holding hands, and Becky swore she heard that little girl's voice say, 'Goodbye.'

From Sefton Park, we next move north to Knotty Ash to document another ghost of the unexplained variety. On the evening of Thursday 17 October, 1968 at a house on Thingwall Avenue, Knotty Ash, two sisters - Sheena, 22, and Laura, 17, attended a huge party. At one point in the party, Sheena noticed that her teenaged sister was missing, and she went in search of her, and had to elbow her way through quite a few lecherous and intoxicated males until she spotted Laura at the top of the first flight of stairs in the hallway, lingering outside a bedroom. 'What are you doing hanging round here?' asked Sheena, and Laura said, a 'very handsome lad' of about 18 had peeped out of the bedroom - and he'd had a woollen scarf around his neck, the ends of which covered his private parts - for he had nothing on. He was naked. He had beckoned Laura, who was now a bit tipsy and giggly, to come into the bedroom. Sheena dragged her young sister away from the bedroom door. As chance would have it, someone in the kitchen had just been telling Sheena the house was haunted by the ghost of a lad who had hanged himself on the premises with a red scarf eleven years ago, and Laura told Sheena the story.

Laura said the boy she had seen had definitely not been a ghost, and that he was solid. 'Sheena, he's in there now,' Laura said, pointing to the bedroom door from the stairs, and she broke free from her protective sister and ran up the stairs and along the landing.

'Laura! Don't go in there!' yelled Sheena, and she ran after her drunken sister.

Laura yanked open the bedroom door – and found the room inside empty. The double bed there was neatly made and there was no sign of the naked young man. Laura looked around the side of the wardrobe as her sister yelled at her to leave the room, and the teenager even looked under the bed. The boy had gone, and this gave Laura the creeps.

At a Christmas party at the Thingwall Avenue house that same year, the ghostly lad popped his head out from the same bedroom door as last time and beckoned another female guest – this time a woman in her early thirties named Jemima and she saw he had on a red scarf and looked as if he was stripped to the waist, and being a bit tipsy from consuming a lot of champagne, Jemima went in the bedroom she saw the young man, naked and hanging from the curtain rail by the long scarf. Just before Jemima screamed the body started to urinate, and then it slowly vanished. Jemima's screams brought the party to a standstill and three male guests ran up the stairs and asked her what the matter was. She told them about the naked man hanging from the curtain rail but when the three men went into the room they found it empty. The head of the household, a man named Leslie, seemed very ruffled by the mention of the ghost with the scarf, and he said he had heard of the ghost before but had no idea whose ghost it was. Leslie had asked the neighbours on Thingwall Avenue who had lived there long before he'd moved there (which was five years before) if there had ever been a suicide at his home, and they had all said as far as they knew, there hadn't.

When a well-attended New Year's Eve party was in full swing at the house on Thingwall Avenue on Wednesday, 31 December, 1969, the ghost got up to its old tricks again. On this occasion at 11:15pm, a naked man who looked as if he was aged 19 or 20 ran naked from the hallway of the house, through the crowd of startled guests, and sprinted up the stairs. He entered the very same bedroom where he had beckoned females from twice before, and minutes later he popped his head out, and again he was wearing a red scarf about his neck. Two girls, both aged eighteen, who had been talking to their boyfriends on the landing with drinks in their hands, saw the naked young man gesturing for the two of them to come to him, but seeing he was nude, except for the long red scarf, they drew their boyfriends' attentions to the man, and the two lads gave their glasses of ale to their partners and went to have words with the offensive guest, but he slammed the door on them. The two young men burst into the bedroom and saw the same shocking sight that had been seen on the last occasion. The nude man was hanging from the curtain rail by the scarf noose, and his tongue was protruding. The feet of the suicide seemed less than five inches from the floor. Then the figure vanished. One of the girls who followed her boyfriend into the room dropped his glass of ale in shock.

News of the nude ghost of Knotty Ash spread around the city, and people speculated on why the troubled spirit was hanging itself after drawing people to that room. Had the ghost worn clothes, we may have been able to date it by its attire, but the only item it carried was that long red woollen scarf, and that was very hard to date. The family moved out of the Knotty Ash house in the 1970s and a couple moved into the place, but the ghost was not seen during their tenure. However, in the 1980s, a couple moved into the house and on the first night at their Thingwall Avenue home, they had a housewarming party that was attended by twenty-odd people – and lo and behold, there were screams of laughter as the unknown streaker ran from the kitchen, across the hall and up to the bedroom, but the screams of laughter turned to shrieks of terror when they found the nude "gatecrasher" hanging from the curtain rail. What was strange about the haunting on this occasion was the fact that no curtain rail existed in the bedroom; vertical blinds hung there instead – and yet people had distinctly seen the end of the scarf tied to a curtain rail.

They say the baffling ghost of the suicide still occasionally appears at the house, but why the ghost goes through the same routine, is unknown, as is its identity.

We move to more recent times now, to what seems to be the ghost of a young lady who met a tragic end – but who on earth is she?

On the misty, drizzly evening of 17 September 2014, at around 10:20pm, a 37-year-old Tuebrook man named Ian was patiently standing at a bus stop on Queens Drive West Derby, close to where the entrance to Holly Lodge Girls' School was, when he was joined by a pretty blonde girl of about 18 to 20 years of age in a smart pink coat, a short dark skirt, black tights and possibly Converse trainers. They were the only two people at the stop. Ian was mindful of the issue (which had been mentioned a lot in the news of recent in the light of several murders of females) about women feeling unsafe at night when they were alone, so he deliberately kept some distance away from the young blonde and he avoided eye contact with her. Ian was a very sociable man but knew his friendliness could be misconstrued, especially this time at night.

'When's this bus coming?' the girl asked, in a soft well-spoken voice, and Ian in turn asked, 'The 60 or the 81?' but received no reply.

The girl then cried out, 'Oh, my head!' and blood trickled from under her fringe into her eye, and Ian also saw what looked like a wound on the top of her blonde head.

'Oh my God - who did that, love?' he asked, stepping forward, and the girl was suddenly not there anymore. She had literally vanished before Ian's eyes. He stood there in shock, and then he looked down and he saw the wet imprint of the vanished girl's shoes – little diamond and lines from what had possibly been her Converse trainer soles, left from her walking from the wet pavement onto the dry ground under the bus shelter. It was the only trace of the girl.

An old man arrived at the stop seconds later, and Ian said to him, 'I've just seen a ghost,' and straight away the elderly man sombrely asked, 'Did she have blood on her face?'

Ian slowly nodded. The man said he'd seen her himself one night last year, and he added, 'in fact I think it was around this date in September. A few have seen her, dressed in pink.' 'Yeah that's what she had on, a pink coat,' said Ian.

The man nodded and said, 'Don't know who she is though; God rest her soul whoever she is, she must not be at rest. Here's the bus.' And the man got out his bus pass and Ian sat next to him on the bus for about six stops, going over his recollection of the meeting with the sad ghost. It's a story I'd heard about a few times before from listeners to my slot on the radio, and no one seemed to know who the blonde was or why she had that ghastly head injury. Perhaps someone out there knows the story behind the haunting.

A ghost that haunted a woman when she was in a very vulnerable situation is another example of an unexplained haunting. On Thursday 6 July 1978 at around 6pm, a 24-year-old lady named Catherine was minding her sister Ruth's home on Mossley Hill's Archerfield Road (which, incidentally, is the road with one of the displaced Calderstones standing at the end of the road near the junction with Booker Avenue). Catherine loved the old-fashioned vintage marble bathtub in the spacious bathroom, and so she leisurely filled it, put some bubble bath mixture in, stripped, and stepped into pure bliss. The sun was shining through the windows from the back garden at a low angle, throwing golden light on the white tiled walls which featured rose designs, and there was a eucalyptus bath bouquet hanging in a seagrass basket above the tub. There were philodendrons, violet campanula bellflowers and peace lilies in that bathroom which made it feel like a green sanctuary of relaxation to Catherine.

But then two things happened; two rather strange things. Catherine thought she saw someone peeping in at her through the window to her right. The movement was only detected by Catherine's peripheral corner-of-the-eye vision. She was considering getting out the bathtub to pull the roller-blind down, even though it would stop that spiritual stream of sunlight shining into the bathroom, but then there was a distraction from the decision; bubbles inexplicably started to rise out of the tub and they floated in the air. Catherine felt the atmosphere change; she felt someone's eyes upon her. Then she saw a figure appear at the end of the bathroom: the figure of a man who was dressed in the attire of a hooded monk. He looked around at the bathroom, then gazed in awe at Catherine, and she was too afraid to even try and get out of that bathtub. He walked slowly towards her in his chocolate brown hooded habit and she could even see his cobalt blue eyes. He leaned forward and gasped something that sounded like, 'Diabolus tentat me,' which, translated from Latin, is: 'The Devil tempts me.'

For some reason, unknown to this day, Catherine felt the monk was a lost harmless spirit, and she held out her foamy hand to him, but he recoiled, startled by the friendly gesture, and instantly vanished. Catherine casually got out of the tub and wrapped a long bath towel around herself and went to the lounge of the house and she sat there, thinking of what she had seen. She was surprised at not feeling scared of the ghost, and actually hoped she would see the monk again, but she never did. When Catherine's sister Ruth returned from a short stay down in Brighton, Catherine told her, 'I saw a ghost in your house,' and her sister and husband looked at one another, and the sister asked, 'It wasn't a friar, was it?'

It turned out that her sister and brother-in-law had also seen the ghost a few times in the garden, but never in the bathroom or in any part of the house. As far as I know, there were no monasteries on Archerfield Road, which deepens this mystery.

And finally, here's a sinister case of an unexplained haunting, but it is strange in that the haunting is connected with the appearance of an apparently solid object: a toy car.

On Wednesday 3 August, 1966, 13-year-old Joe and his 11-year-old sister Sharon boarded the Number 79 bus to their Wavertree home after a visit to Woollies on Church Street, and Sharon found a brand new "Dinky Supertoy" box containing a model of a pink car, lying on a seat at the back of the bus. Sharon excitedly picked up the toy car in its box and showed it to her brother, saying, 'Look what I found – and it's finders keepers.'

Joe tried to grab the car but Sharon was too quick and she withdrew it from his grabbing hand and she teased him saying, 'All mine! Joe's got a cob on, cos he can't have the car-har!' Joe said the car was a boy's toy and argued that he should have it, and if he didn't get it he'd tell their mum. Sharon loved playfully taunting her younger brother and Joe whined about how the Dinky car should be his all the way to the children's home on Thingwall Road. On the doorstep, just as Sharon and Joe were about to go into the house, Sharon handed the car to her brother, who snatched it out of her hand.

That night around twenty minutes past midnight, Joe was shaken awake by what he described as a "toy clown" in a pink outfit with polka dots, and it said, 'You took my car you naughty boy!'

Joe saw that the chalk white face of the clown had black solid circles around its eyes, as if someone had given it a couple of shiners, and the face was also dotted with tiny blood-red heart symbols.

'Mum!' yelled Joe, and the clown slapped his face with a clammy hand and melted away into the darkness. The boy woke the household with his screams. His mother said he'd had a nightmare, but the pink Dinky Supertoy car had gone, and the boy's parents and Sharon heard weird laughter coming from Joe's room nights later. The three of them went into Joe's room and saw that he was laughing and talking in his sleep in a strange voice. Then Joe's mother said, 'What's that on his face?'

Joe's face had dozens of little red heart-shaped symbols on his cheeks, nose and forehead – identical to the ones he had seen on the terrifying ghostly clown. The boy's father, against the wishes of his mother, shook Joe awake, and the hearts on his face quickly faded away. The boy had no recollection of talking and laughing in his sleep.

On Saturday 3 October that year, Sharon and her mum boarded the 79 bus after a day out and – yes, you've guessed it - there was the pink Dinky Supertoy in its box on the same seat. Sharon wouldn't go near the toy - but a lad of about 13 saw it and said it was his. I wonder if that boy was visited by the clown...

A GIRL NAMED JULIE

I've changed some names and details in this story for legal reasons. Back in 1965, most people in England observed Duck Apple Night on the last day of October. Apples were suspended from threads of cotton that had been pinned or tacked with small nails to door frames, and children – and some adults – had to seize the dangling bruised apples (which shillings and tanners had been inserted into) with their teeth – and then came apple-bobbing; big green apples with coins embedded into them immersed in a bowl of soapy water or a bucket. To own them you had to pick them up with your mouth, but it was fiendishly difficult; much harder than you imagined; if you missed the apple you were likely to have your face shoved in the soapy water. And then there were chestnuts that were baked in ovens or sometimes the more adventurous would place them on an iron shovel that would be placed on the coals of an open fire, and those chestnuts would explode with the heat and fly across the room like bullets. The children of Irish, Welsh and Scottish parents in Liverpool often made lanterns out of hollowed-out swedes and turnips – pumpkins were virtually unheard of in those times – and the Celtic kids called Duck Apple Night "Hallowe'en" – derived from the Scottish pronunciation of All Hallows Eve – but in Huyton in 1966, a woman named Mary, her two daughters – Eve (aged 13) and Sally (aged 10), and their stepfather – an American man named Ralph – were celebrating Halloween with actual pumpkin lanterns Ralph had brought into the country from Illinois, and along with the pumpkins on this magical night there was American candy corn, home-baked apple pies, cakes from Sayers, hot sausage rolls, lemonade and sarsaparilla. Mary, Ralph and the children put on fancy dress costumes to get into the Halloween mood. Mary and her daughters dressed as witches, and Ralph dressed as Frankenstein but he gave up when the bolts on his neck kept falling off because the glue wasn't sticky enough. Ghost stories were told by candlelight but the tales were more silly than frightening. At 7:30pm, Cheryl, the 17-year-old "babysitter" came over to look after Eve and Sally while Mary and Ralph spent a few hours at the local pub. Eve was thirteen and felt offended at her mother asking Cheryl – who was only four years older than Eve - to 'mind' her but she had to accept the arrangements. At 8pm, there was a knock at the door, and Cheryl answered to see a girl of thirteen named Julie. The babysitter recoiled at the sight of her as if the Devil had called, for Julie was regarded as a very strange girl and her mother was reputed to dabble in witchcraft. 'What do you want?' Cheryl asked the raven-haired, dark-eyed girl, but Julie said nothing for a moment, and there was a faint grin on her face. 'Death visited your home tonight, Cheryl,' she said in a calm yet eerie voice.

'What are you talking about? Cheryl asked, and found herself afraid to hear the answer.

'I saw Death standing on your doorstep, just after you left,' answered Julie, and she glanced past the babysitter at Eve and Sally. 'They found your mother dead in the kitchen.'

'You're lying,' said Cheryl, her voice faltering, 'you just want me to go home so you can come in. What a horrible person you are.'

Cheryl then noticed a crowd standing in front of her home and she grabbed her coat and left the house after warning Eve and Sally not to let Julie in, but curiosity got the better of Eve and she opened the door. Julie cheekily walked past her into the hallway. Eve asked, 'Has Cheryl's mum really died?'

'Yeah!' laughed Julie, and she went into the living room and picked up a bakewell tart on the table and asked, 'Can I have it? I love cakes with glazed cherries.'

She bit into it before Eve could reply, and then she said to the girls, 'It's Halloween – not Duck Apple Night; this has always been the one night when you can talk to the dead and even bring them back. I know how to as well.'

'No one can bring the dead back,' said Sally, 'it's impossible.'

'Jesus did, didn't he?' said Julie, looking annoyed, 'so you're wrong.' And then Julie treated herself to the lemonade and more cakes and she found some candles when she went mooching about in the kitchen – and she arranged the candles in a circle on a coffee table, and she scribbled weird symbols on scraps of paper and placed them in the circle.

'What are you doing?' Eve asked, curious yet nervous, and Julie said she was going to conjure a 'dead'un' up. Something caught the peculiar girl's eye – a magazine about murders. It had been brought from America when Ralph had first come to the UK to marry Mary. Julie flipped through the magazine and pointed to an identikit of a rapist and murderer who had never been caught in Santa Cruz. Julie said the man was dead and in Hell – but then she tore out the magazine page featuring the killer's identikit and put it in the middle of the circle of candles. Julie spoke in two voices simultaneously in a strange harmony, and Eve told her to stop because Sally was terrified. After a few minutes, Sally screamed as someone rapped on the window. It was a grinning man – and his face was identical to the identikit picture of the killer.

'I *told* you I could raise the dead!' said Julie, her face full of candlelit glee.

'Open the door, kiddies!' said an American voice outside. There was a pause.

'Eve, I'm scared,' Sally told her sister, and a tear welled in her eye.

'It's okay, Sally no one can get in,' Eve told her younger sister, and as she hugged her, there was a terrific bang as the door flew off its hinges and landed in the hallway. The man entered the living room and chased Eve, Sally and Julie around the table, and then the children ran out – into a fog. The resurrected killer chased the terrified kids across Huyton, and then, at 10:30pm he was heard to cry out in agony, and he burst into a vivid reddish flame – and vanished. At that moment, back in the house, Mary and Ralph had returned home, and Mary had thrown the torn-out page featuring the killer onto the fire. Cheryl visited the house and told Mary and Ralph how Julie had called to say that her mother had died – when in fact she had just fainted (as she had a low blood pressure condition). Eve and Sally returned home exhausted and in tears, and Mary told Julie to stay away from her daughters in future. I often wonder what became of Julie.

A TALE OF TWO
POSSESSIONS

Mention the word 'possession' and most immediately think of *demonic* possession, which I have witnessed, and it is very real, but I have many cases on file where the possession did not (as far as I could tell, anyway) involve a demon, and here are two such cases.

In March 2018, a 23-year-old girl named Haili bought a pink vintage square-neck dress with blouson sleeves from a shop on Etsy, and from the moment she tried it on, Haili felt very confident, whereas she was usually quite an introverted girl. Haili liked the dress so much, and found, for some unknown reason, that it had – as she put it – 'such a feelgood aura' she decided to wear it when she next went out on the club scene in Liverpool city centre, and this was on a Saturday night. Haili went out with her "posse" - 3 girls she'd known since college, but Haili soon embarrassed the trendy trio by continually badgering the DJ at a well-known club to play songs that were all from the 1990s. Haili had been born in July 1995, and yet she kept harping on about specific hits from the Nineties – songs that were somewhat before her time to put it mildly. All the same, the DJ enthused to Haili and said he was a "90s freak too" and people at the club laughed as Haili sang the Shaggy hit *Mr. Boombastic* - and she was word perfect as she recited all of the lyrics of the song. Haili then pestered the DJ to play Livin' Joy's *Dreamer*, TLC's *Waterfalls*, Baby D's *Let Me Be Your Fantasy*, and Des'ree's *You Gotta Be* and so many other vintage songs. Haili's friends were taken aback by her odd dance moves, as she was usually a very unimpressive dancer, and that was when she did dance – she was usually the wallflower at the club who rarely ventured onto the dancefloor. Outside the club, a girl approached Haili and said she was psychic, and that she'd seen 'a blaze of purple light' around her as she walked to the club, and the girl said she had a feeling a "close soul" had been walking with Haili. Haili just smiled and wondered if the girl was on ecstasy, and she got a cab home. As soon as Haili took the dress off, her personality reverted to the usual introverted state. Haili now felt a little down as well. She put the dress on a hanger and placed it in her wardrobe, then went to shower before retiring to bed and going straight to sleep. The next morning, Haili's best friend Sophie called her on her mobile and asked how she knew the words to *Mr. Boombastic* - and Haili said she didn't; she had no recollection of singing that song at the club or any of the others that Sophie mentioned.

When Haili's Nan saw the dress a few days later, she said she was sure it was the exact type of dress Haili's mum had worn in the 1990s, before her tragic death in late December 1995. When Haili tried the dress on again, it had no effect on her, and she is sure that somehow, by some fortuitous coincidence, it is the very dress her own mum sometimes wore when she went out clubbing, and so the girl has it packed away in her wardrobe, a link to a mum she never got to know.

Here is the second case of a possession – but possession by what is hard to say; I feel something took over the personality of a young man in the last century.

Every Saturday at noon, 25-year-old Simon Telford came into the Lyons Café at 59 Church Street - where the Pandora jewellery store is now – but this was in 1920. The excessively self-conscious Simon would come in and have coffee and some Maison Lyons Chocolate Biscuits and gawp at the overworked waitress Daisy, but he'd never say a word to her, so imagine when he came strutting into the café on a sunny Thursday morning on 1 July that year in a new well-tailored suit and his coal black hair slicked back with Macassar oil; picture the staff's faces when Simon grabbed Daisy's hand and said, 'This is your day off. All work and no play makes Jill a dull girl, and you my girl, are exceedingly dull – so I have come to brighten you up.'

And Simon took off her cap and apron and he led a blushing Daisy out of the café and all astonished eyes were upon her.

'I regret resorting to these strong-arm tactics Daisy, but faint heart never won a fair lady,' said Simon, and 18-year-old Daisy felt weak, felt kidnapped, but was so drawn to this bizarre new masterful version of a young man who had struck her as cute when he sat tongue-tied and lovelorn in the corner of the Lyons Café. She accompanied Simon, attracted to him like a pin to a magnet as he pulled her by the hand across Ranelagh Street to Central Station, and at 10 am the train took them to Southport. He French-kissed the waitress and literally took her breath away, and a lady, disgusted by the "carrying on" of the couple left the carriage. Two elderly men who sat facing the couple were too embroiled in a discussion about politics to notice the young lovers, and Simon happened to hear one of the elderly men talking about the striking ship engineers who had hoisted the Red Flag in Glasgow. The old man said, 'Those traitorous bastards should be hanged drawn and quartered! The country is unstable at the moment, and we've just had a police strike,' and the other old man replied, 'Just put them up against a wall and shoot them.'

Simon broke off from kissing Daisy, who sat there in the padded seat of the carriage with her eyes closed and a blissful look upon her angelic face. 'Don't stop, Simon,' she moaned.

A bearded, smartly dressed man reading a book was sitting diagonally across from the couple, and he started eyeing Simon with a suspicious look.

Simon stood up in the carriage and delivered a firebrand speech in which he called for the Royal Family to be deported and for the United Kingdom to become a "classless republic" – and there were gasps of shock from the two old men, and one of the pensioners yelled, 'Not in my lifetime, young man!'

Simon grinned and said to the oldster: 'Your lifetime will soon be over old chap, so you have no need to worry.'

'You impertinent idiot!' said the other old man to Simon, 'How dare you address my friend in such a discourteous manner! You coward! I'll have the law on you!'

Simon laughed at the threat from the pensioner and told the other people in the carriage, 'This country has never been so near to revolution. Cometh the hour, cometh the man! All throughout history, when a crisis looms, a hero always appears – I am that man!'

Daisy's huge eyes gazed so admiringly up at Simon from her seat, and she giggled and told him, 'You're my hero, Simon.'

Simon clenched his teeth, clenched his fist and raised that fist above his head, and he ranted, 'Though we may be commoners, our blood runs purer, more authentically English than that of any German monarch! He discarded his German heritage and adopted an English facade – calling himself Windsor! I bow to none! Get off your knees and arise from your subservience to join me on this crusade!'

'Someone have this traitor arrested!' cried the old man Simon had insulted.

Simon raved on: 'As long as idiots idolise and worship the Caesars and Napoleons and Kings and Popes, the Caesars and Napoleons and Kings and Popes will take control of the masses and rule their lives!'

Meanwhile, the bearded man in his thirties, smartly attired and previously engrossed in his book, seemed to react to Simon's speech as if the words struck a chord in his psyche, and he lunged forward. Seizing Simon's left hand, he deftly removed a ring adorning his middle finger - an opulent golden band embellished with a detailed ivory cameo depicting the profile of a strong-jawed man. The very moment the ring slipped off Simon's finger, he instantaneously transformed into the meek and unassuming character Daisy was accustomed to observing at Lyons Café. 'The ring of confidence; very dangerous,' said the man who had removed it, and he asked Simon where he had obtained it.

'An old man gave it to me; he was sitting on a bench in Newsham Park,' whispered Simon. The bearded man then asked, 'Tell me, did this man in the park happen have a slight German accent?' And Simon nodded. The man pocketed the ring. Simon never asked for it back, and sat timidly holding hands with Daisy.

The two old men got off the train at the next stop, and one of them struck Simon's arm with his walking stick before he left the carriage.

Daisy later asked the man who had taken the ring from Simon to return it to him, but the man shook his head and continued reading the book.

'You have no right to take what isn't yours,' said Daisy, and the man placed a purple silk ribbon in the book and closed it before turning to the waitress.

'That ring belonged to an occultist, back in the Regency period,' the man told Daisy, 'and you may wonder how I know this; well, I am well-versed in the occult. That ring has been on the finger of many a ruthless murderer, and it also has a tendency to drive the wearer mad. I believe it was worn by the infamous German philosopher Friedrich Nietzsche in the last century, and it turned his mind and drove him to believe that God had long perished and that the only way to get what you want is by trampling over people and obstacles and even killing to get it; Nietzsche called this concept the Will to Power.'

Daisy looked at the man blankly and he shook his head and sighed, believing the girl could not comprehend what he was telling her about the dark history of the ring.

The man got off the train at Southport and told

Simon Telford: 'I saved you from becoming a monster. You were possessed while you wore that ring. I am going abroad next week – to live in a little town called Meissen, and there I will bury the ring and perform a ritual and hope it never sees the light of day again.

Simon often wondered whose face had been carved in that mysterious cameo ring; did that bearded man bury it? Or did that ring end up on the finger of someone in Germany? The man had said he was going to Meissen, a town that is less than a hundred miles from Berlin, where nineteen years later, a dictator arose who tragically applied the idea of Nietzsche's Will to Power.

THE FIGMENT

On May 29 May 2023, a long-lost blue ring binder folder packed with many unpublished stories of mine (as well as files I was researching) was mysteriously returned to me by a person or persons unknown. The folder had gone missing in 2002 at a radio station. It was left on the doorstep of my office on Rodney Street and according to a few witnesses, the person who dropped it off went back to his vintage Jaguar and drove off. I have no idea who that person was or how he came to be in possession of those long-lost files. One of the stories in the files I'd been researching was a bizarre case from the 1950s that came my way via a number of letters sent to me at the radio station where I was presenting a slot each week on the paranormal. Here's the basic gist of the story.

A man, we'll call him Mark, was brought into a police station in Liverpool because of bizarre and violent behaviour at a doctor's surgery. A policeman chased him from the surgery into a church where he had disrupted a sermon with very colourful language. Mark was asked to give his name and address to a detective in an interview room, and he was also asked why he had caused the bizarre disturbances. What mark said in reply resulted in him being classed as a man with a serious mental health problem – and in the 1950s they were not as enlightened as we are today as regards to mental health. Furthermore, they were literally ready to put a straightjacket on Mark after they heard his extraordinary testimony. Mark told the police he had thought he was Mark for many years, a certain person who lived at an address in Liverpool, but then he had realised through some strange memory that he was in fact the "figment" of some *thing's* mind, and he said many people are such figments of this entity without even knowing it.

Upon hearing this statement from Mark, the detectives automatically assumed he was suffering from some mental illness and so they brought in a psychiatric nurse who joined in the interview, and she took notes on Mark's replies.

Mark stated in a well-spoken voice: 'The thing that made me, or dreamt me up, made a few mistakes – it does that now and then, and in my case it left parts of my body "out" – I was hit by a car, and somehow it caused me to remember that I'm just a figment of this thing – I don't think it's human and it's been doing this for a long, long time.'

'When you say "left parts of your body out" – what do you mean?' asked the psychiatric nurse, the ballpoint of her pen hovering a few inches over the yellow form she was making notes upon.

'Well, I have no insides now – I'm just hollow,' said Mark, 'and that's very rare, but it does happen, because sometimes the thing gets distracted and it slips up and leaves something out so you don't look authentic. I know all this sounds far-fetched but it's the truth and I just want someone to believe me so they might be able to wake everyone up to the thing and stop it running our lives. We're physical manifestations of its thoughts. If it forgets us we die; that's why you often hear of people vanishing without a trace and you never find them.'

'And you had a doctor by the throat trying to tell him all this?' asked a bemused detective, looking at a sheet.

'That was when I first realised I had no insides,' said Mark, 'it frightened me, and I thought I was going mad. I asked the doctor to take a look at me, but he wouldn't and said I'd jumped the queue in the surgery.'

'Can you show us what you mean by having no insides?' asked another detective, and Mark nodded and said, 'Can I borrow your pen?'

A gold-plated fountain pen was given to Mark and he uncapped it and impaled his face with it, inserting the nib end into his left cheek first, close to the corner of his mouth. The pen came out the other cheek. The policeman standing guard on the door grimaced, the psychiatric nurse felt queasy and one of the detectives muttered, 'Seen that done in India after the war. Sleight of hand.'

Mark pulled the pen out and opened his mouth wide. 'See?' he said, sounding odd, speaking with his mouth open that wide, 'No teeth, no tongue – nothing. I'd show you more but I'd have to strip to the waist.'

The detective leaned forward to Mark and snatched back his pen, wiped it with a handkerchief, even though there was no blood on the pen, and then he said in a voice devoid of emotion, 'You will be taken to a ward for a physical and mental assessment with this lady,' and he nodded to the psychiatric nurse. She and two police officers took Mark to a sterile-looking room, and hanging in the air in that room there was the aroma of an antiseptic substance of the kind you'd smell in a hospital, and here, the psychiatric nurse received the greatest shock of her life. Mark stripped to the waist – and there were what could only be described as large sections of his chest and abdomen missing; they were holes, and it was plain to see there was nothing inside of Mark, just a reddish brown space. He put his fist in to prove this was not "sleight of hand" as the detective had claimed earlier, and the nurse cried out to the policeman standing by the door. He was utterly transfixed by the surreal sight of the holes in the man's thorax and the hand reaching about inside of the impossible cavity in the abdomen. Mark sat there on the couch and said: 'The thing knows it's slipped up now, I can sense it because I'm part of its thoughts, so it'll rectify the mistakes it's made soon and I'll be erased. I don't know whether it will recycle me or whether this is the end.'

And the figure on the couch seemed to melt for a few moments and made a weird rasping sound from its mouth, and then it was gone, and there was a sickly sweet smell left lingering in the air.

It is said the incomprehensible incident was almost covered up, but because the whole episode was so bizarre, parts of the account got out from some of the witnesses, but no one has ever made sense of Mark's comments. Some said he was saying that we are all just figments of some supermind in this strange universe while others believed he was just talking about himself and perhaps a few other people who are not aware that they are just some type of projection of a higher intelligence. Some even believed the whole thing was down to someone who hypnotised everyone. It really is a bizarre one and I am still researching the account.

LAUGHTER IN THE CEMETERY

In December 2019 a couple – a 39-year-old teacher named Greg and a 23-year-old secretary at a housing association named Jenny, started having an affair. They had met, of all places, in a supermarket, where they had chatted about the store never having a certain brand of wine, and both felt drawn to one another at that first encounter. After meeting for the third time at that supermarket, Greg asked Jenny if he could take her out for a meal, and said his home life was depressing, and he came clean and said he had a wife, but was unhappily married. Jenny said it was the same story for her too; she had married early – at eighteen – and now her husband took her for granted and often went out to the pub with his mates, leaving her at home on her own.

After that first night out together at the restaurant, Greg said he actually felt as if had been born again, and Jenny had laughed and said that was a dramatic thing to say, but Greg assured her that it was true. And so began the affair.

About a week after the commencement of the affair, Greg believed his wife suspected him of seeing someone and had hired a private detective to follow him. His suspicions had been alerted one day in January 2020 when he had been driving to Southport with Jenny and had noticed a maroon van which followed his car all the way to the seaside town.

Wherever the couple went, that maroon van – and sometimes a dark blue Ford Fiesta - seemed to follow them. Greg became so paranoid about being watched, he posted a letter to Jenny on his way to work one day in February 2020, telling her to meet him in Allerton Cemetery at 6pm at a certain landmark. This was a ridiculous and dangerous request, but Greg was so paranoid about being followed and reasoned no one would be able to follow him to a cemetery without being seen, and he just had to see Jenny to kiss her, to hold her, to chat and make plans about their future without looking over his shoulder. Greg lived not too far from the cemetery and left his home under the pretence of going to get cigarettes but he walked to Allerton Cemetery, and being February it was quite dark. He got there early and about fifteen minutes afterwards he saw Jenny arrive at the gates – with a woman.

'Who the hell is that?' Greg asked when Jenny arrived at the rendezvous point.

'My mate Michelle – she won't tell a soul, honest,' said Jenny, and she waved at the silhouette of Michelle, who waved back and walked away. 'I've known her since I was ten;' Jenny told Greg, going on tiptoes to kiss him, 'she only lives with her boyfriend round the corner from here.'

'The whole idea for this cloak and dagger business was so no one would know we were meeting,' said Greg, and sighed, and Jenny hugged him and said, 'Oh shut up Greg, she won't blow us up – she's deep as the ocean. I was scared coming in here to meet you – not very romantic is it?'

Greg passionately kissed her and then he led Jenny a little further into the cemetery and the moon broke through the muddy-coloured clouds, highlighting the skull-white marble headstones and contrasting the shiny black gravestones. Greg got very carried away kissing Jenny and he pushed her against a tree and he said, 'I missed you so much. Maybe I should just tell her.'

'Greg, calm down, please,' said Jenny, pushing back from the tree, and she thought she could hear his heart pounding in the crystallized stillness of the cemetery. His warm breath was billowing from his mouth now into the frigid wintry air.

'You look so beautiful in the moonlight,' said Greg, and Jenny burst out laughing and Greg smiled and said, 'I know; I can't believe I just said that.'

'Cringeworthy,' said Jenny, and they kissed, and Jenny whispered, 'Don't even think of trying it on in here. We'd die of hypothermia. Let's go to a hotel down the town.'

They then heard what could only be interpreted as ripples of laughter, and Greg was so startled, he pushed Jenny away quickly and her head flew back. 'What was that?' he asked, and his eyes scanned the moonlit cemetery.

'Voices, and people laughing,' whispered Jenny, 'let's get out of here Greg.'

'Probably ket-heads and yobbos,' muttered Greg – he could see no one. He formed a faint smile and looked back at Jenny, saying, 'Sound travels weird at night; it was probably drunks laughing miles away.'

Ha ha ha ha!

It sounded almost like a laughter track in an old TV sitcom.

'There it is again,' said Greg, just after he'd kissed Jenny's eyebrow.

Jenny swore and said, 'That's it, we are leaving here now, and if you don't want to go, I'll leave here on me own.'

Ha ha ha ha ha Oh!

The laughter sounded nearer now.

'Where the hell is it coming from?' asked Greg – and then he saw a large group of silhouettes because the moon's light increased as the clouds scudded away from its face. Greg pointed to the figures. 'There they are – look!'

Jenny turned and saw the mass of silhouettes. She suggested it might be someone holding a ghost walk or a vigil, but why would they all be laughing? It didn't make sense. It was clear they were not ghosts – they just looked like solid people, men and women and a few kids were among them too. Greg wandered towards them, curious as to what was going on, trying to eavesdrop, and Jenny reluctantly walked behind him.

And then they saw the person making the crowd laugh; he was standing at the centre of the gathering and they were all facing him. His outline was unmistakable; the wild hair, the melodious voice, the way he was delivering his lines – and Jenny, who has perfect eyesight, thought the man held a feather duster, but then the moon went behind a cloud and the people and the figures dimmed.

Jenny and Greg said the same thing at the same time.

'Ken Dodd.'

They looked at one another. The couple vaguely recalled the comedian being buried in a local cemetery in Liverpool, but when this was, they did not know, nor could they remember what cemetery Dodd had been interred in. What the couple *did* know was that they should leave immediately, and they hurried from the vast place of the departed – or not-quite-departed in this case. It was as if Dodd was perhaps entertaining an audience of deceased people.

The couple ran out of the cemetery, and there outside was a man in a maroon van. Possibly the private eye Greg suspected of following him. He swore at the white-haired man sitting in the van and walked into the well-lit avenue clutching Jenny's hand.

Ken Dodd had been buried in Allerton Cemetery in March 2018, and the couple are not the only ones who have seen his ghost. A few years before, on the sunny Thursday afternoon of 1 November 2018, a 20-year-old girl named Alexandra was waiting at the bus stop on Springwood Avenue outside of Allerton Cemetery. Alex had just been to pay respects to her Nan who was buried at the cemetery. She had called her father on her mobile and told him she'd be waiting at the bus stop outside the cemetery gates. As she stood there, Alex saw everything darken as heavy clouds obscured the feeble sunshine, and then she had the intense feeling of being watched; she literally felt eyes on the back of her head and she turned to see a man in a white suit standing by the gateposts of the cemetery, looking at her. She looked away and wished her father would get a move on.

'Lovely day, isn't it young lady?' said a voice behind her, and Alex turned to get a good look at the man. She nodded and smiled at him; she thought he seemed confused, as he was gazing at the floor with a puzzled look. And then in an instant - he was gone - vanished before her eyes. The girl hurried away from the bus stop and kept walking and looking back and she heard a loud beep which gave her a start. It was her father, and he pulled up in his car and asked her why she wasn't by the bus stop; he said he thought she'd been abducted and had started to panic. Alex jumped in the vehicle and told him about the white-suited ghost. Just under a week after this, Alex saw a picture of Ken Dodd in a newspaper and shuddered; she was certain it had been his ghost she had seen at the cemetery gates. Alex looked up Ken Dodd on Wikipedia and learned that the comedian had died in March of that year and had indeed been buried in Allerton Cemetery. Alex's father said she'd just seen someone who looked like him, but Alex had seen the figure vanish - it had been a ghost; that she was sure of, and that man had looked exactly like the picture of Ken Dodd she had seen on Wikipedia. Another famous comedian (who was also an impressionist, singer and actor) has been seen in the cemetery where he was laid to rest – West Derby Cemetery – and this ghost is that of the outrageous Freddie Starr. When I first heard reports of Freddie's ghost, I was a bit sceptical because I had believed he had been buried in Prescot Parish Church, but I later discovered he had been laid to rest in his mother's grave in West Derby Cemetery.

One woman said his solid-looking ghost passed her on a foggy afternoon in January 2023 in West Derby Cemetery and she had said 'Hiya Freddie,' then realised the star had died some years ago. He had winked at the woman but was walking around as if he was in a daydream. Two men in their fifties visiting the cemetery in early February of that year also claimed to have seen Starr in broad daylight in a black jacket and dark trousers, and he had white hair. One of the men said to his friend, 'Isn't he the spit of Freddie Starr?' and the other man said, 'I've seen him before, I think he's a relative,' but then the two men were shocked to see that the figure had gone. Seconds before, the man had been standing with his head bowed, perhaps looking at a grave. He had literally vanished into thin air. If it was Freddie, I wonder what brought him back?

TALES OF THE
TIME BARRIER

First of all, there is no time barrier – so why do I mention it in the title of this chapter? I am being ironic and I am saying that the so-called barrier to time travel is imaginary; it's psychologically fabricated like a lot of barriers in our lives. There used to be a sound barrier – and that was imaginary too. Until 14 October, 1947 no aircraft had travelled faster than the speed of sound (which is about 767 mph) – and then, upon that aforementioned date in October, an American test pilot named Chuck Yeager travelled faster than the speed of sound in the X-1 rocket plane, instantly showing that it was possible to fly faster than a sound wave – faster than a speeding bullet. Up to that point there were many scientists in the aviation industry who believed supersonic travel would not be possible because planes had undergone too much stress as they neared the speed of sound and some had even crashed because air molecules in front of the plane could not get out of the way as the craft neared the speed of sound and these molecules had been compressed into the plane, and that had exerted a tremendous stress on the plane's structure. However, constant experimenting with different streamlined shapes of planes in wind tunnels eventually paved the way to supersonic travel, and scientists realised the sound barrier had been more of a psychological concept rather than a physical barrier. Nowadays supersonic air travel is ready for a comeback after the heyday of Concorde. The SR-71 Blackbird military plane flew at more than three times the speed of sound and now there is talk of hypersonic jets (and unfortunately hypersonic missiles); hypersonic speed is one that exceeds five times the speed of sound, and there are plans on the drawing board for hypersonic airliners that could travel from Liverpool to New York in an hour. There are probably young EasyJet pilots now flying out of Liverpool John Lennon Airport who will one day qualify as astronauts as their planes fly into orbit at phenomenal speeds.

And so, the *sound barrier* is a term you will rarely hear today, and it will be the same with the *light barrier* one day, despite what the myopic closed-mind scientists of today say. Perhaps nothing can move through space faster than the speed of light so we have to find ways of altering space itself, maybe with gravitational waves. Once upon a time, scientists believed Isaac Newton's laws were perfect – until Einstein came along and proved that the Newtonian laws of physics were wrong on the very small scale – as observed at the Quantum Physics level of reality, and it won't be long before a new science – perhaps even aided by artificial intelligence – comes into being; I think of this as the Third Physics, after Newtonian and Einsteinian Physics, and the Third Physics will allow faster than light travel and superluminal communication, it will circumvent the associated paradoxes that may arise by exceeding the speed of light, and the physicists of the Third Physics will know *why* light and gravity waves move at their specific speed, and this constant may well have something to do with the properties of space and the 'shape' of the universe. Who knows what momentous discoveries regarding the nature of time lay ahead? We often forget: science isn't finished yet – it is an ongoing study that never ends.

The fact that we move through time at a rate of one second per second is undisputed proof that time travel is a reality, and sometimes, some poorly understood conditions arise which send people much further into the future – and the past – and we call these occurrences timeslips for want of a better word. This chapter is concerned with these timeslips and, as well as looking at cases where people have stepped into the past, I will also be looking at the intriguing descriptions of our future world which have been seen in timeslips. Over the years I have received a lot of reports of slippages in time in which the witness – or witnesses – have found themselves in the future, and many of these types of timeslip are remarkably consistent in that they seem to show a future where Britain is a tropical republic. When I first mentioned some of these timeslips decades ago, they were looked at with some scepticism because climate change was not taken seriously by most people at that time, and the idea of Britain becoming a republic looked very unlikely, as it was thought that a majority of people in the UK were all for the Royal Family – but that attitude has changed *drastically* in the 21st Century, with the younger generation opting for a disbandment of the House of Windsor and the formation of a democratic republic. With social media, the widespread voices of dissent – from the young and old - are now being heard, and it would seem that *some form of change* in our society is imminent. On top of that we have calls for Scotland to become an independent country, and the same goes for Wales.

Bearing in mind this sea change in public opinion towards royalty and the creaky political system, the following timeslip incident intrigues me.

In October 2012, a 22-year-old lady named Bethany left the bakery where she worked on her lunch break, intending only to go for a stroll to get a breath of fresh air for a few minutes. She still had on her work overalls and as she strolled up Lyceum Place – the passageway that runs up an incline from the Central Shopping Centre (outside Central Station) to Bold Street, she experienced a timeslip. The exact spot on Lyceum Place where Bethany stepped into the future was two square manhole covers at the top of the incline. The slip began with the classic signs – a feeling of pressure on Bethany's ears, everything sounding muffled for a few moments, and then came the noticing of things that just didn't seem right. Most timeslips last between a few seconds to a couple of minutes, but this one was unusual, because Bethany was gone for about six hours. She found herself in the future, and the fashions of people around her had not looked that different from the fashions of 2012, but the cars looked futuristic to Bethany. One thing Bethany saw does not make seem to make sense, but she is absolutely clear on this; Bethany saw a gleaming white car which had the name Orion on it, and it was moving along silently, as if it was electric, and she is sure the vehicle had the Ford logo upon it. There was a Ford Orion which went into production in the last century in 1983, but that vehicle was discontinued after ten years. Perhaps the car Bethany saw was either a quiet vintage Ford model, or a custom-built electric or hybrid version, built by someone for purely nostalgic reasons.

Bethany has General Anxiety Disorder, and when she realised she was no longer in her familiar time, she panicked, hyperventilated and almost fainted. Two young men, Oliver and Theo, went to Bethany's aid and took her into a café in the Lyceum on Bold Street, where she was given mineral water. They asked her where she lived and offered to give her a lift home but Bethany believed she'd be sectioned if she said she was from another time and said she was okay and needed no assistance. However, the bakery employee then realised she had left her wallet and her phone in her locker at work, as she had only intended to get out of the place for some fresh air because she had felt a panic attack coming on. She calmed herself down and listened to the conversation of Oliver and Theo and established that they were university students, and Oliver took her to a campus where there was American-style election posters everywhere campaigning for a woman (possibly surnamed named Sultana or Santana) – for President. Bethany was then a simple girl with no interest in politics, but she understood, from the snatches of conversation, that Britain was now a republic. Oliver took her to a café on the campus where Bethany was shocked to see cannabis-infused drinks, which she declined. Oliver talked about an upcoming "Eco March" through the city and in passing he mentioned something about the 'Revolution' having been plotted in the main universities across the country and how so much more work needed to be done to amend the 'constitution'.

Bethany thought of her twin sister, Bella, and became upset. Curiously, while Bethany was missing, Bella felt her sister was in danger and kept having waking visions of her being with two young men, and she sensed that something was very unusual about the situation, and that Bethany was near yet so far in some sense. Perhaps it was some extra sensory perception (ESP) phenomena working across time. ESP experiments were conducted by one of the Apollo astronauts in 1971, and it is thought that telepathic communication between minds may not be hindered by vast distances, so perhaps ESP can span the dimension of time in the same way that it can cross the vast distances of space.

Bethany's stay in the future came to an abrupt end after about six hours as she was walking past a building that seems to have been the Yoko Ono Lennon Centre on the corner of Grove Street, Edge Hill, a building that would not be opened until 2022. Bethany had been walking past the centre with Oliver when she saw the building vanish, along with Oliver; she had heard his voice grow fainter and then he was nowhere to be seen. Bethany saw that a triangular green with a path running from Oxford Street to Grove Street going through it now existed where the building had stood seconds ago.

Three days after this extraordinary experience, when Bethany was alone at her house in West Derby, she was visited by two men who claimed they were detectives, and they knew she had been involved in a timeslip. Each of the men showed a plastic card bearing what seemed to be a silver hologram sticker showing their face, and one of the cards bore the name

Michael Stendek with the words "Detective Inspector" in bold below it, and Bethany also noticed what looked like raised Braille dots to the left of the man's photograph. The men interrogated Bethany in her kitchen and seemed to want to know the names of all the people she had met during the timeslip and other details. They warned Bethany to tell no one about her experience because 'such an unlawful disclosure would be a very serious crime and it would result in imprisonment.'

The officious men left after Detective Inspector Stendek said they would be in touch again in a few days. Bethany had a feeling the men were impostors; there was just something 'off' about them that she couldn't put her finger on, and so she contacted the police by phone and a police officer stated that no detectives had been sent to Bethany's home, and that they were unable to trace anyone in the force named Michael Stendek, which deepens the mystery of this case. The two men were never heard from again. I interviewed Bethany at length, and what set her apart from the occasional liar and attention seeker was her wish not to be identified. I sometimes have a sixth sense when I'm ascertaining whether a person is a liar or a fantasist, and Bethany seemed – to me, anyway – to have experienced something truly inexplicable. Bethany mentioned seeing cannabis-infused drinks in a café on a university campus during her visit to what seems to have been the future, and this observation immediately reminded me of the following timeslip account, which is said to have happened the year before Bethany experienced her shift in time.

In October 2011, a 24-year-old lady named Lucy left

Primark in Liverpool city centre with her boyfriend Adam and decided to try the new coffee shop on the corner of Church Street and Parker Street - and Lucy was a bit disoriented as she could have sworn Schuh (the shoe store) was at that location but Adam drew her attention to the name of the coffee shop: The Marijuana Dispensary. He went into the shop, and feeling the urge to pee he went to a door marked with the baffling sign "G Toilet", and when he returned, Lucy nodded to a bearded man sitting at the counter and whispered to Adam, 'He works here. I asked him if it was legal to put cannabis in coffee and he didn't even reply.' So Adam looked at the menu and asked the young vacant-looking member of staff if he could have two "Pot Luck" lattes - and received no answer. The man just sat on a stool, gazing past the couple as if he was in a daydream.

'He looks stoned,' said Adam, 'maybe he's been drinking the coffee.'

Adam and Lucy then left in a huff, disgusted by the dreadful customer-unfriendly service and that evening, Adam happened to mention The Marijuana Dispensary to his friends in his local pub, and his mates assured him there was no such café at that spot on Church Street - the Schuh store was there they told Adam, and his friends said that there was no place in the British Isles where marijuana was legal barring certain official cannabis-based medication, perhaps. Adam insisted there *was* such a café and he was so confident that the place existed (after all, he *had* been inside the café) he said he'd give £100 to anyone if the Marijuana Dispensary was a figment of his mind – and the mind of his girlfriend, who had also visited it with him. Will, Adam's best friend, drove him downtown to Church Street - and there was Schuh the shoe store - and there was no trace of any coffee shop called The Marijuana Dispensary. Lucy believed she and her boyfriend had somehow walked into some café in the future, when cannabis has been legalized, perhaps. Lucy thinks the timeslip angle might explain why the staff was ignoring her and Adam during their visit to the "Dispensary" that day – perhaps the staff couldn't see or hear them because of the one-way nature of the timeslip, whereas Adam and Lucy could clearly see the staff and their controversial shop. Here is another fascinating account of a future establishment being visited via a possible timeslip.

People from all walks of life who have found themselves apparently stepping into another era have told me again and again how crossing the 'time barrier' was not marked by lightning bolts flashing around them and they were not enveloped by a swirling vortex of plasma – that is how Hollywood depicts time travel. I'd say quite a few 'timewalkers' do not even know they have entered another period until they notice someone dressed quaintly in old-fashioned clothes, or realise a building they were looking at had long been demolished. In the case of a 70-year-old man named Alfie, he seems to have nonchalantly walked unaware into a future period that has not yet arrived – but I feel it's not that far away. One bitterly cold afternoon in December 1992, Alfie went to Mathew Street to catch up with his old mate Ted, and he noticed a new pub called "Le Scouseur Bar" – so he went into the place and thought someone was pulling his leg. A tall man at the bar was wearing curlers, and next to him stood a pretty young lady with luminous, colourful clothes, and to this woman, Alfie smiled, nodded at the man in rollers and said, 'Is he for real?'

The lady returned a puzzled look, then looked Alfie up and down. He talked about the recent Derby game to the barman and asked for a pint of lager – and the barman looked at the fiver in Alfie's hand and shook his head. The tall gent with the curlers started laughing at Alfie, and said, 'Lager? Try this!' And he offered the elderly man a cocktail with glowing cubes. Alfie shook his head but the man insisted, so Alfie sipped the drink, and in seconds he started to giggle. Alfie then saw something very odd – the football match on the huge wall-sized screen featured male and female players.

'What in God's name – ' Alfie said, smirking at the screen.

'Newcastle and Tottenham,' said the man, who later told Alfie his name was Ozzy. 'What do you think of Happy?' Ozzy asked, nodding to the drink. Alfie thought the drink had been spiked and turned and hurried out of the bar. He later bumped into Ted, who was sitting on his usual stool at his usual pub on Mathew Street, and Alfie told him, in-between outbreaks of uncontrollable chuckling because of that drink, what had just happened to him in the bizarre pub. Ted said he had never heard of a place called Le Scouseur Bar, and he joked, 'Have you been smoking something, Alfie?'

'I'm serious mate,' Alfie told Ted, holding his sides because he felt he was going to emit a belly laugh.

'Sure you don't want to go to the Royal [Hospital] and get checked over?' Ted asked his friend with a concerned expression.

Alfie shook his head and grinned then grimaced, and he said, 'Ted, come with me and I'll show you this joint; you can see it with your own eyes – it's bizarre; a fellah had rollers in like a judy, honest.'

'You're going round the bend, you are,' replied Ted, 'have you been on the Aussie whites again?'

'Oh for God's sake, Ted, just remove your lazy arse from that stool and come and see the place; talk about sedentary...'

'Come on then,' Ted got off the stool and walked out the pub, and he followed Alfie around Mathew Street, but Le Scouseur Bar was nowhere to be seen.

'This is bleedin' bizarre,' said Alfie, standing on the corner of Whitechapel and Mathew Street, 'unless it was on Temple Court.'

'I'll be in court for doing you in if you don't shut up about this nonsense,' said Ted, losing his patience; he was losing valuable drinking time on this wild goose chase for a non-existent bar his barmy friend had obviously imagined.

'It wasn't nonsense, Ted, it was a real place!' retorted Alfie.

Ted said to a well-known drunk named Johnny, who just happened to be staggering past, 'Hey mate, settle an argument for me will you?'

'Oh don't be asking him,' moaned Alfie, 'he doesn't know what day it is.'

'Who – who doesn't know what day it is, eh?' said the offended Johnny in a slurred voice, 'I know perfectly – perfectly – what day it is; it's er...'

'Never mind that, Johnny,' interrupted Ted, 'all I want to know is this: is there a pub called Le Scouseur

Bar on Mathew Street? You know every boozer in town and if there's anyone who'd know where that pub was, it'd be you.'

'Are you – are you insinuating I'm a plonky or something?' Johnny asked, grabbing hold of a lamp post to steady himself. He glared at Ted. 'I might just go and see Rex Makin round the corner and get you done for defamation of character, pal.'

'Never mind all that Johnny,' sighed Ted, 'have you *ever* heard of a pub called Le Scouseur bar?'

'Yes, yeah,' said Johnny.

'Ha! See? I told you Ted!' said Alfie, quite animated now.

'Where is it then?' Ted asked Johnny, who shrugged.

'You asked me if I had heard of it, well that's a trick question isn't it?' said Johnny, baffling Ted and Alfie. He continued, 'I heard about it from you, just then, so yeah, I have heard of it.'

'Oh my [expletive deleted] God,' growled Ted. 'Johnny, have you ever seen a pub of that name on Mathew Street?'

'What name?' Johnny asked, looking genuinely confused.

'We're wasting our time with him,' said Alfie, walking away. Alfie looked for that strange pub till the day he passed away, and never found it again. If it was indeed a timeslip showing a pub of the future, and possibly a future that is not that far away, we may one day see Le Scouseur Bar opening on the world-famous Mathew Street.

The following account of a possible time-displaced item seems to agree with the chronology of the future suggested by other timeslips. In 1999 a 32-year-old man named Simon found a 100 kg parcel outside his shop on The Colonnades, Albert Dock one morning. The parcel had strange coded symbols on it and clearly said "By Drone" (and no one knew what a delivery drone was in 1999). The address the parcel bore was the "Omega Parliament Building L3 4AA". The geographical origin of the package was printed on the parcel as: Houses of the Oireachtas, and the post code was D02 XR20. In other words, the parcel was from the Parliament of Ireland building in Dublin. Simon showed the parcel to his usual postman, who said it had not been sent by Royal Mail – but by some private parcel delivery business called Arrow Republic Mail, which he had never heard of. Likewise, no one in The Colonnades of the Albert Dock had ever heard of the "Omega Parliament Building". Simon asked the postman if he could open the parcel and was told that he couldn't, technically. He would have to contact the sender first and tell them about the unsolicited goods – but there was no name of a sender on the parcel. Simon telephoned the Irish Parliament and was eventually told that no one there had sent any parcel to the Albert Dock, and no one had heard of the Omega Parliament Building in Liverpool either. Then the parcel vanished. I mentioned the strange incident on *The Billy Butler Show* and a security guard called me on air with a very interesting story. He had been a guard at the Albert Dock shortly after it had opened, and one night on his rounds near the Colonnades he got lost. He found himself in a huge bright domed structure – and in glowing letters over the grand arched entrance it said Omega Parliament Building. Various speakers from political parties were debating in this building, and the guard became bored by the discussions and left the place to tell a colleague about 'the new building'. The guard's co-worker said there was no big domed building anywhere near the Albert Dock and so he went with his colleague to see this Omega Parliament Building but it couldn't be found. The guard who had seen the building and ventured into it to hear the stuffy parliamentary debates was so affected by the strange incident, he took time off work and asked his doctor if he had a mental health problem – but not in those words; it was 1999 and a stigma was still attached to all things associated with mental health. The guard's actually question to his GP was, 'Am I losing it?'

The doctor recommended taking it easy and having a fortnight's rest. The guard later returned to work and never saw the enigmatic domed building again.

If the Omega Parliament Building is in our future and not some parallel world, this hints that Liverpool will either have a northern parliament in the near future, or, chillingly, perhaps something will happen to London which results in the transfer of the capital to Liverpool? Could that something be some enemy state's Intercontinental Ballistic Missile wiping out London in a nuclear attack?

In early July 2023 I interviewed a man named Rob who got in touch with me via the *Liverpool Echo* after reading my column in the newspaper about the Bold Street timeslips. I checked out all of the details Rob supplied about his alleged timeslip experience and they seem to vindicate that something strange happened to him. I contacted his former employer who said that Rob *did* report in sick after saying something bizarre had happened to him in March 1987 in the Bold Street area, and I also checked up on a few other people Rob mentions in his story and they confirmed he had told them of his experience in early April 1987 and they had thought he was joking at first or possibly pulling an April Fool joke. Here's the gist of the story, although there are a few things Rob told me which I have withheld until I research the claims in more depth.

In March 1987, a man in his thirties named Rob was heading for Central Station to see if he could travel to Aigburth to visit a relative. He had just been to Dixons on Ranelagh Street to look at some home computers. He was not thinking of anything remotely paranormal, but when Rob was about to walk into the railway station he felt ill, and dizzy, and abandoned the trip to Aigburth and walked lethargically up the incline leading from the railway station to Bold Street. This is the very same incline Bethany was walking up when her timeslip experience - detailed earlier in this chapter - started, and this location was also the spot where one of the first timeslip cases I looked into took place in the 1990s when an off-duty policeman stepped into the 1950s. The case of the timeslipped policemen has since gone viral and is often repeated inaccurately on social media and some television shows. The official name of this timeslip hotspot is Lyceum Place, and it is about 65 feet in length and 15 feet wide. It is named after its close proximity to the much-neglected Lyceum, a Neoclassical building of sandstone that was built in 1802 to serve as a newsroom and a library; it was England's first subscription library, but later became a gentleman's club. Since then it has been a post office, a building society, a co-operative bank and several drinking establishments, including Life Bar and Prohibition. The threat of demolition is constantly hanging over this beautiful Grade II listed building and in all seriousness I lay a terrible curse on anyone who demolishes it. At the time of writing, the facade of the deserted Lyceum is covered with a ghastly board featuring 'artwork' and collages of photographs.

Back to Lyceum place; Rob walked up this passageway from Central Station to Bold Street and one of the first things he saw was a palm tree in front of what should have been Radiant House, the original head office of British Gas, but instead, Rob saw a whitewashed building – and what on earth was a palm tree doing in front of it? This thought crossed his mind as he walked tentatively onto Bold Street. Rob saw palm trees to his right and recognised none of the shops. He also became aware of an unbearable warmth which he likened to walking around in Florida. He walked down Bold Street and crossed into an almost unrecognisable grassed over Church Street, and saw most of the people were dressed in white - the men in white suits and white wide-brimmed hats, and women in white skirts (but a few in trousers of that colour too); they also had wide white hats on. Rob thought he was going mad, and started to panic. He heard a low pitched sound down the bottom of Church Street and saw it was some type of monorail coming from the direction of James Street. This monorail stopped at a station near what must have been Whitechapel and Rob saw the words "Anglesey to Manchester" on the front of the monorail. He lit a ciggie to calm himself and got some hostile looks from passers-by for doing so. Rob passed through what seems to have been a very flowery park near Derby Square, where the Queen Victoria Monument normally stood (but it was absent), and the plants there were huge tropical ferns and strange brightly coloured flowers. A policeman walked past Rob and gazed at the cigarette in his mouth and glared at him, so Rob threw it on the floor and stepped on it, and the policeman, who was dressed in white with a strange helmet, looked him up and down. Rob turned and walked the way he had come and became soaked with perspiration. He could not find Central Station; there was a huge store which had a variety of what looked like (humanoid) robots in its tinted blue windows. Rob walked around for ages trying to find Central Station and then something bizarre happened; as Rob reached what would be Lewis's Corner (where Ranelagh Street meets Renshaw Street) he heard his eardrums pop and found himself on Renshaw Street in what seemed to have been the aftermath of an air-raid in World War Two. He saw ruined buildings, fires, and rubble across the road, and an acrid aroma was hanging in the air, but then bizarrely, he heard a man's voice shouting him. It was a friend who was still in 1987 and he was standing outside of what was then the Newington pub (now The Blarney Stone), and Rob walked over to his friend, an electrician named Alec, and said, 'Have you seen this?' and Rob turned to point at the World War Two scene but it had gone; the street had reverted to modern times. Alec had not seen anything strange; he had merely seen Rob walking in a confused state along Renshaw Street. Rob gave Alec a brief summary of what had happened to him, and Alec could see Rob's clothes were soaked with sweat. The two men went into the Newington pub and Rob had to go the toilet and swill his face and remove his denim jacket because it was soaked. Alec listened to Rob, who thought he had lost his mind and assured him that he must have been in some type of 'timewarp'. Rob was so shook up by the incident he called his boss at work and said he wouldn't be coming in (he worked nights at his job) and he told his employer everything that had happened. If this incident did happen as Rob describes it, then it may have been a glimpse of a future that has been reported to me before – a tropical Liverpool caused by climate change. What's also interesting about this slip in time is the way it changed to the days of World War Two before Rob found himself back in 1987. I'm still researching this intriguing story.

And now for some timeslips into the past, and I'll start with a fascinating account that came my way via a call to BBC Radio Merseyside in response to my weekly spot on the *Billy Butler Show*. The call came from a former highways cleaner named Kevin. In March 1999, Kevin, aged 32, and fellow road sweeper Len, aged 50, met on the corner of Bold and Slater Streets, where their routes overlapped. The men had known one another by sight for about three years in their occupation but never socialised outside of work. Kevin had been sweeping Bold Street and Len had been on Slater Street, and it had been a drizzly and pretty uneventful day. Kevin had used a pressure washer to clean chewing gum from a pavement up near Leece Street earlier in the morning, and now, as the afternoon progressed, he was looking forward to knocking off around 4pm to drive back to the cleansing depot. In recent weeks Kevin had been suffering from bouts of depression and was seriously thinking of going back to college to further his prospects for a better job. The two men chatted on the corner near Slater Street about sport, and during their conversation, Kevin noticed Bold Street had *changed* and it baffled him. Then he saw Slater Street looked quite misty and there were barefooted children running around and a shabby-looking man in a battered top hat came out of nowhere and looked the men (who were wearing yellow high-vis jackets) up and down, and this scruffy fellow was then joined by a woman in 19th century attire, and two other men who came from Wood Street round the corner. Len and Kevin were surrounded by these backdated people and Len wondered if they were film extras to some Victorian movie being shot locally, but Kevin felt they were ghosts, but he could not understand why the street also looked old-fashioned. The two men from Wood Street produced knives and looked at the top-hatted man and the latter said what sounded like "Bald-headed hermit," to Len - but Kevin thought the man in the topper had said "Herbert" - anyway - the two knifemen lunged at Kevin and Len, and Len, knowing a little martial arts, punched one of the men, knocking his hat off, and he tried to parry the knife-wielding hand and somehow the blade was knocked back and it cut the man's other hand. Len saw the blood drip onto his own jacket and jeans. Kevin kicked the crotch of the man attacking him, and then a well-to-do-looking man in a topper appeared from Bold Street and shouted something the street cleaners could not understand, and the whole surroundings reverted back to 1999 in a flash. Kevin saw a startled modern-day youth standing a few yards away, looking at him and Len (who still had blood from his attacker on him). The sweepers contacted Granada Reports to tell them of their bizarre and frightening experience – but no one got back to them – and so the men then telephoned the newsdesk of the local press – but no one came to interview them. The men put the weird incident down to something supernatural, and only thought about timeslips much later when they read an article I'd written on the Bold Street activity in the *Merseymart* newspaper. Len said the bloodstains on his jacket and jeans faded within minutes and did not leave a trace. When I mentioned the incident on local radio, a woman who had worked as a secretary for a legal firm in the city centre told me she had witnessed the entire incident, and she gave details that were later confirmed by Kevin and described the two men accurately. The secretary, who was 19 at the time, had seen the figures involved in the melee vanish into thin air. This timeslip is unusual in that blood was spilled – a person from the a future time – from the point of view of the 19th century attackers – accidentally caused a person in the past to suffer physical injury (in this case a knife wound). This would seem to prove – against the reasoning of modern physicists – that we can change the past. Such acts are deemed to be paradoxical by scientists, so that if you go back in time you theoretically cannot shoot dead your father because you wouldn't exist in the first place (discounting that the shooting took place before your birth) – but the incident in 1999 seems to make a mockery of this 'rule'. In theory, someone could travel back into the past and kidnap Hitler as a baby and bring him up in the 21st Century, thus preventing World War Two – but such a theory may not work. The time traveller could return from the 1890s and find that World War Two still happened; another dictator named Goebbels was the Fuhrer and being more stable than Hitler, almost won the war. Another possibility is that World War Two still went on from 1939 to 1945 as before, with Hitler committing suicide in the Berlin bunker, because the traveller, by kidnapping the baby Adolf had created a parallel world where things turned out different – but unfortunately the time traveller returned, not to the altered course of history, but to the one he was familiar with.

So, if we scour the newspaper archives relating to Liverpool, we may not find a report of a man in a weird yellow (hi-vis) jacket causing a mugger to stab himself because the incident happened in a newly created alternative history. This is all theoretical of course. Let us return to some more timeslip reports in which the past was apparently opened up to the people of the present.

On a sunny day in early September 2009, a 22-year-old Liverpool John Moores University dropout named Larissa was travelling northwards with her boyfriend Lee in his battered old Volkswagen camper van along Hall Lane in the district of Lathom, Ormskirk. Lee decided to stop for an impromptu picnic and the couple camped in a field close to some farmland. They sat on a pink gingham sheet eating sandwiches when Larissa noticed something odd – it looked like a cumulus cloud, but it was not in the sky, it was on the ground in a field about 500 feet away, and as the couple looked on the cloud flattened out but did not dissipate. Traffic slowed nearby on Hall Lane as motorists took in the odd spectacle. Larissa got up and went to have a closer look, and Lee told her to stay put in case the cloud was some gas or chemical fertilizer leak, but off Larissa went – and when she didn't return after fifteen long minutes, Lee drove the camper van to the cloud – and he saw it fade away. Larissa was nowhere to be seen. He immediately pulled out his mobile and dialled her, then heard her iPhone ringing behind him – in the pink holdall Larissa had packed all her stuff into. She'd been sitting next to that tote bag (as she had called it) as she picnicked with Lee. He got out of the camper van and looked around and it was plain to see that Larissa was nowhere in sight, and she could not have gone anywhere.

Larissa, meanwhile, found the fields crawling with what looked like Parliamentarian soldiers of the type who fought in the English Civil War (1642–1651), and at first the girl thought the whole thing was one of those re-enactments put on by vintage military enthusiasts. Larissa saw an old woman with a white "mop hat" and long shawl and a dress made of rough-looking dark brown material that went to her feet. She looked Larissa up and down, and then she shouted something to one of the "Roundhead" soldiers on a horse. He rode over to Larissa, dismounted, narrowed his eyes as he gazed at her, then made a grab at her and scrutinized her arm and chest tattoos. He then smiled as he felt her orange and green hair.

'Get your hands off me,' said Larissa, and she looked back, hoping to see Lee and the camper van – but the fields were dotted with soldiers.

An older, corpulent soldier with a Vandyke and rosy cheeks came on the scene, and seeing Larissa, he asked the soldier holding her, 'What is this?' and then he embraced Larissa, who was now trembling; at this point the awful realisation that she had gone back in time made Larissa feel nauseous.

'The green lady - or a witch,' one of the soldiers remarked and chuckled, and the man holding her added, 'and a fair witch at that.'

'Who are you?' asked the older, stocky soldier. Larissa had a feeling he was a captain or lieutenant from his swaggering overconfident nature.

'I don't have to tell you anything,' said Larissa, annoyed now because he was feeling her orange and green hair with a look of fascination.

The soldier held Larissa's face in his hands and puckered his lips as if he was going to kiss her, but then he clenched his teeth and his hands slid down from her face and gripped at her neck. 'Hark, strumpet!' he seethed, 'Respond to my inquiry, sorceress! By what audacity dost thou dare converse with me in such insolence?'

Larissa felt his large rough hands gripping her throat, and she was afraid to speak, to utter a word in case he strangled her. His piercing blue eyes contrasted against his face, which had now become flushed with anger.

'Wench – ' he started to say, but then he faded away and Larissa heard his faint voice cry out, 'Whence did the enchantress abscond?' and another voice said, 'Verily, she hath eluded our grasp!'

And then they were all gone, along with a mansion Larissa had seen in the distance. That would have been Lathom House, a stronghold of Royalists until it fell to

Cromwell's troops during a siege in December 1645. Larissa spotted her boyfriend in his van and started crying. When Lee got out the van and ran to his girlfriend, asking where she had been, she tried to talk but kept sobbing. Lee looked at her neck and said, 'What are those marks?'

On Larissa's delicate neck were reddish patches with slight bruises that darkened over the next few days – the marks left by the gripping hands of a man who had lived 364 years ago. When Larissa finally managed to tell Lee what had happened, he bundled his girlfriend into the van and frightened her by saying, 'I'm a bit psychic – I've never told you that before, and I have this feeling they [meaning the Civil War "ghosts"] are still around us now, watching us, and they might try and snatch you again.'

Larissa is not sure if what happened next was some form of autosuggestion brought on by Lee's creepy comments, but as she was getting into the camper van, she felt someone touch her behind and mutter the word 'witch' – and it had an echoing quality to it. The couple left the area and have not been back to that field in Ormskirk since.

Early in 2023 I had an interesting chat with a priest who told me how, in December 1977, his mother, Elizabeth, aged 70, was shopping (looking for gloves and a scarf) on Bold Street with her two daughters, but slipped away from them as they stopped to chat to a female friend. Elizabeth entered a lovely old shop that looked as if it was lit by gaslight, and a grey-haired spectacled man came out the back of the shop dressed in rather old attire, and for a moment, Elizabeth wondered if he was a ghost, but he was obviously solid, and he said, 'Good afternoon madam; are you browsing or seeking anything in particular?' to which Elizabeth replied, 'I'm looking for a decent pair of gloves and a scarf, actually.'

'Ah, I'm afraid you won't find them in here;' the man replied, 'this is an antiques shop, bric-a-brac and the like. May I suggest Faraday & Sons? They're at Number 4 Bold Street and they sell very reliable gloves,' and the man pointed to his left, indicating the direction of the shop.

'Thanks,' said Elizabeth, and she looked at the window of the shop, and saw people outside were not dressed in the fashions of the Seventies, and she just had a weird feeling she had gone back in time. When she reached the shop door she saw she was right - there was no sign of her daughters - just people dressed in old fashioned clothes, and she could hear horse clip-clopping along in the distance. Elizabeth opened the door, and the daughters were standing there, still chatting. Elizabeth stepped back, closed the door - and the daughters vanished, and again she saw the street as it was in some bygone time. Elizabeth turned and looked at the spectacled man, who was standing there with a look of suspicion on his face, and she said, 'Excuse me, but can you tell me what the date is?'

'It's the eighteenth,' the man slowly said. He thinned his eyes as he looked at Elizabeth and she got the impression he thought she was going to try and perpetrate some con-trick. In a self-conscious manner, feeling a bit silly, Elizabeth said, 'What *year* though?' And the man returned a perplexed expression, and he answered, 'The 18th July, 1918,' then smiled, as if he thought Elizabeth was joking, and added, 'Thursday.'

Elizabeth said, 'Oh my God,' and she stepped outside the shop, walked unsteadily to her daughters and shook the arm of one of them, and said, 'You're not going to believe this,' but her daughter seemed annoyed, as she was talking to her friend and replied, 'Hang on a sec, mum.'

The other daughter asked her mum what the matter was, and Elizabeth dragged her to the shop, which had now been replaced by a shop that sold Airfix models and other toys.

Elizabeth's daughters knew their mum was not an imaginative type so they could not explain what had happened. Incidentally, in 1918, the retail store J Faraday & Sons was indeed located at 4 Bold Street, just as the man in the antiques shop had stated when directing Elizabeth to the store to buy gloves and a scarf. Our present science will find it exceedingly difficult to explain how a woman in 1977 was able to walk into an antiques shop in 1918, but Elizabeth assured her daughters it really happened and these types of timeslips are still being reported to me every week. Some people report the timeslip to me immediately, but some keep it a secret for a while and then tell me or tell friends and relatives who in turn contact me, but I've noticed that by talking about the timeslip phenomenon in books, newspaper articles and even posts on social media, a lot of people are realising there is no stigma attached to talking about the subject. Once upon a time, people would be ridiculed or have their mental health questioned if they claimed to have been in another time, but nowadays there's a fascination with the subject. I even have people asking

397

me where they are most likely to experience a timeslip because they have had enough of the trials of modern life and would happily live in the 1960s or some other bygone age, and what's odd is that these people are not all mature nostalgic types, hankering for an age they once lived in; some of them are young people who were born in the 1990s and even later. This brings us to the next incident, which seems to have been some slip in time back to the 1960s or possibly the early 1970s. On Tuesday 22 March, 2011, three sisters, aged 14, 16 and 18, slept over at their aunt's house on Woolton's Blackwood Avenue, and because their cousins were also visiting at the same time, all the bedrooms in the house were taken, so the three sisters had to sleep in the same bed. They all got to sleep by around 1am, but then at 2:30am, the trio all experienced a shivery feeling which woke them up at the same time, and the girls felt as if the room was moving. Then the three sisters saw the dour bedroom wallpaper change to a flowery pattern, and the room was bathed in rainbow light. At first, the oldest sister though the coloured light was the headlights of a passing car shining into the room, but the spectrum of light moved left and right, up and down, and then twelve strangers appeared and they were all dressed in 1960s or early 1970s clothes. The oldest sister clearly recalls there were seven men and five women present. These people seemed to be at a party and the girls could hear music playing. The dozen people didn't notice the sisters at first, but one spectacled man with a short pointed black vandyke beard said, 'Where did *they* come from?' before making a very inappropriate remark about the girls, who started to shout for their aunt. The man with the glasses smiled at the teens and started to climb onto the bed, and the sisters clung to one another as the spectacled man walked on all fours across the bed – and then in an instant the man vanished and the room became dark again. The auntie of the girls and two of the girls' cousins from a nearby room came into the room and immediately the aunt detected an aroma of marijuana. None of the girls even smoked and even the oldest one only had the occasional drink at Christmas. The girls told their aunt about the room changing and the strangers they'd seen and the two cousins who came to the room said they had heard loud music coming from the girls' room and a man's voice. The auntie had lived at the house for twenty years and had never seen anything ghostly on the premises in that time. On the bed, one of the girls found an emerald earring which was later identified as an Albert Weiss earring, manufactured in the 1960s. This is a peculiar incident, but I suspect the twelve people who appeared in the bedroom were not ghosts in the usual sense; I think they may have 'come through' from the past through some timeslip mechanism. It would explain how the wallpaper changed – the room was reverting to an earlier interior. It's strange how one remnant from that slip in time – the earring – managed to stay in 2011. It's rare for something to come through from a timeslip and stay in the present for any length of time, but in the summer of 2006, a 20-year-old girl named Emmaline was walking along Wood Street on her way to the Philharmonic pub when she suddenly saw old-fashioned vehicles and people dressed in clothes that seemed to indicate the 1960s. Emmaline walked on, thinking perhaps the street had been turned into a movie set by some film company (a not unusual occurrence in Liverpool) but when she turned a corner, Emmaline was shocked to realise she had on a purple dress - a dress she had never seen before in her life. She'd had a white tee shirt and jeans on, but now the jeans and the shirt had gone and she had on the dress. She still had on her pair of Converse All Stars. Emmaline went to see a friend in Grand Central on Renshaw Street and told her what had happened, and being a hypochondriac, Emmaline thought she was suffering from some time of premature dementia, as she had no recollection of buying the dress and putting it on and started to panic, but her friend Lisa said the label on the dress said Foale and Tuffin - a 1960s firm that were part of the Swinging Sixties fashion scene, and the dress looked brand new. The dress label read 'size 16' and even though Emmaline was a 12, it fitted her snugly, but some 1960s sizes do not correspond with modern ones. I wonder what happened to Emmaline's modern tee shirt and jeans - where did they go? It's a strange case, even as timeslips go.

One of the most intriguing cases of a possible timeslip came my way many years ago in 2001 when I was a regular guest on BBC Radio Merseyside's *Billy Butler Show*, talking about local mysteries (usually of a supernatural nature) each week. My afternoon slot proved to be very popular and of the million listeners who tuned in, quite a lot sent me letters, emails or sometimes telephoned me on air, and the following story came my way when one listener visited the radio station before I was due to go on air. The listener was Peter O'Hare, and he told me about a weird experience his father – Peter O'Hare (senior) had.

In the summer of 1930, Peter O'Hare – who hailed from Huyton – had to get out of New York for reasons he never explained. O'Hare had been a merchant seaman who had decided to stay in the Big Apple in 1928, the year before the calamitous Wall Street Crash, and he fell in with local hoodlums. O'Hare wrote regularly to his mother in Huyton but after February 1929 the letters ceased abruptly. There were rumours which reached Liverpool's underworld grapevine that O'Hare had somehow been involved in the infamous St Valentine's Day Massacre in Chicago. By July 1930 O'Hare had bleached his hair white, was living the life of a hobo and, desperate to leave the States, he stowed away on the Liverpool-bound Cunard liner *Laconia*, together with a Birkenhead gambler named Ralph Jones. The *Laconia* left the New York docks with Jones pretending he was a third-class passenger and sleeping in an unoccupied cabin, while the cautious O'Hare slept under a canvas-covered lifeboat. Three days into the voyage, Ralph Jones won a small fortune at a poker game, but when he went to the ship's purser to claim his winnings, the purser carried out the routine procedure of checking Ralph's name against the passenger list – and he saw it was absent. 'Wait there, Mr Jones,' said the purser, obviously on his way to report Jones as a stowaway. Jones fled, and hid in the lifeboat Peter O'Hare was hiding in. O'Hare was furious, as he thought the first thing the ship's officers would do would be to search the lifeboats – but instead, something extremely bizarre happened. Everything went quiet, and O'Hare noticed it first; there were over 2,000 passengers on the *Laconia* and yet the two stowaways could not hear a single voice. Jones lifted the canvas and peeped out. The deck was deserted – and stranger still, that deck and all of the fittings looked different. Despite O'Hare trying to pull him back into the lifeboat, Jones got on the deck and said, 'Where's everyone gone? Have they abandoned ship? Are we sinking?'

O'Hare left the lifeboat, intending to punch Jones to stop him from attracting the attention of the ship's officers, but he saw his colleague was right; there wasn't a living soul about – and O'Hare also noted that the ship now bore no resemblance to the *Laconia*.

'This is very fishy – very fishy indeed,' murmured O'Hare, and Jones grabbed his arm and said, 'O'Hare – is this someone's idea of a joke?' and he nodded at the name on the lifeboat. It read *S.S. Titanic*.

O'Hare took a deep breath. He pinched his own arm, thinking he was perhaps still asleep in the lifeboat and dreaming this – but it was no dream. 'It can't be the *Titanic* – obviously it can't; she went down nearly twenty years ago.'

'She did,' said a stunned Jones, 'so, unless this is one of her lifeboats – maybe they salvaged it;' and he couldn't finish the sentence.

O'Hare inspected the other lifeboats; they all had the name *S.S. Titanic* on them at one end and "Liverpool" at the other. This was taking a joke too far – or the men were really on the *Titanic*. This was the thought of Peter O'Hare. He and Ralph Jones walked the deck, which seemed much longer than the deck of the *Laconia*. Then Jones saw the name *RMS Titanic* on life rings mounted about the place, and those four huge black-topped funnels above – an orangey shade of buff – did not look right. 'This can't be,' said Ralph Jones, his superstitious nature getting the better of him, 'this is a trick of the Devil.'

'Talk of the Devil and he'll appear,' O'Hare suddenly remarked, 'who's this fellah?'

The figure of a man stood on the promenade deck about 70 yards away. Jones had the superior eyesight of the two, and said the stranger had on a cloth cap. The stowaways walked slowly towards him, and O'Hare slyly produced a revolver, which surprised Jones. As the duo drew nearer, they could see the man was young – late teens, early twenties – with a round baby face. He put his hands up when he saw O'Hare's revolver.

'Do you know we're on the *Titanic*?' the young man asked in a Scottish accent. It transpired he had been a stowaway too, and that his name was John Dempsey, trying to get home to Lanarkshire. He was as baffled as O'Hare and Jones, but O'Hare searched him anyway. The three of them explored the deserted liner, and Jones saw the fine food and wine laid out on the dining tables, but was simply too scared to touch the food and drink. Then Dempsey yelped. He said something had brushed past him. The men then heard faint voices – people in conversation – people laughing, and an aroma of tobacco. Now and then the trio would see shadowy figures darting about and then Jones bumped into something which had a feminine scent, and this unseen presence said, 'Oh! What was that?'

Jones panicked and ran up to the deck with O'Hare and Dempsey following. Jones cried: 'We're on a ship full of ghosts! I've got to get off!'

O'Hare struggled to explain his take on the uncanny proceedings. 'It's as if these people are there, but in another time; it's like the way the blade of a fan seems to vanish when it turns fast.'

'I wonder if it will hit the iceberg?' said Dempsey, 'because it hit an iceberg – the *Titanic* did.'

'I *know* what happened to the *Titanic*, and I want to get off this ship now!' shouted Jones, grabbing the handrail. He looked out to the infinite sea – nothing on the horizon but sky. Dempsey said they could try and steer the ship and Jones snapped, and screamed at him to shut up. Then the deck was suddenly full of flickering shapes, and voices; the passengers of 1912 were slowly returning. Jones ran to one of the lifeboats and hid in it. He said the Lord's Prayer over and over and O'Hare got in the lifeboat with the revolver. He too was beginning to believe that Jones was right – that perhaps some demonic force was at work. Then they heard a crash, and screams and the canvas flew off the lifeboat, lifted by a gale. O'Hare and Jones were back on the *Laconia*. They made it to Liverpool with a tale no one would believe. Dempsey was discovered in a lifeboat and ended up in Walton Gaol. I have checked these claims out and found them to be true, printed in black and white in the old newspaper archives. In his later years, Peter O'Hare often told the story to his son, and stuck to the theory that through some 'fault in the running of time' (as he put it) he and two men had ended up on the world's most famous liner, and the passengers on that doomed vessel had, for some reason, been at some higher frequency of reality, so they appeared as flickering shadows.

I've changed a few names in the following story for

legal reasons. One of the strangest and most intriguing cases in my almanac of the paranormal concerns a down-at-heel self-appointed private investigator in his late forties named Manley, who, in 2007 was listed in a telephone directory of local businesses with the wrong phone number. Through some misprint, the telephone number of Phil Manley's one-man detective business was placed under the entry for a well-respected private inquiry agency, and so, one Saturday in July 2009, the rock-bottom private investigator, living on coffee and tobacco with a chronic gambling problem, took a call from a woman (who sounded well-to-do) named Virginia who thought she was ringing Discreet Investigations Ltd. Virginia wanted a private detective to follow her daughter because she was 'knocking around with some very strange people at night.' Phil met with Virginia at his 'office' (his brother's flat) over a cake shop on Church Street, and accepted the simple job, for which he would receive £60 per day plus expenses. Phil intended to draw this job out for that kind of money. Virginia gave him some photographs of her 14-year-old daughter Toni and said: 'She's been hanging around with some very strange people for the past couple of months; I think they may be Goths. They dress in old-fashioned black clothes and Toni has started doing the same. She also goes missing with these people, sometimes for days on end.'

'So you can't control her?' Phil asked.

'I've tried to,' Virginia replied, 'but I'm a single mother and Toni is very headstrong. I've tried to lay down the law, but she ran away once when she was thirteen, and it was all over an argument we had. Toni asked why she couldn't stay out all night like her friends. It really scared me when she ran away; she stayed with a friend for two days. I was frantic. The people she's associating with now are, well – different – there's just something odd about them.'

'Have you actually met these people?' asked Phil.

'I was walking through town once – I'd been shopping with my sister - and I saw Toni on Hanover Street, she was all dressed up like a Victorian woman, and there was a girl with her, a blonde girl, quite pretty, and she was dressed the same. And there were two lads with them, they looked slightly older than Toni, and one had on a top hat and a cloak, and the other young man wore a bowler hat and he had on a chequered suit. I shouted to Toni but she just ignored me, and they all walked on.'

'And you think these people she's hanging around with are a *bad* influence?' Phil Manley asked.

'Yes I do;' Virginia replied glumly, 'they've changed her. Toni used to be so bubbly, always laughing, and now – well – she never even smiles, and she doesn't want to be with me. I asked her to have a birthday party at her home when she turned 14, and I told her she could invite her friends around, but she didn't want that.'

Phil fiddled with his small black notebook, and then he asked: 'Do you think she might be doing drugs, or maybe having – relationships with these people?'

Virginia paused for a while before she gave her reply. 'I think she's on the pill, she won't tell me; she's got some sense regarding sex but I don't know if she's into drugs. That's what I want you to find out. I have this feeling she might have got into some cult; I just have a bad feeling about these people she's seeing; I told the police about my suspicions about her being involved in a cult and they did nothing. Toni seems to be brainwashed by the people she's hanging around with, and she looks at them like they're her family. They seem to all hang around outside that place – Grand Central on Renshaw Street.'

'Well, Virginia, I'll get to the bottom of this; I'll blend in later down at that place you mentioned – Grand Central. I'll watch her every move, and I'll find out who she's hanging about with and so on.'

After his client Virginia left, Phil studied the racing pages of a tabloid, and went to the William Hill bookies next door to the Newington pub on Renshaw Street. Phil then went around the corner, and despite his assurance to Virginia about blending in to observe Toni and her associates, he made no attempt to keep a low profile. He stood outside Grand Central – an alternative shopping complex on Renshaw Street – leaning on a lamp post, smoking a roll-up and pretending to read a tabloid. At 4pm, he saw Toni, dressed all in black lace, in a long bell-shaped dress which looked quite Victorian. She came from Newington (not the pub, the thoroughfare) across the road and stood about ten feet away, glancing at the huge clock over the doorway to Grand Central. Two lads dressed in old fashioned clothes, including top hats, came out of the Grand Central building and chatted to Toni. Phil eavesdropped. One of the young men in toppers held Toni's black gloved hand and kissed her knuckles. He said, 'Greetings fair Antonia, let us...'

And Phil could not hear the rest because of the loud squeal of a passing bus's tyres as it came to a halt at a nearby bus stop.

Antonia and the two bizarrely dressed men walked across Renshaw Street and went down Newington until they reached Back Bold Street, a dark alleyway that runs parallel to Bold Street. Phil gingerly followed, keeping himself about 20 feet from the three teens, and he saw them turn a corner into the Back Bold Street, so they were now behind the Oxfam shop. He reached that corner seconds later and he could see the silhouettes of Toni and the two youths going further down Back Bold Street, and then they turned left at one point, and Phil thought they had gone through a doorway into a backyard. He crept down the alleyway until he reached the spot where he believed the three teens had gone through a backyard door – but there was no such door there – just a brick wall. Something very strange happened here; as Phil stood there, wondering where Toni and her friends had gone, he heard voices coming from the wall, and he thought he could see shadowy forms on the brickwork. When Phil took a close look at the wall, he saw that it did not seem solid; the bricks seemed to shimmer and some seemed gaseous. Was it a trick of the darkness? Phil took out his lighter and clicked it, and the small blue and white flame confirmed that the wall was indeed made of something that was not solid; it was swirling like a vapour. The teens had gone. Phil reached out with his left hand – and he felt that hand go through the wall as if it was made of air. He leaned further in, and saw Bold Street as it would have looked in the days of Jack the Ripper; it was night time, and there were gas lamps with flickering flames, horse-drawn hansom cabs, cobbled roads, top-hatted gents, and there was Toni and her friends – and now a blonde girl with her hair up in a bun, who was also dressed in the same old-fashioned clothes as Toni, joined them. Phil stood in the shadows of some archway, and watched as two more girls approached Toni, and the two of them, were wearing what looked like black straw boaters and typical 19th century female clothes – long skirts that went down to the ankles of their boots.

In shock, Phil whispered to himself, 'What the hell is going on?'

Two more Victorian lads joined the group, and then Toni turned around and saw Phil leaning against the jamb of the arch. Phil slowly realised, that in his modern blue jacket and jeans and white trainers, he'd easily stand out, and sure enough, Toni pointed him out, and those two lads in toppers who had accompanied Toni from Grand Central came running towards him brandishing walking canes. Phil turned and ran, and hesitated at the wall he had passed through. He reached out with his right hand and it went through the wall, and then he leaped straight through it and ran off up Back Bold Street. Being a heavy smoker and a man who never exercised, Phil was soon out of breath, and he ended up walking from the alleyway onto Newington, glancing back all the time, but he could not see the two youths with their top hats and canes. Phil went into the public telephone box facing the Newington pub and called Virginia to tell her of his extraordinary discovery; that Toni was knocking around with Victorians and that there was some type of portal which she was using to go back to their time period. Virginia accused him of being drunk; she had never heard of anything as far-fetched in all of her life.

'You can come down and look at the wall for yourself,' insisted Phil Manley, but Virginia hung up. When he got back to his office, Phil listened to the answer-phone message from Virginia. She told him he would not receive a penny from her. Phil returned to Back Bold Street the next day in the morning, and by the light of day, he inspected that insubstantial backyard wall he had walked through into another time – and now it had reverted to a mundane and very solid brick wall. Phil hung around the entrance of Grand Central but never saw Toni and those two outlandishly dressed men ever again. I told Phil that the wall he had gone through had quite a history, and explained how I had written about what seems to have been a portal within that back alleyway wall in *Haunted Liverpool 33*. Here is a rather inadequate and short summary of the strange account in my book. I received an email from an ex-private detective named Paul, now residing in Holland. He regaled me with an intriguing tale involving a timeslip incident on Bold Street, our local hub of timewarps. In 2010, Paul was hired by the CEO of a large second-hand goods chain to probe into the dubious activities of a Liverpool man known as Danny, who regularly flooded the resale shops with *astonishingly pristine* vintage items from the 1960s. The enigma deepened as Danny always seemed to disappear mysteriously in an alleyway – and that alleyway was Back Bold Street. Despite his doubts, the private detective Paul persisted in shadowing Danny until he confronted him, demanding an explanation. Astonishingly, Danny confessed that a wall in the alleyway occasionally served as a way into the past –

usually the 1950s or 1960s – and during trips to those 'bygone' periods he would steal various goods and bring them back to the present to sell them as vintage items. Danny managed to evade being arrested and vanished without a trace from the Liverpool underworld scene in very uncanny circumstances. Paul had told many people about the incredible activities of the time-hopping thief, but no one would believe a word he said, and I suppose we can't really blame people for doubting the story; it would be like expecting a Victorian to believe that 6 kilograms of metal (the weight of six pineapples) could destroy half of London – when in fact 6 kilograms of plutonium was used in the atomic bomb that decimated Nagasaki in 1945. Looking further ahead, 1 kg of antimatter, which can now be made in very small amounts, would have a destructive power equal to 43 megatons of TNT if it reacted with 1 kg of ordinary matter. This would be sufficient to vaporize Moscow or New York and their surrounding areas. The Victorians would have a very difficult time believing in the destructive power of such small amounts of substances – they would not be able to see beyond their belief barrier – and that brings us back to the time barrier where this chapter first started. All the barriers are coming down in the 21st Century; gender barriers (equal pay for all genders), disability barriers, language barriers, and technological barriers (like Moore's Law – the observation that the number of transistors in an integrated circuit doubles every two years – was once seen to present a barrier to the development of silicon chips, but now scientists can build transistors on the nano scale and may soon be able to use modified atoms and even create DNA-like structures to make more ultra-sophisticated chips). The time barrier concept died on 14 September 2015, with the discovery of the first time-warping gravity wave. The only barrier to time travel now is not a physical one, but the failure of a scientist's mind to find ways of moving through time, perhaps through a fuller understanding of quantum physics, with a little help from artificial intelligence.

BERRY STREET'S
GHOSTLY COUPLE

I remember this case clearly from 2003, and cannot believe twenty years have elapsed since it was reported to me by two of the people featured in the story – Ben and Gary, both car mechanics who worked in a garage in the city centre not far from St Luke's Church. One autumnal day in 2003, when the mechanics were on their lunch break, Gary noticed a very pretty lady who looked as if she was in her twenties, possibly early twenties. She had long auburn hair and striking blue eyes. Gary said to Ben, 'Seen that bird over there? Nice looking girl isn't she?'

'Nice looking girl? What's got into you? You usually use really coarse language when you point out birds,' said Ben, and he looked over at the girl in question.

'Nah, she's a decent girl her, the sort your mam would love to see you going out with,' said Gary, and Ben smiled and said, 'She's alright I suppose. Looks well-to-do. You wouldn't have a chance with someone like her mate. She wouldn't see anything in a grease-monkey.'

On the following day the two mechanics saw the woman again as they had their elevenses, which consisted of Ben having biscuits and coffee and Gary smoking a cheroot. They both noticed something odd. The girl seemed to be wandering about near Berry

Street in an aimless manner. She also kept looking at other women and seemed to be copying them. Ben noticed this behaviour first. A woman was looking in a shop window, standing on her tip-toes in a certain posture – and that brunette lady the mechanics were observing did the very same thing. Another woman yawned and fanned her yawning mouth with her hand – and the dark-haired lady did the exact same thing.

'Why is she doing that?' Ben asked Gary without taking his eyes of the pretty impersonator.

'Maybe she's got a screw loose,' said Gary, his cheroot levering up and down in his mouth as he spoke.

'Aye, aye, she's coming over here;' said Ben, 'pull that belly in, mate.'

The woman walked past the men near the entrance to the garage and Ben said, 'Excuse me love,' and the woman jumped, as if startled by Ben's voice. Ben smiled and said to her, 'You look very smart if you don't mind me saying so. Do you work round here? Saw you here yesterday, like.'

Gary rolled his eyes at his friend's corny attempt to strike up a conversation with the lady.

The woman looked Ben up and down and said: 'Pardon me, sir; I am unacquainted with you, and it is of no relevance to you whatsoever where I engage in labour. I - I must express my astonishment at your audacity to address me in - in such a manner! Good day to you!'

And she walked on along Berry Street, heading south, and was soon out of sight in the crowds.

'What the friggin' hell was all that about?' an astonished Ben asked, and Gary butted in and said,

414

'Didn't I tell you she wasn't playing with a full deck? Your gob when she said that, priceless mate.'

'And I was trying to be nice and that,' said Ben, and Gary, seeing that he really did look ruffled, said, 'Do me a favour lad; when you see a bird, don't use that line about her looking smart – it sounds cringey and creepy.'

'Says the women expert who's single and living with his mam,' retorted Ben.

'Ooh, touchy – just 'cos I told you you're a melon,' said Gary, blowing cheroot smoke in his friend's face.

The mechanics got back to work, and later that afternoon, Gary said to his friend, 'Ben, you're not going to believe this; there's a fellah outside who wants to see you, and he's got a top hat on.'

'What?' asked Ben, wiping his hands on a green oil rag.

'Honest-a-God mate,' said Gary, grinning, 'he said, "Excuse me sir, I'd like to talk to your associate," and he sounded dead posh and weird.'

'If this is a wind-up Gary, I'll give you such a smack,' said Ben, 'I'm way behind here – '

'On our kid's life, he's out there now,' said Gary, smirking, and he walked behind Ben to the pavement outside the front of the garage. Ben saw his friend was telling the truth; there was indeed a man in a top hat, dressed impeccably in Victorian-looking clothes.

'You wanted to see me? What can I do for you?' said Ben, looking the strangely dressed man up and down.

In a loud, well-spoken voice, the man replied, 'Sir, I must apprise you of the impropriety you have displayed by persistently encroaching upon the company of my betrothed.'

'Eh? What?' said Ben; he genuinely had not the slightest idea what the crank was talking about, and Gary giggled behind his colleague.

The top-hatted man continued. 'Such impertinence from a person of your humble station does not sit well with me. You will desist from any further engagement with her, for I assure you, should you dare to transgress again, the scars you shall bear shall serve as a lasting reminder of your audacious actions!'

And the man seemed to produce a knife from nowhere like a sleight-of-hand magician.

'You – you better know how to use that blade mate,' stammered Ben, and Gary stepped back in shock. A stunned and scared Ben continued, 'Cos if you try and stick me with that it'll be the last thing you do. Now get out of here before I call the bizzies!'

'Come 'ed Ben, let it go, he's a divvy!' said Gary, and the man glared at Ben, then closed the clasp-knife and walked away.

A man in his forties in a tea-green belted raincoat who had been standing nearby watching the bizarre exchange between the man in the top hat and Ben said to the mechanics, 'Now that was odd. He said "Such impertinence from a person of your humble station..." etcetera – that's like something someone would say in the 19th Century. I think we might have just seen a ghost.'

'Are you serious?' asked Gary, 'Are you in on it with him?'

'Yes I am serious and no, I am not in on anything with anybody,' said the man, 'I'm just a passer-by and it just struck me as weird, his patter and the old-fashioned clobber he had on. I could just about get the gist of what he was saying.'

'Which was what?' Ben wanted to know.

'He was saying you'd been flirting with his girlfriend,' said the man.

'What girlfriend?' Ben shouted, and Gary tapped his arm and said, 'The woman you chatted to earlier – the one who you said looked smart.'

'Anyway, lads,' said the passer-by, 'I'm going for a pint. If that fellah *is* a ghost, get hold of a copy of the Bible, I believe they can't abide with it. Ta ra!'

And the man walked off.

'Do you think he was a ghost, Ben?' asked a worried Gary.

'Nah – I think it's someone winding us up, but I don't know why;' said Ben, 'we probably won't see him again.'

'I hope so. I'm bringing me Nan's Bible into work tomorrow, and her St Christopher medal,' said Gary in all seriousness.

And on the following day at 3pm, Ben was under a car in the MOT bay when Gary came over and shouted, 'Ben! That fellah in the top hat is back and he's with that bird you talked to.'

Ben's head popped out from under the car. 'What?'

'Honest mate, they're standing outside linking arms. She's wearing a bowler or something and she's got this outfit on, it looks like something out the 1960s and he's standing there looking smug. He looks gone in the head to me, mate, like he's on hard drugs.'

'Did he say he wanted to see *me?*' Ben asked.

Gary shook his head and said, 'No, but he's standing there as if he's going out of his way to be seen.'

'What's their game?' Ben got up and went to have a

look from the front of the garage. The man in the topper smiled at Ben, and pulled the woman Ben had chatted to yesterday close to him and said, 'Come, come my dearest, let us leave this lamentable place and join the company of individuals of a superior ilk. May we find solace and congeniality amidst a more refined echelon of society!'

And the oddly-attired couple walked off.

'If he starts coming round here again with that knife I'll have to put him down,' Ben told Gary – who did a strange thing. Gary walked after the couple, despite Ben shouting for him to come back. The mechanic kept jumping into doorways whenever the couple glanced back, and he followed them as far as an old building known as the Blackie, a former church which is now an arts centre. It stands on Great George Street. Gary saw the couple walk behind the Blackie. They went down a lonely alleyway named Sankey Street, and here, Gary saw the couple vanish. They were there one moment, walking along, linking – and then they were gone. Gary walked to the spot where the figures vanished, and then he turned around and headed back to the garage in delayed shock. He told Ben what he had seen, and his workmate thought he was joking at first, and was waiting for the punch-line to a long-winded joke of the kind Gary was prone to tell. But Gary was deadly serious. He assured Ben he had seen the couple vanish with his own eyes.

'It's been a trick of the light,' said Ben, 'they'll have walked round a corner.

'It *wasn't* a trick of the light or them going round a corner, Ben, I saw this before in broad daylight; they were ghosts,' said Gary, and the next day he brought his Nan's Bible into work but he couldn't find her St Christopher medal. The two mechanics lived in mortal fear of being visited by the couple, but thankfully they never set eyes on them again. Just who that couple was remains unknown. I mentioned the incident on the radio and a man named Bob who used to run a café on Berry Street told me he had seen the couple, long before the mechanics encountered them. Bob gave an excellent description of the uncanny couple and said he had the feeling they were ghosts from different time periods. He believed the man was probably Victorian or Edwardian and that the woman was from a later period. Sometimes she wore the attire of a 1920s lady with the cloche hat and at other times she wore 1960s outfits that were like something Mary Quant had designed, and Bob has also seen the woman imitate other women's gestures and even their speech. He had only realised the couple were ghosts when he had seen them vanish near Bold Place one evening as he was locking the café up. Bob sat in the window seat of his café one afternoon and watched the couple kissing across the road, and they seemed to be so deeply in love. Who they were when they were alive and why they became attracted to one another after death still eludes me.

WARNINGS

Sometimes ghosts do not serve any purpose at all; they appear, they frighten and then they return to that mysterious obscurity where they seem to live in a kind of hibernation; but sometimes ghosts issue advice and warnings to the living, and these warnings and cautions can be subtle or as clear as crystal. This chapter is about just a few of these warnings from beyond.

We'll start in late May 1997 on a sunny morning at 9am; a 19-year-old Tuebrook girl named Jenny Rogers went to the National Express coach station at the back of London Road, ready to get the bus down to London to meet her boyfriend James, who was returning from work in Germany (where he'd been a bricklayer on a building site for three months). Jenny and James planned to go to shopping at Harrods (where Jenny intended to buy her mum a birthday present), and then the couple would have a meal at the Savoy before calling in at Ronnie Scott's Jazz Club, and then Jenny and James would book into a swanky hotel for the night. Anyway, Jenny got to the coach station a bit earlier than planned, just in case the coach turned up before it was officially due and she stood there under a canopy, waiting patiently for the bus on this hot summer's day, and a man was standing about twenty feet away with his back to the girl and under the awning he looked like a silhouette in the bright morning sunlight that was reflecting off the white livery of a parked National Express coach; a coach that would soon set off to Leeds. This man started singing a very strange and unsettling song that went:

Jenny Rogers left her ciggie burning, and in the bed upstairs, her sleeping folks were turning, and the sofa went up in flames, Oh Jenny, you only have yourself to blame...

It sounded like a country and western song the way the lines were delivered – as a real depressing dirge, and Jenny went cold because she recalled she could not remember putting the cigarette out that she had been smoking as she had sat on the sofa in the living room, inspecting her made-up face in a hand mirror before she left. To the silhouetted man, Jenny said, 'Who are you?' and he never replied, he just hummed and whispered, 'You only have yourself to blame.'

Jenny was a real worrier at the best of times, and so she swore and went home, fearing that she might have caused a fatal fire by leaving a lit ciggie on the sofa. When she got home, her stomach somersaulted because she found the sofa smouldering; it had been caused by her cigarette, which had rolled off the edge of the ashtray that she had left on the arm of the sofa. Jenny dowsed the sofa with water and then went upstairs and roused her mother and father, who had been enjoying a sleep in because they'd both taken a day off work. She told them about the cigarette almost causing a blaze and her father was furious at her. Jenny returned to the coach station an hour late, and she had to explain to a woman at the National Express ticket office that there had been a fire in her home and the ticket lady was surprisingly sympathetic. She issued Jenny with a new ticket for the next bus to the capital. Jenny's boyfriend was understanding and believed

Jenny's story as she had never lied to him in the four years he'd known her. He was just so glad to see Jenny after living away from her for three months. Who that eerie silhouetted singer at the coach station was remains a mystery. Jenny feels the shadowy man was possibly a ghost who had saved her parents from dying in a house fire.

Here's a story of a ghost that seems to have opened a girl's eyes.

In July 1998, a girl in her twenties named Nicola was living at her boyfriend's house on Acheson Road, Old Swan, and on this warm night she was sitting alone, thinking about her relationship with her abusive boyfriend (who was out drinking with his mates) when she heard faint music; she recognised the music - it was a song her mother always played when she was a kid, called *Young Hearts Run Free* - and it was a big hit for singer Candi Staton in 1976. Nicola could not work out where the song was coming from; the radio was switched off, and so was the TV, and yet the music sounded as if it was in the room. A glowing figure of a young lady, perhaps of Nicola's age, appeared in front of her, naturally startling her. When the part of the lyrics of the song "love really don't love you" was sung, the ghost waved her pointed index finger six times at Nicola in time to the syllables of the words. The ghost then seemed to float backwards into the wall and vanished. The music of the song faded away. Nicola was scared, and yet she got the gist of the ghostly girl's message - love really didn't love Nicola in her relationship - and so she packed her stuff and got out of that house, and on her way to her mum's she saw her boyfriend having sex with a woman against a tree on Lisburn Lane.

Nicola's boyfriend saw Nicola walking past and stopped having sex, and the young lady he was with said, 'Who's she?'

Nicola shouted back, 'I used to be his girlfriend!' and walked on. Her boyfriend called around that night at Nicola's mum's house, claiming he'd been drunk and on drugs when he was with that girl, but Nicola's mother swore at him and told him to keep away.

The identity of the female ghost seen at the house on Acheson Road is unknown. Nicola later met someone else and is still happily married to him. In the next story of a supernatural forewarning, the ghost's 'message' took some time to sink in. In the 1990s a girl in her twenties named Kyrie saw an old neighbour she had known as a child named John being hit by two cars at Tarbock Island, Huyton, and she held his hand as he died at the roadside. The experience traumatised Kyrie, and it took a few months before she stopped having nightmares Then, about five months after the incident, she was living with her boyfriend David in Mossley Hill, and one day she went to do a bit of shopping at Tesco on Mather Avenue, and there, coming towards her down the aisle was John, the old man who had been killed in that horrific car accident earlier in the year. This man was no lookalike, and he even wore the same tweed suit and trilby he had worn on the day he was killed, and as he brushed past the shocked girl he said, 'Hello Kyrie,' then continued on his way. He was not carrying a basket or pushing a trolley, and he just walked on, and Kyrie felt faint. She took a deep breath, and a woman serving at one of the checkouts noticed that Kyrie looked unsteady on her feet, and she mouthed the words, 'You okay love?'

Kyrie nodded, but the checkout lady said something to a security guard and he came over to see if Kyrie was alright. At this point Kyrie saw that John, the old man had gone. He had been walking away one moment and then he was gone - vanished. Kyrie later learned from an employee at the supermarket that the old man's ghost often came into the store, wandered around for a while, then either walked out of the place again or vanished on the premises. I know from experience that a lot of ghosts re-enact the same routines they did when they were in human form – they really can be creatures of habit, and John is probably one of them. A few days after the encounter with the ghost of the old man, Kyrie told her boyfriend David that she was sick of living in Mossley Hill; she found the area boring and felt as if she was stuck in a routine. Kyrie said she wanted to move to the city centre, and Rodney Street in particular; things just seemed to be more alive down there. David said he preferred the suburbs and hated the city centre; it was too noisy, according to David. Kyrie persisted, saying she thought they should move but one of David's relatives called and that put an end to any further discussions on the subject.

That night, Kyrie dreamed she was in her local supermarket, Tesco, and she was walking about like a zombie in the dream, picking up the same old food items and Kyrie found she was stuck in a repetitive loop, going to the checkout and then walking back into the store, as if she was stuck in a film that kept rewinding back to the beginning. And then, John, the old man whose ghost Kyrie had seen in the supermarket, suddenly appeared in the dream and he said to her, 'Change brings life. Go to Rodney Street or you'll walk these aisles till you're an old woman, and you may even walk them when you are dead.'

Kyrie awoke with a start and recalled the dream, which was unusual for her as she often forgot what she had dreamed about after she'd awakened. She felt John's ghost had been trying to tell her not to get stuck in a rut. He had been such a man of routine, he was still carrying out the same repetitive quotidian rituals in death as he had in life, going to the same supermarket and so on. Kyrie's mind was made up – she wanted to move from Mossley Hill to Rodney Street and that was that. She nagged David until he finally acquiesced and the two of them went looking for flats on Rodney Street, and eventually found one. Kyrie felt as if she had broken free of the invisible shackles of her routines at last. A very similar ghost – but not of a person – inspired another young lady to pursue her dreams and to kick the mind-numbing nine-to-five existence that was stressing her out. This strange incident happened in August 2009, when a couple from Liverpool, Sera (short for Seraphina) and Jon, went to visit Formby beach, and here Sera spotted something she had not seen since she was a kid, and Jon thought she was joking at first; it was a white seal, an exceedingly rare creature. Sera seemed to believe the creature was a ghost, as she was now 30 and she had seen that seal when she was 7 years of age, and no one had believed her.

Now Jon saw it too and he said, 'You're right, I can see it, it must be an albino.'

Sera shook her head and said, 'No, it's *him*, and he

has blue eyes like sapphires Jon; I've got to go and see him,' and she stripped down to her underwear - against Jon's wishes - and she ran into the glittering sun-flecked sea, and Jon, who couldn't swim, ran after her till the water was up to his chest, and he saw Sera and the white seal vanish into the sea's sun-glare and the foam of the rolling waves, and he screamed and shouted for her to come back and up to that point, Jon never realised how much he loved Sera – he was terrified she'd be swept away.

Sera experienced something very strange from her viewpoint, the sea became calm, and ended up resembling a mirror of clouds, and she could see the white seal swimming off. It looked back at her a few times, and she wanted to cry, because she wanted to touch him. The stillness was very eerie now, and then came the big shock; when Sera looked back – the shore had gone. There was no Formby – no land, just a flat horizon – just a mirror of the sky. Sera started swimming back the way she had come, hoping to see the shore but it was as if the country had vanished below the waves. Sera started to feel a weakness in her limbs and lungs after a time she could not measure, and she started crying and thinking of Jon, and then she saw him appear ahead of her, up to his waist reaching out to her. The beach was back. He waded out to her cursing and he shouted and ranted at her for going away into the sea, and yet he held her and dragged her to the sands, and Sera heard gulls, and what sounded like a distant bell, perhaps on a buoy, and far off voices of out-of-sight people walking along the beach. She has not seen that little white seal since, and still thinks it is a supernatural being, or perhaps some archetype of peace. Sera's encounter with the white seal seemed to open up her creative side, and she realised she wanted to leave the rat race of the 9 to 5 treadmill and do what she had always enjoyed, and that was pottery, painting and just making things. She opened a shop on Etsy, and Jon even bought her a potter's wheel and built her a studio in a huge hut in their garden. Sera feels her health – and her mental wellbeing – would have suffered had she continued her all-consuming job, which was programming for a finance company. Now she is so contented in her life, and all because of an 'old friend from the sea.'

And now for a warning via a violent 'vision'.

In July 1997, four men were doing up a flat in Aigburth, and when the place was finally finished, Gene, the man who had got the men the job turned up and had a look at the quality of the workmanship and he said, 'Yeah, that's brill, nice one lads, I'll get your wages off Mr Bristow in the morning.'

'Er, make sure Mr Bristow pays us in cash – readies - Gene, no bouncing cheques or I'll be round on the bounce to him,' said the foreman of the gang, Frankie, a no-nonsense man from Kirkby. Gene nodded and left the house and two of the men left with him, getting a lift home from Gene in his van. Frankie and his friend Danny were about to leave when Frankie noticed a hole in a wall that had been plastered three days back, and he was livid.

'Who the hell did that?' he asked, gazing at the hole, which was about four inches in diameter. Danny saw it and said, 'That'll have been that halfwit Terry, messing about with some dowelling this morning, pretending some wooden pole was a light-sabre,' Danny recalled, although he had not seen the pole poke a hole in the wall.

'Well, that's my early dart snookered,' said Frankie, and he peeped into the hole and said to Danny, 'Hey, look at this.'

Through the hole, Frankie could see an old fashioned kitchen of the type his grandmother had cooked in when Frankie was a kid. The walls were tiled pear-yellow with pictures of pots, pans and ladles. The cooker looked as if it dated to the 1950s and some of the pots on it were of shiny copper. Danny came over and peeped through the hole and said, 'That can't be next door's kitchen, mate, the party wall isn't that thin.'

Frankie looked through the hole again and whispered, 'There's a lady in there. She looks like somethin' out the 1950s. She's got rollers in and she's wearing one of those old aprons or a pinny, whatever you call them.'

'What?' Danny tried to shift his mate out the way to look but Frankie wouldn't budge.

'She's doing the washing up – this is nuts,' said Frankie, and he stepped aside and Danny looked through the hole and saw the woman too. She was attractive, aged about twenty to twenty-five maybe, and Danny turned to Frankie and said, 'She looks familiar; I feel as if I've seen her before. Shall I shout to her?'

Frankie shrugged.

'Excuse me love,' said Danny raising his voice, but the woman didn't even look at him.

'That must be some hole to go through a party wall,' said Frankie.

'Love!' shouted Danny, but the woman didn't even

react. Danny turned to tell Frankie she couldn't hear him and Frankie shoved Danny out the way, saying, 'You're not shouting loud enough, man, give it some welly.' Frankie the cupped his hands around his mouth and yelled into the hole, 'Hey girl! Hey love!'

The woman walked away singing, 'Once I had a secret love', from the old 1953 Doris Day song, *Secret Love*.

'Frankie, is she a bleedin' ghost?' Danny suddenly asked, and Frankie turned to him and said, 'Don't be daft, she just dresses a bit antwacky. Some people are into all that 1950s clobber. Anyway she's gone. We better get on with blocking that hole up and plastering over it, pronto.'

'The weird thing is that she never heard us, and I feel as if I've seen her before somewhere. I think there's something very odd about this, mate,' said Danny. Frankie saw he looked scared – and that was something he thought he'd never see; Danny was such a tough nut, a part-time bouncer.

'I'll kill that bleedin' Terry when I see him tomorrow,' said Frankie, trying to change the subject.

There was an ear-splitting scream – which came from that wall – and from that hole – and when the two plasterers took turns in gazing through it they saw that woman in the rollers and dated attire had sustained a violent attack by the amount of blood she was covered in. Danny could see the stab wounds in the woman's chest oozing blood, and he thought he caught a glimpse of a blond man with a thick beard who fled from the kitchen. Danny ran out of the room and went next door. He hammered on the door and an old lady answered.

'Someone's being attacked in your house, in your kitchen!' said Danny, and the old woman said, 'I live alone. There's no one else here.'

'There is!' Danny insisted, and then Frankie arrived at the doorstep too.

'She's a ghost, the woman you saw,' said the old lady, 'she's been seen before. The window cleaner won't clean my windows because he saw her in the kitchen. She's just a ghost.'

'I'm sorry, love,' said Frankie, over Danny's shoulder, and gently led his friend away down the path.

'She's just a ghost – not real!' shouted the old woman, and closed the door.

Danny would not stay at the house, and Frankie said he'd patch up the hole himself, but when he looked at the wall, the hole was gone.

Frankie rushed outside and waved to Danny as he was about to start his car in the drive. 'It's gone!'

'What?' Danny asked, rolling the window down.

'That hole in the wall – it's gone, not a trace of it,' said Frankie, palms up, gesturing the Gallic shrug.

'I *told* you there was something spooky about that;' said Danny, 'I'm glad this job's finished. If there's one thing I'm scared of it's the supernatural.'

When I first heard this story, I thought that was it – the men had seen some replay of a murder that had happened, back in the 1950s, going by the woman's clothes and the decor of the kitchen. But I discovered that there was more to this case. A year after the incident at the house in Aigburth, Danny started seeing Kerry, a 21- year-old student, and she just happened to be into vintage fashion and the 1950s in particular. Danny and Kerry moved into a ground-floor flat in Aigburth, near to Sefton Park, and Kerry said to Danny, 'Seeing as you're a decorator, can you do the kitchen up like a 1950s kitchen?'

Danny said he could and told Kerry to pick the vintage wallpaper for the period kitchen she had in mind. 'Can we have tiles instead of wallpaper, pretty please?' she asked, and Danny smiled and said, resignedly, 'Whatever.'

A few months later, Danny put the last pear-yellow tile with the little pictures of pots, pans and ladles into place, and expertly applied the grout. When the adhesive of the tiles had hardened, Danny surprised Kerry by bringing an old genuine 1950s range cooker into the kitchen and it was of a pale yellow, which matched the tiles. Danny's friend George fitted the cooker – which had been bought from an eBay seller - and Kerry bought vintage kitchen wear – enamel pots, copper pans and so on. The place soon looked like an authentic kitchen from the heyday of Elvis.

And then, a few months after this, Danny had a blazing row with Kerry, she had been seen with a student from her college named Ambrose, and Danny had heard she was going out to see him tonight. Kerry denied this and said she was going out with two girls from the college. She stood there in the vintage kitchen in her pink old-fashioned rollers, dressed in a floral pinafore, and she told Danny she didn't want to be with someone as possessive as him. At this time, Danny had grown a beard and as he started to row with Kerry, he caught a glimpse of his reflection in the kitchen window, and he had just reached for a knife – but he threw it in the sink when he heard a song come on the radio which chilled him to the bone. It was

Secret Love by Doris Day – the song he and Frankie had heard when they had looked through that baffling hole in the kitchen wall. The kitchen they had seen was this one, and the woman in the rollers was Kerry – and the murderer Danny had glimpsed was his future self – a blond bearded man. And now the song playing on the radio underlined this terrifying revelation. Danny hugged Kerry and said he was sorry for being paranoid.

'As if I'd go and see someone behind your back,' Kerry sobbed, her face squished into Danny's chest as he hugged her.

'I'm so sorry Kerry, I'm just bad-minded sometimes, and I'm terrified of losing you, that's all,' Danny told her in a broken voice.

The couple stayed together and later married. To this day, Danny feels that the murder he and Frankie had seen in that Aigburth house had been some warning from someone in the hereafter – but who was doing the warning remains a mystery.

The last case reminds me of the following one in some aspects. In July 2010, two sisters, Helena and Maren, decided to leave their cramped flat in a tower block overlooking Sefton Park and clubbed together to rent a house on Mossley Hill's Meredale Road, and from the moment Maren set foot inside the house she had a bad feeling about the place, but Helena said the place had a lovely atmosphere and that she could now have enjoy a proper garden instead of the window box in the hi-rise flat. Maren said she had the feeling someone was watching from the back garden. Helena put her sister's feeling of bad vibes down to her morbid imagination, but on their first night at the house, Maren said she could hear someone singing, and this was about 11:30pm. Then Helena heard it; she strained her ears and said, 'It sounds like that song our mum used to sing when we were kids - *Rivers of Babylon.*

'It is,' said Maren, 'and it sounds like it's coming from the back garden.'

Maren was right; the sisters went into the kitchen and listened; it was right outside in the back garden. The light was switched off in the kitchen but the sisters could see no one in the garden through the wide window. Helena switched the light back on and went to the toilet upstairs, and Maren stayed in the kitchen. The singing had stopped. She could see someone out the corner of her left eye - that person was outside the kitchen window, close to the pane. Maren's eyes darted left, and she recoiled in fright. A blonde woman was standing there. 'By the Rivers of Babylon, there we sat down...' she started to sing, and Maren ran out the kitchen and upstairs, then onto the landing and almost collided with Helena, who was coming out the toilet. She told her sister she'd seen the singer - right outside the kitchen window, and she had just known she was a ghost.

Helena said, 'Calm down, Maren, it might have just been a drunken neighbour,' but then the two girls looked down from the top of the stairs and saw the rectangle of light across the hallway floor, caused by the kitchen light shining through the kitchen doorway, and now there was a shadow - a shadow of what looked like a long haired woman moving forward in that rectangle of illumination on the hallway floor. The figure of a blonde woman came ever so silently into the hallway, and the horrified girls saw that the unknown lady had bloodstains on the front of her dress, mostly by the chest, as if she had sustained some terrible wounds there.

The figure started singing *Rivers of Babylon* again, then fell to its knees before landing face down in the hallway with a thud. The figure then very slowly faded away. The girls left the house that night and managed to get their deposit and first month's rent back from the landlord, telling him his house was haunted and that they'd go to the local newspapers if he didn't pay up - and he never denied the place was haunted. Helena and her sister Maren were in the Rose of Mossley pub a month after they had left the house on Meredale Road, and they were telling a woman about their spooky experience in a quiet corner of the pub when a grey-haired man in his fifties chipped into the conversation.

To Helena, the man said, 'I'm sorry to butt in, but I couldn't help overhearing your story about the singing ghost. I heard — and I don't know if it's true or just a myth — but there was supposed to be some weird serial killer going round years ago, and I'm going way back to the Seventies, like.'

'Ooh,' said Helena, 'I'd like to hear *this*.'

The man stood nearer to the table where the three women were seated and said, 'Yeah, what I heard was that some fellah who was a bit of a Bible thumper, had a thing about women singing that *Rivers of Babylon* song.'

'Didn't he like Bony M or something?' Maren asked with a lopsided smirk.

The man gave a painful looking smile and explained:

'Well what it is, is this: that song is based on a 2,500-year-old Hebrew poem – a Psalm, like. The lyrics of the song were adapted from Psalms 19 and 137. If I remember correctly, the verse in the Bible goes: By the rivers of Babylon, there we sat down, yea we wept, when we remembered Zion.'

'And how does this have anything to do with the ghost these two young ladies saw?' asked the bemused woman sitting between Helena and Maren.

'Well, as I was just going to explain,' answered the man, looking rattled by the woman's attitude, 'this fellah – the killer – didn't like people singing the Lord's psalms, so if he was walking by and he happened to hear anyone singing that song, he'd mark them for death.'

'What a load of codswallop,' said the woman at the table, and she threw back her head and drank the remains of a gin and tonic.'

'It *does* sound a bit far-fetched,' Helena softly told the man, and she saw a nervous tic pulse in his left cheek and his eye twitched.

'So, this killer just walks past houses were people might be singing the *Rivers of Babylon* and then he goes ape?' asked Maren, and the man said, 'Maybe he heard them in pubs or in a club, I don't know; I'm just telling you what I heard years ago.'

'Well you heard rot,' said the lady at the table of the sisters, 'and they were probably winding you up.'

'Well you believe what you want to believe,' said the man, and he gazed at his watch then walked away and was lost to sight in the crowded bar.

Maren started singing the *Rivers of Babylon* song, but her voice was way out of tune and it sounded like a

435

totally different melody. Helena laughed and pointed to her sister, saying 'Ah, you've had it now, you'll be marked for death.'

Maren then went the toilet, and as she was sitting in the cubicle, someone tried the door. 'It's engaged!' Maren shouted, 'I'm in here!'

The person on the other side of the door said, 'Bitch.' It sounded like a male voice.

Maren stood up and fixed her clothes and she shouted, 'Who is that?'

The person kicked the door, and Maren screamed, and then she heard heavy footsteps walking away.

Maren peeped out the cubicle, and then she ran out the toilet and went to the bar to tell Helena what had happened, but her sister said she had seen no one come out of the toilets in the last minute or so. The sisters went home – they were now living off Rose Lane in Mossley Hill. Maren kept looking behind her as if she thought she was being followed and Helena said, 'Maren, no serial killer is following you. That story that fellah came out with is a load of crap. Maybe he just got off on trying to scare us.'

'Someone knocked on that toilet door though, and it was definitely a man,' said Maren, grabbing her sister's arm.

At 2am, Maren came into her sister's bedroom and found her already awake. 'Helena, someone's just posted a Bible through the letterbox.'

'I heard a noise which woke me up,' said Helena, thinning her eyes at the light shining into the bedroom from the landing. 'A Bible?'

'Yeah, I didn't touch it; it's still on the floor of the hallway,' said Maren, 'I put the bolt on.'

Helena got up and looked out the bedroom window – Rose Lane was deserted and as quiet as the grave. Helena left the room in her bare feet and padded down the stairs to the hallway. There was a black leather-bound Bible on the bristly brown mat. Helena picked up the Holy Book and opened it, and on the first blank page, someone had written, 'READ THIS YOU WHORE' in red block letters.

'Should we go to the police?' Maren asked, shocked at the message in red.

'No, this is just someone playing a prank on us;' Helena replied, 'probably someone in the pub who overheard the story of the ghost.'

'Well I don't find it funny,' said Maren, and she went to put the kettle on. The sisters didn't go back to their beds until the light of dawn came creeping across the sky. They rose around noon and over coffee and toast they talked of the strange delivery in the wee small hours. Maren had the man in the pub down as the culprit who had delivered the Bible. He had just seemed weird to her, quoting passages of the Old Testament and coming up with that scare story about a killer driven by some religious mania.

'I don't think it was him, somehow,' reckoned Helena, pausing her lips above the rim of the coffee mug.

'Well who then?' asked Maren, and even now, with the sunlight of mid-day blazing into the kitchen, she seemed afraid.

'Maybe that man in the pub was telling the truth;' said Helena, 'perhaps there is a killer going round who targets what he sees as blasphemers.'

Maren looked perplexed. 'But that fellah in the Rose

said the killer was going back in the Seventies; he'd have to be an old man or dead by now, surely?'

'It all depends how old he was in the Seventies,' said Helena, 'he might have been in his twenties, which means he'd just be fifty-odd now.'

'You're scaring me,' admitted Maren, and she yelped as some junk mail was posted through the letterbox.

'Well you're an adult, Maren, you can't hide your head in the sand. Maybe we *should* go to the police.'

Maren thought about the suggestion. 'They'd probably say the whole thing is a joke, and we can't mention the ghost we saw in our last place – they'd throw us out the station for wasting their time.'

'Well let's just let this whole thing blow over and hopefully it'll all end up as a bad memory,' said Helena.

The sisters decided to go to town. They didn't have much money but they thought that even window shopping and the odd coffee and a bite to eat in a café would be a welcome distraction from the 'bogeyman' figure they were building up in their minds. The sisters visited Liverpool One and then they went to the Midland Hotel pub on Ranelagh Street, and who should walk in but the man who had first told them the story about the serial killer who was down on women for singing Biblical psalms. His eyes widened when he saw Helena and Maren sitting there. Helena left her table, walked up to the man, and before she could speak, another drinker said to the man, 'What you havin' Peter?'

'So, *that's* your name, eh? Peter,' said Helena.

'No thanks, I'm not staying long,' Peter told his generous friend, then turned to Helena and asked, 'That's my name, yes, what about it?'

'Well, Peter, do you often go around in the dead of night posting Bibles through people's letter-boxes?' Helena asked.

'What on earth are you talking about?' said Peter, narrowing his eyes, and those eyes darted left to look at Maren, who was seated at a table.

Helena poked him in the chest with her index finger as she said, 'Someone posted the Bible through our door this morning and they wrote a note in it saying "Read this you whore". If there's any more of this crap I'll be going straight to the police. I've got your first name now, and it'll be easy to get your surname.'

Peter's face turned red with rage. 'Look love, keep taking your medicine and leave me alone, alright? You've obviously got issues going on in that brain of yours.'

To the man who offered Peter a drink, Helena asked, 'What's your friend's surname?'

'Why don't you ask him?' the man suggested.

'This stupid bird thinks I'm terrorising her or something,' Peter told his friend, 'got a persecution complex or something and is going to report me to the police.' And then he turned to Helena and said, Well, seeing as I have nothing to hide, I'll tell you my full name and even my National Insurance number and blood group if you want. My name is Peter Phoenix Scott.'

Helena returned to Maren and sat down, but Maren suggested leaving, saying the man was creeping her out. The sisters left the pub and hailed a hackney cab which took them straight home to Mossley Hill. As soon as they entered their house, Helena went upstairs to the toilet and Maren went into the bedroom to change into something more comfortable. From the toilet, Helena heard her sister emit a subdued shriek, and so she went to see if she was okay. When Helena went into the bedroom, she saw Maren with her hands to her face, looking in horror at the bed. The duvet had been pulled back because Maren had noticed something under it. That something turned out to be a huge old crucifix or the type you'd find hanging on a church altar. The cross measured about four feet in length.

'Oh my God – he's been in here,' said Helena, and Maren said, 'And he might still be in here!'

The sisters went to the police and told them what must have sounded like a long-winded barmy tale. The police seemed to think someone was just playing a prank on the sisters, but that someone would have needed a key to gain access to the house as there was no sign of a forced entry. Helena and Maren no longer felt safe at the house, so they moved in with a cousin in Speke. For a few nights at the new address, someone telephoned the house on its landline in the early hours, and when the phone was answered, heavy breathing was heard. The caller had withheld their number and was never traced. Since then, the sisters have not heard from their sinister persecutor, and they go cold whenever they hear that Bony M song.

Here's a rather short but moving account of a classic warning from the sphere of the dearly departed. In late June 2009, a 17-year-old girl named Madison was waiting for her boyfriend (also aged 17) and his three mates near Hanover Street. Madison's boyfriend kept borrowing his dad's car (unknown to him) and he would take Madison and his 3 mates on a spin around the region, sometimes speeding down a certain badly lit country lane that stretched from Halewood to Widnes with the headlights switched off. Tonight Madison had been promised the front passenger seat instead of being squished between her boyfriend's mates in the backseat. They were going to tear down a few motorways and maybe even play chicken by driving towards oncoming cars to get the old adrenaline going - but - on this unusually cold night for June, Madison was waiting for her boyfriend when she had a really bad feeling that something terrible was going to happen. She also had the sensation of being watched, and she turned and was utterly shocked to see what had to be a ghost - the ghost of Tim - he had been her older brother, the brother she had looked up to, but he had tragically died in a car crash 7 years ago. He was covered in blood and Madison drew a sharp intake of breath when she saw him standing there, and then she said, 'Tim, is that - ' but before she could finish the sentence he slowly turned his sad face away from her and he vanished. Madison felt all choked up, and she believed this was some warning for her not to get into the car with her boyfriend, and she ran off to the gyratory to get the bus home. Madison's boyfriend texted her as she was still on the bus, asking where she was. She never answered, and then she saw her boyfriend in his father's car, driving parallel to the bus. Madison had to duck down and lay sideways across the seat to avoid being seen by him and his mates. That night, her boyfriend lost control of his father's car near Speke and totalled it - and he was lucky he wasn't seriously injured, and he had his seatbelt on — unlike the lad who had been sitting in the front passenger seat

– where Madison would have sat; he was thrown through the windscreen and went over a fence ringed with barbed wire into a field. His face was scarred after that night, although his 'mates' all thought it was hilarious. Madison realised she would have been scarred for life had she gone for a spin that night, and perhaps she might have even been killed. She lit a candle for Tim in her window that night.

And finally, here is a case where some supernatural being inadvertently warned a girl of someone with a murky secret.

At a house on Old Swan's Oakhill Road in 2004, a 17-year-old girl named Mirabelle was putting on her make up at her prized mirror (which she'd bought from eBay) when there was a thunderstorm. The girl's mother came in and told Mirabelle to draw the blinds as it was 'unlucky to look in a mirror and see your face by lightning.' Mirabelle returned a condescending look and said, 'Er – no.'

Her mum gazed at her own face in the mirror and said, 'Look at those bags under my eyes. I remember being your age and thinking I can never be old.'

'Well you are now,' joked Mirabelle, 'only kidding. Stop depressing me, mum.'

Her mother left the room and Mirabelle gazed into the oval looking glass and lightning flashed into the room, and for a split second the teen was blinded by the electrical radiance. Then she saw strange after-images in the mirror. Then came the thunder, and the house literally shook from the chimney pots to the foundations. Mirabelle's cat jumped off the bed and ran downstairs to snuggle in with the Labrador, who was quaking in his basket at the thunder roll. Upstairs meanwhile, Mirabelle could still see green and blue shapes in the mirror, and for some random reason, she thought of the anonymous love letter she had received the day before yesterday, and she jokingly said to the mirror, 'Mirror, mirror, show me the face of my secret admirer; who is he? Show me, show me.'

And she smiled, but then something happened to wipe the smile off the teenager's face. The mirror became cloudy, and in the clouds, Mirabelle saw the face of a girl who was in her class at school – Jess. The face started to dissolve after about ten seconds. Mirabelle went downstairs to her mum with one false eyelash on and told her what had happened. Predictably, her mother said, 'You've always had a vivid imagination.'

Mirabelle emitted a grunting sound and said: 'Mam! I didn't imagine this – it was a clear image of Jess. Does that mean she wrote the letter?'

'Has she ever shown you any signs of liking you?' her mother asked, raising one eyebrow up and down, messing about.

'Seriously – what do you think?' Mirabelle asked. Her young brother, who was drawing with a Sharpie pen on a notepad as he lay across the sofa, started to listen in.

Mirabelle's mum whispered, 'I'm not a psychologist, I haven't a clue. Do you like her?'

'Yes, of course I do, she's a friend,' Mirabelle replied.

'No, I mean – you know – *like* her, like her,' said her mother, and Mirabelle blushed.

'I don't know – I don't think so, not in that way,' replied her daughter, 'I thought some fellah had written that letter because the handwriting is terrible.'

'Oh look, Mirabelle, I'm not getting involved in your love life,' chuckled her mum, and her young son asked, 'Does some girl fancy Belle (as he called his sister) mum?'

'Stop earwigging, you,' his mum told him.

'You're supposed to give me advice like a life coach,' said Mirabelle, and she left the living room in a huff and went back upstairs.

'Me? A life coach? I've never had a life,' complained her mother.

A very eerie thing happened when Mirabelle went to the mirror. A whispering voice from it said, 'Can you hear me?'

Mirabelle froze, then answered, 'Yeah – who is that?'

'I'm the girl in your mirror who showed you your secret admirer;' said the whisperer, and then she added, 'if I show myself will you be scared and run away?'

Mirabelle could feel her chest moving as her heart pounded. 'No,' she said.

The image of a smiling girl who only looked about twelve years of age appeared in the mirror, and she had on old-fashioned clothes and the room reflected in the mirror looked like a room of long ago, possibly Victorian, with a solitary oil lamp. 'Hello,' said the girl in the mirror.

'Who – who are you?' Mirabelle asked, backing away.

'I told you who I am. Draw those blinds, I don't like too much daylight,' said the girl behind the quicksilvered glass. After the thunderstorm, the sun was out again and shining into the bedroom.

Keeping her eye on the apparition in the mirror, Mirabelle went to close the blinds.

'If you swear you'll be my friend I can show you things happening a mile off,' said the girl, 'and I can tell you anyone's secrets, be they good or dark. I know secrets about your neighbour that would shock you.'

'Swear to be your friend?' said Mirabelle, feeling that this would entail something bad. She just sensed this.

'It doesn't really hurt,' said the girl in the glass, 'you just prick your little finger with a pin and wipe some blood on the mirror. Just a tiny drop.'

'No,' said Mirabelle immediately.

The girl stopped smiling and seemed surprised. 'Why ever not?'

'What would you need my blood for? Only something evil would want that,' Mirabelle told her.

'I am not evil! Goodbye!' said the girl, and she vanished and now Mirabelle saw her own face, reflected in the mirror. She opened the blinds and went downstairs to her mum, who was in the kitchen with the neighbour, a towering stocky man with a shaven head. Mirabelle was so afraid, she told her mother everything the 'ghost' in the mirror had said, including the claim that it knew people's secrets, 'good and dark' – and how it said the neighbour had secrets that would shock her.

'Oh Mirabelle, not all this again,' groaned her mum, and she smiled at the neighbour and said, 'she watches too many horror films.'

At the mention of a neighbour having secrets, the neighbour in the kitchen looked very shocked, and he said, 'That sounds like an evil spirit, especially asking you to put your blood on the mirror.'

'Thank heavens someone believes me!' said Mirabelle, glaring at her mum.

'I'll take the mirror away if you want, and dispose of it,' said the neighbour, adding, 'my son-in-law's a priest.'

'Oh take no notice of Mirabelle,' the girl's mother told the neighbour, but he completely ignored the advice and said to Mirabelle, 'Show me this mirror.'

'Come on,' Mirabelle said with a sideways tilt of her head, inviting the man to follow her up to her room.

The neighbour went up to the bedroom and saw the mirror. Downstairs, Mirabelle's mum shouted, 'I'm going to tell your father about the way you're carrying on, my girl! This is not normal!'

'This is the mirror,' said Mirabelle, pointing at the oval walnut framed looking glass, 'I got it off eBay.'

'It definitely has an aura about it,' said the neighbour, 'I'm a little bit psychic, see.'

'Oh, and can you sense something?' Mirabelle asked, highly intrigued.

'Yes,' said the man, 'do me a favour and go downstairs and get some salt. There's a spell I know for cleansing mirrors of evil spirits.'

'This is so exciting,' said Mirabelle, 'how much salt?'

'Just a few teaspoons will do,' said the neighbour, his eyes scanning the bedroom for some reason as he spoke, as if he was looking for something.

'Righty-o!' Mirabelle rushed excitedly from the room and bounded down the stairs. She reached the bottom step and her mum said, 'I can't believe the crap you're coming – '

But her words were dramatically interrupted by the sound of a mirror being smashed upstairs.

Mother and daughter ran up the stairs and reached the doorway of Mirabelle's bedroom. The neighbour stood there, looking at the smashed mirror with an expressionless face.

'What happened?' Mirabelle asked. She saw her left platform shoe lying on the floor, and there were fragments of the mirror everywhere; on the floor and on the bed and on the dresser, some glinting in the strands of sunlight on the carpet. One silvery shard was sticking out the insole of Mirabelle's platform.

'That shoe flew across the room and smashed into the mirror,' said the neighbour, and he did not sound convincing. Both Mirabelle and her mother had the feeling he had thrown the heavy platform shoe through that looking glass. But why?

After that day, the neighbour never came near Mirabelle's family; before then, he had been round almost every day and Mirabelle had even offered to help him tidy up his garden. Within two weeks he had moved from the street and told no one why he had moved or where his new home was. Mirabelle told her mother she believed he had smashed the mirror because he was afraid that the girl in the glass would tell her what his dark secret was. 'I think the secret he had was *very* dark,' Mirabelle told her mother.

She was probably right.

Printed in Great Britain
by Amazon